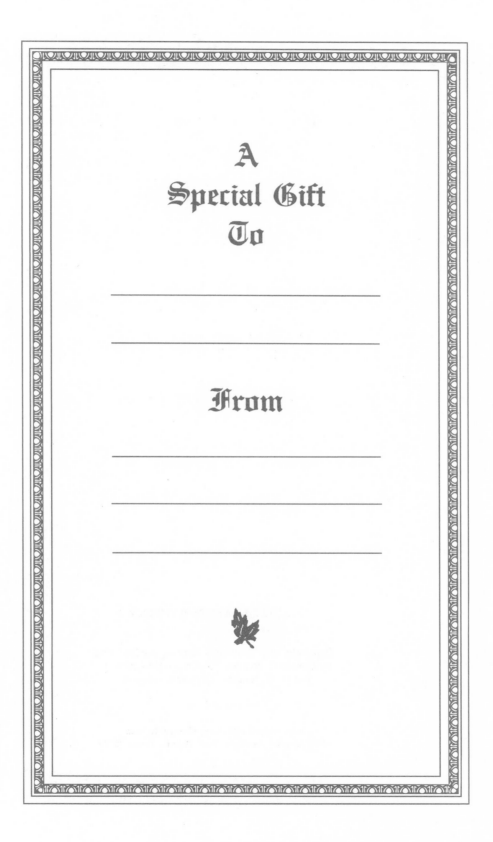

A
Special Gift
To

_____

_____

From

_____

_____

_____

Standard Edition: ISBN 0-915720-74-4

Printed in China

Brownlow Publishing Company, Inc.
6309 Airport Freeway, Fort Worth, Texas 76117

Leaves of Gold

An Anthology of

PRAYERS
MEMORABLE PHRASES
INSPIRATIONAL VERSE AND PROSE

From the Best Authors of the World,
Both Ancient and Modern

EDITED
BY
CLYDE FRANCIS LYTLE

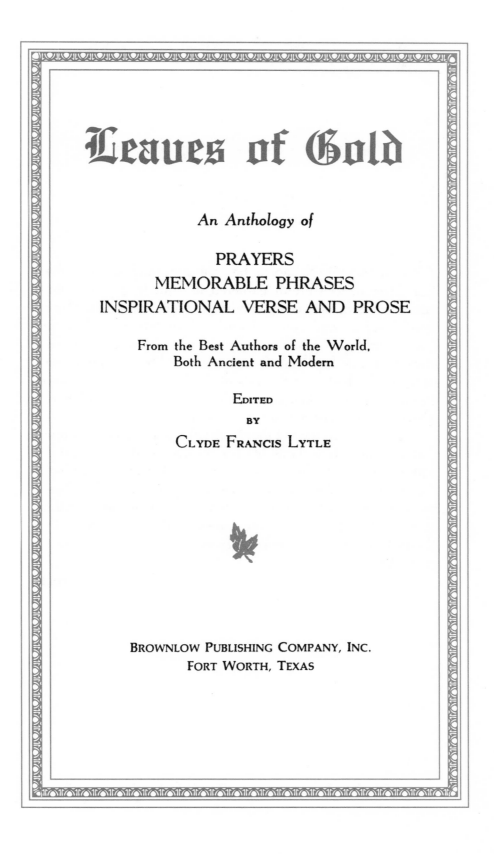

BROWNLOW PUBLISHING COMPANY, INC.
FORT WORTH, TEXAS

The Heart's Haven

CIVILIZATION had its beginning around an open fire. Here at its warmth gathered the family group to find safety, comfort, and companionship. Trace the origin of our word *fireplace* and you will find it definitely related to the Latin word *focus*. There is the explanation of what home has always meant; for home is the center of life,—no mere residence of the body but the axis of the heart; the place where affections develop themselves, where children love and learn, where two toil together to make life a blessing.

To picture in a word the depths of want, we say of a man that he is homeless. True, life is a journey, and we are all on a pilgrimage. But when distance has lost its enchantment and the ardor for adventure has cooled, when danger has been bravely faced and wonder satiated, hearts long for a resting place and find in the ruddy glows of the hearth-fire "the charm from the skies" that hallows life and gives refuge to man's tired soul.

—THE EDITORS

Leaves of Gold

Foreword

POOR indeed is the man whose mind is not enriched by some phrase of lasting truth and beauty which serves to restore his soul in the exigencies of life. Each of us needs in his heart's treasury the memory of a lovely line to renew fellowship with the great and noble of this earth—and, indeed, almost as great as the ability to write a line of strength is the ability to use that line to higher levels of emotion and achievement.

To discover afresh in truth expressed with elemental force our eternal kinship with God is a universal urge. "Leaves of Gold" had its origin in the recognition of this impulse. From those who spoke with authority have been chosen words in which the Word becomes flesh to dwell among us. Here are maxims, phrases, anecdotes, passages, proverbs and essays from the best minds among men; here are words of wisdom and thoughts of comfort for all mankind.

Consolation is the objective of "Leaves of Gold"; to provide a key to things of the spirit as inspiration for daily living, its design.

With unrelenting crescendo, the symphony of a life replete with melodic progression, hastens to its finale. And a friendship that is ours to share, with its "largos" and "allegros" moves ever-lasting; onward, in sweet memories.

Contents

I. ACTION

TWO DIVISIONS OF SOCIETY—There are two methods of human activity—and according to which one of these two kinds of activity people mainly follow, are there two kinds of people: one use their reason to learn what is good and what is bad and they act according to this knowledge; the other act as they want to and then they use their reason to prove that that which they did was good and that which they didn't do was bad.—*Leo Tolstoi.*

STANDARD OF JUDGMENT—Men are not to be judged by what they do not know, but by what they know, and by the manner in which they know it.
—*Vauvenargues.*

CHRISTIANITY— is not a voice in the wilderness, but a life in the world. It is not an idea in the air but feet on the ground, going God's way. It is not an exotic to be kept under glass, but a hardy plant to bear twelve months of fruits in all kinds of weather. Fidelity to duty is its root and branch. Nothing we can say to the Lord, no calling Him by great or dear names, can take the place of the plain doing of His will. We may cry out about the beauty of eating bread with Him in His kingdom, but it is wasted breath and a rootless hope, unless we plow and plant in His kingdom here and now. To remember Him at His table and to forget Him at ours, is to have invested in bad securities. There is no substitute for plain, every-day goodness.—*Babcock.*

TWO ALTERNATIVES—We shall meanly lose or nobly save the last hope of earth.—*Abraham Lincoln.*

TRAINING—An athlete was never made by mere instruction. No soldier was ever trained by the mere study of his manual, but by practising his drill. Not the hearers of the law, but the doers are justified before God. We must be going forward, not standing still, simply listening and learning. Where our duty is seen God is revealed. Duty is always the will of God. To see it and not to do it, is a most disastrous thing for the man, as well as being an offense against God.
—*Outlook.*

SERMONS WE SEE

*I'd rather see a sermon than hear one
    any day,
I'd rather one should walk with me
    than merely show the way.
The eye's a better pupil and more will-
    ing than the ear;
Fine counsel is confusing, but ex-
    ample's always clear;
And the best of all the preachers are
    the men who live their creeds,
For to see the good in action is what
    everybody needs.
I can soon learn how to do it if you'll
    let me see it done.
I can watch your hands in action, but
    your tongue too fast may run.
And the lectures you deliver may be
    very wise and true;
But I'd rather get my lesson by observ-
    ing what you do.
For I may misunderstand you and the
    high advice you give,
But there's no misunderstanding how
    you act and how you live.*
—EDGAR A. GUEST.

"Sermons We See" is from the book "The Light of Faith" by Edgar A. Guest, copyright 1926 by The Reilly & Lee Co., Chicago.

RIGHTEOUSNESS is the fulfillment of God's creative purpose in a man's whole life. It begins with the soul, the real eternal self, that is instinct with the life of the God from whom it came. It is the response of the highest in man to the claim of God.—*Percy C. Ainsworth.*

A Persian Proverb

He who knows not,
   And knows not that he knows not,
      Is a fool—shun him.
He who knows not,
   And knows that he knows not,
      Is a child—teach him.
He who knows,
   And knows not that he knows,
      Is asleep—wake him.
He who knows,
   And knows that he knows,
      Is wise—follow him.

SUPERFLUITY — True eloquence consists in saying all that is necessary, and nothing but what is necessary.
   —*La Rochefoucauld.*

PERSONALITY—It is not what he has, nor even what he does, which directly expresses the worth of a man, but what he is.—*Henri-Frederic Amiel.*

KISMET—I do not believe in a fate that falls on men however they act; but I do believe in a fate that falls on them unless they act.—*G. K. Chesterton.*

DOING VS. DREAMING — Do noble things, not dream them all day long: And so make Life, Death, and the vast Forever one grand, sweet song.
   —*Charles Kingsley.*

THE HARVEST—Sow a thought, reap an act; sow an act, reap a habit; sow a habit, reap a character; sow a character, reap a destiny.

WHO LIVES MOST?—We live in deeds, not years; in thoughts, not breaths; in feelings, not in figures on a dial. We should count time by heart-throbs. He most lives who thinks most, feels the noblest, acts the best.
   —*Philip James Bailey.*

Worth

It is not what the world gives me
In honor, praise or gold;
It is what I do give the world,
So others do unfold.

If by my work through life I can
Another soul unfold,
Then I have done what cannot be
Made good, by praise or gold.

One tiny thought in tiny word
May give a great one birth,
And, if that thought was caused by me,
I lived a life of worth.
   —*Richard F. Wolfe.*

DIVINE SERVICE—Unless we perform divine service with every willing act of our life, we never perform it at all.
   —*John Ruskin.*

GROWTH—All growth depends upon activity. There is no development physically or intellectually without effort, and effort means work. Work is not a curse; it is the prerogative of intelligence, the only means to manhood, and the measure of civilization.—*Calvin Coolidge.*

WHAT IS WORTHWHILE?—The world is blessed most by men who do things, and not by those who merely talk about them.—*James Oliver.*

The life of man is made up of action and endurance; the life is fruitful in the ratio in which it is laid out in noble action or in patient perseverance.—*Liddon.*

One thing, and only one, in this world has eternity stamped upon it. Feelings pass; resolves and thoughts pass; opinions change. What you have done lasts—lasts in you. Through ages, through eternity, what you have done for Christ, that, and only that, you are.

—*F. W. Robertson.*

It is well to think well; it is Divine to act well.—*Horace Mann.*

Existence was given us for action, rather than indolent and aimless contemplation; our worth is determined by the good deeds we do, rather than by the fine emotions we feel. They greatly mistake who suppose that God cares for no other pursuit than devotion.—*E. L. Magoon.*

SIN, by its deadly infusions into the soul of man, wastes and eats out the innate vigor of the soul, and casts it into such a deep lethargy, as that it is not able to recover itself.—*J. Smith.*

DISCIPLINE — Thank God every morning when you get up that you have something to do which must be done, whether you like it or not. Being forced to work, and forced to do your best, will breed in you temperance, self-control, diligence, strength of will, content, and a hundred other virtues which the idle never know.—*Charles Kingsley.*

DO SOMETHING—Observe what St. Paul did at Athens. He did something. He was not the man to stand still and "confer with flesh and blood" in the face of a city full of idols. He might have reasoned with himself that he stood alone; that he was a Jew by birth; that he was a stranger in a strange land; that he had to oppose the rooted prejudices and old associations of learned men; that to attack the old religion of a whole city was to beard a lion in his den; that the doctrines of the Gospel were little likely to be effective on minds steeped in Greek philosophy. But none of these thoughts seem to have crossed the mind of St. Paul. He saw souls perishing; he felt that life was short, and time passing away; he had confidence in the power of his Master's message to meet every man's soul; he had received mercy himself, and knew not how to hold his peace. He acted at once, and what his hand found to do he did with all his might. Oh, that we had more men of action in these days!—*Ryle.*

BEST

Like the star,
That shines afar,
Without haste
And without rest,
Let each man wheel with steady sway
Round the task that rules the day,
And do his best.

—*Goethe.*

REALITY—I will be a man among men; and no longer a dreamer among shadows. Henceforth be mine a life of action and reality! I will work in my own sphere, nor wish it other than it is. This alone is health and happiness.

—*Henry W. Longfellow.*

DECISION—The decisive man walks by the light of his own judgment; he has made up his mind; and, having done so, henceforth action is before him. He cannot bear to sit amidst unrealized speculations; to him speculation is only valuable that it may be resolved into living and doing. There is no indifference, no delay. The spirit is in arms: all is in earnest. Thus Pompey, when hazarding his life on a tempestuous sea in order to be at Rome on an important occasion, said, "It is necessary for me to go: it is not necessary for me to live." Thus Caesar, when he crossed the Rubicon, burned the ships upon the shore which brought his soldiers to land, that there might be no return.
—*Paxton Hood.*

THE MINISTER is to be a live man, a real man, a true man, a simple man, great in his love, great in his life, great in his work, great in his simplicity, great in his gentleness.—*John Hall.*

THE PREACHER who deals with the great truths of holy character must impersonate those truths. There is power inherent in truth; but it is often like electricity, needing a conductor to develop it. The preacher who best commends the truth of the gospel to his hearers is he who has translated that truth into his own life, until his life is full of it and redolent of it.—*Anonymous.*

PATIENCE
Let us, then, be up and doing,
With a heart for any fate;
Still achieving, still pursuing,
Learn to labor and to wait.
—*Henry W. Longfellow.*

MASTERPIECES—When love and skill work together expect a masterpiece.
—*Ruskin.*

WHICH ARE YOU?

An attender or an absenter?
A pillar or a sleeper?
A wing or a weight?
A power or a problem?
A promoter or a provoker?
A giver or a getter?
A goer or a gadder?
A doer or a deadhead?
A booter or a bucker?
A supporter or a sponger?
A soldier or a sorehead?
A worker or a worrier?
A friend or a fault-finder?
A helper or a hinderer?
A campaigner or a camper?
—*The Baptist.*

FORTUITOUS—The greatest pleasure I know is to do a good action by stealth and have it found out by accident.
—*Charles Lamb.*

THOUGHT—To act is easy; to think is hard. . .—*Goethe*

DAY DREAMING
I sleep
through my years, in
the shadow of my puny
cosmos, while I should be dusting
the stars.
—*Kermit Oswald.*

GOALS—I find the great thing in this world is, not so much where we stand, as in what direction we are moving.
—*Goethe.*

SCULPTORS—All in their life-time carve their own soul's statue.
—*Thomas Buchanan Read.*

II. ADVERSITY

BURDENS—I compare the troubles which we have to undergo in the course of the year to a great bundle of fagots, far too large for us to lift. But God does not require us to carry the whole at once. He mercifully unties the bundle, and gives us first one stick, which we are to carry today, and then another, which we are to carry tomorrow, and so on. This we might easily manage, if we would only take the burden appointed for us each day; but we choose to increase our troubles by carrying yesterday's stick over again today, and adding tomorrow's burden to our load, before we are required to bear it.—*John Newton.*

SUFFERING — Suffering overcomes the mind's inertia, develops the thinking powers, opens up a new world, and drives the soul to action.—*Anthony H. Evans.*

HIS YOKE IS EASY—A man was carrying a heavy basket. His son asked to help him. The father cut a stick and placed it through the handle of the basket so that the end toward himself was very short, while the end toward the boy was three or four times as long. Each took hold of his end of the stick, and the basket was lifted and easily carried. The son was bearing the burden with the father, but he found his work easy and light because his father assumed the heavy end of the stick. Just so it is when we bear the yoke with Christ; He sees to it that the burden laid on us is light; He carries the heavy end.—*John T. Faris.*

AFFLICTIONS—No affliction would trouble a child of God, if he knew God's reasons for sending it.—*Morgan.*

CARES—Just as there comes a warm sunbeam into every cottage window, so comes a love-beam of God's care and pity for every separate need.
—*Nathaniel Hawthorne.*

Sorrow

Go, bury thy sorrow,
  The world hath its share:
Go, bury it deeply,
  Go, hide it with care.
Go, bury thy sorrow,
  Let others be blest;
Go, give them the sunshine,
  And tell God the rest.

OPPORTUNITY

*With doubt and dismay you are
  smitten,
You think there's no chance for you,
  son?
Why, the best books haven't been
  written,
The best race hasn't been run,
The best score hasn't been made yet,
The best song hasn't been sung,
The best tune hasn't been played yet;
Cheer up, for the world is young!*

*No chance? Why, the world is just
  eager
For things that you ought to create.
Its store of true wealth is still meager,
Its needs are incessant and great;
Don't worry and fret, faint hearted,
The chances have just begun.
For the best jobs haven't been started,
The best work hasn't been done.*
—BERTON BRALEY.

Copyright by Berton Braley, all rights reserved.

SPIRITUAL INSIGHT — Illness knocks a lot of nonsense out of us; it induces humility, cuts us down to our own size. It enables us to throw a searchlight upon our inner selves and to discover how often we have rationalized our failures and weaknesses, dodged vital issues and run skulkingly away. For only when the way straitens and the gate grows narrow, do some people discover their soul, their God, or their life work.

Florence Nightingale, too ill to move from her bed, reorganized the hospitals of England. Semi-paralyzed, and under the constant menace of apoplexy, Pasteur was tireless in his attack on disease. The great American historian Francis Parkman is a triumphant prototype of all such conquerors of pain. During the greater part of his life, Parkman suffered so acutely that he could not work for more than five minutes at a time. His eyesight was so wretched that he could scrawl only a few gigantic words on a manuscript, yet he contrived to write nearly 20 magnificent volumes of history.

Even pain confers spiritual insight, a beauty of outlook, a philosophy of life, an understanding and forgiveness of humanity—in short, a quality of peace and serenity—that can scarcely be acquired by the "owner of pure horse flesh." Suffering is a cleansing fire that chars away much of the meanness, triviality and restlessness of so-called "health." Milton declared, "Who best can suffer, best can do." The proof is his *Paradise Lost* written after he was stricken blind.

—*Louis E. Bisch.*

TROUBLE—Great minds have purposes, others have wishes. Little minds are tamed and subdued by misfortune; but great minds rise above them.

—*Washington Irving.*

COMFORT OF PURE THOUGHT —The scholar only knows how dear these silent yet eloquent companions of pure thoughts and innocent hours become in the season of adversity. When all that is worldly turns to dross around us, these only retain their steady value. When friends grow cold, and the converse of intimates languishes into vapid civility and commonplace these only continue the unaltered countenance of happier days, and cheer us with that true friendship which never deceived hope nor deserted sorrow.—*Washington Irving.*

Joy Cometh in the Morning

They are not long, the weeping and the
  laughter,
  Love and desire and hate:
I think they have no portion in us after
  We pass the gate.

They are not long, the days of wine and
  roses:
  Out of a misty dream
Our path emerges for a while, then closes
  Within a dream.

—*Ernest Dowson.*

LIFE'S TESTS—The tests of life are to make, not break us. Trouble may demolish a man's business but build up his character. The blow at the outward man may be the greatest blessing to the inner man. If God, then, puts or permits anything hard in our lives, be sure that the real peril, the real trouble, is that we shall lose if we flinch or rebel.

—*M. D. Babcock.*

DIFFICULTIES—Life is always difficult in proportion to its intensity and reality.—*Edward Howard Griggs.*

Even This Shall Pass Away

Once in Persia reigned a King
Who upon his signet ring
Graved a maxim true and wise,
Which, if held before the eyes,
Gave him counsel at a glance,
Fit for every change and chance.
Solemn words, and these are they:
"Even this shall pass away."

Trains of camels through the sand
Brought his gems from Samarcand;
Fleets of galleys through the seas
Brought him pearls to match with these.
But he counted not his gain
Treasures of the mine or main;
"What is wealth?" the king would say;
"Even this shall pass away."

In the revels of his court
At the zenith of the sport,
When the palms of all his guests
Burned with clapping at his jests;
He amid his figs and wine,
Cried: "Oh loving friends of mine!
Pleasure comes but not to stay;
Even this shall pass away."

Fighting on a furious field,
Once a javelin pierced his shield;
Soldiers with a loud lament
Bore him bleeding to his tent;
Groaning from his tortured side,
"Pain is hard to bear," he cried,
"But with patience, day by day,—
Even this shall pass away."

Towering in the public square,
Twenty cubits in the air,
Rose his statue, carved in stone,
Then, the king, disguised, unknown,
Stood before his sculptured name
Musing meekly, "What is fame?
Fame is but a slow decay—
Even this shall pass away."

Struck with palsy, sere and old,
Waiting at the gates of gold,
Said he with his dying breath;
"Life is done, but what is death?"
Then, in answer to the King,
Fell a sunbeam on his ring,
Showing by a heavenly ray,
"Even this shall pass away."
—*Theodore Tilton.*

CROSS—In the cross of Christ we glory, because we regard it as a matchless exhibition of the attributes of God. We see there the love of God, desiring a way by which He might save mankind, aided by His wisdom, so that a plan is perfected by which the deed can be done without violation of truth and justice. In the cross we see a strange conjunction of what once appeared to be two opposite qualities— justice and mercy. We see how God is supremely just; as just as if He had no mercy, and yet infinitely merciful in the gift of His Son. Mercy and justice, in fact, become counsel upon the same side, and irresistibly plead for the acquittal of the believing sinner. We can never tell which of the attributes of God shines most glorious in the sacrifice of Christ; they each one find a glorious high throne in the person and work of the Lamb of God, that taketh away the sin of the world. Since it has become, as it were, the disc which reflects the character and perfections of God, it is meet that we should glory in the cross of Christ, and none shall stay us of our boasting.—*Spurgeon.*

BROKEN HOPES—As the tree is fertilized by its own broken branches and fallen leaves, and grows out of its own decay, so men and nations are bettered and improved by trial, and refined out of broken hopes and blighted expectations.
—*F. W. Robertson.*

SPIRITUAL RESOURCES — The man who has no refuge in himself, who lives, so to speak, in his front rooms, in the outer whirlwind of things and opinions, is not properly a personality at all.

He floats with the current, who does not guide himself according to higher principles, who has no ideal, no convictions—such a man is a mere article of the world's furniture—a thing moved, instead of a living and moving being—an echo, not a voice. The man who has no inner life is the slave of his surroundings, as the barometer is the obedient servant of the air at rest, and the weathercock the humble servant of the air in motion.
—*Henri-Frederic Amiel.*

Tears

When I consider life and its few years—
A wisp of fog betwixt us and the sun;
A call to battle and the battle done
Ere the last echo dies within our ears;
A rose choked in the grass; an hour of fears;
The gusts that past a darkening shore do beat;
A burst of music down an unlistening street—
I wonder at the idleness of tears.
Ye, old, old dead, and ye of yesternight,
Chieftains and bards and keepers of the sheep:
By every cup of sorrow that you had,
Loose me from tears, and make me see aright
How each hath back what once he stayed to weep;
Homer his sight, David his little lad!
—*Lizette Woodworth Reese.*

From THE SELECTED POEMS OF LIZETTE WOODWORTH REESE, copyright, 1926, by Lizette Woodworth Reese, and reprinted by permission of Rinehart & Company, Inc., Publishers.

HUMILITY—One of the great lessons seldom effectively taught in college is the lesson of humility. It is usually the first of a long series of lessons we learn in our postgraduate course, when "the cold, cold world" is our instructor. This was subtly suggested in a cartoon appearing once in a New York paper late in June. It pictured a young woman in cap and gown, armed with her college diploma and a sufficient amount of self-satisfied dignity. Confronting her was the grim visage of the old World himself, who remarked rather casually, "Well, who have we here?" "You evidently don't know me," replied the slightly pained young graduate; "I am Virginia Cordelia Smith, A.B." "My dear girl," replied the World, "come with me and I will teach you the rest of your alphabet."—*George Walter Fiske.*

COMPLAINT — Impatient people water their miseries and hoe up their comforts; sorrows are visitors that come without invitation, and complaining minds send a wagon to bring their troubles home in.—*C. H. Spurgeon.*

FAILURE—There are few positions in life in which difficulties have not to be encountered. These difficulties are, however, our best instructors, as our mistakes often form our best experience. We learn wisdom from failure more than from success. We often discover what will do by finding out what will not do. Horne Tooke used to say that he had become all the better acquainted with the country from having had the good luck sometimes to lose his way. Great thoughts, discoveries, inventions have very generally been nurtured in hardship, often pondered over in sorrow and established with difficulty.
—*Paxton Hood.*

OUT OF GREAT TRIBULATION

—No words can express how much the world owes to sorrow. Most of the Psalms were born in a wilderness. Most of the Epistles were written in a prison. The greatest thoughts of the greatest thinkers have all passed through fire. The greatest poets have "learned in suffering what they taught in song." In bonds Bunyan lived the allegory that he afterwards indited, and we may thank Bedford Jail for the "Pilgrim's Progress." Take comfort, afflicted Christian! When God is about to make pre-eminent use of a man, He puts him in the fire.—*Macdonald.*

BURDENS—We have all of us sufficient fortitude to bear the misfortunes of others.—*La Rochefoucauld.*

STRENGTH—We never have more than we can bear. The present hour we are always able to endure. As our day, so is our strength. If the trials of many years were gathered into one, they would overwhelm us; therefore, in pity to our little strength, He sends first one, and then another, then removes both, and lays on a third, heavier, perhaps, than either; but all is so wisely measured to our strength that the bruised reed is never broken. We do not enough look at our trials in this continuous and successive view. Each one is sent to teach us something, and altogether they have a lesson which is beyond the power of any to teach alone.—*H. E. Manning.*

MISFORTUNE—It requires greater virtues to support good fortune than bad.
—*La Rochefoucauld*

LIFE is a long lesson in humility.
—*James M. Barrie.*

THE ROSARY OF MY TEARS

Some reckon their age by years,
　Some measure their life by art;
But some tell their days by the flow of
　　their tears,
　And their lives by the moans of their
　　heart.

The dials of earth may show
　The length, not the depth of years,
Few or many they come, few or many
　　they go,
　But time is best measured by tears.

For the young are oft-times old,
　Though their brows be bright and fair;
While their blood beats warm, their
　　hearts are cold,
　O'er them the spring—but winter is
　　there.

And the old are oft-times young,
　When their hair is thin and white;
And they sing in age, as in youth they
　　sung,
　And they laugh for their cross was light.

But, bead by bead, I tell
　The rosary of my years,
From a cross to a cross they lead; 'tis well
　And they're blest with a blessing of
　　tears.

Better a day of strife
　Than a century of sleep;
Give me instead of a long stream of life
　The tempests and tears of the deep.

A thousand joys may foam
　On the billows of all the years;
But never the foam brings the lone back
　　home;
It reaches the haven through tears.
—*Abram J. Ryan.*

III. AGE

REVALUATION—Age, that lessens the enjoyment of life, increases our desire of living. Those dangers which, in the vigor of youth, we had learned to despise, assume new terrors as we grow old. Our caution increasing as our years increase, fear becomes at last the prevailing passion of the mind, and the small remainder of life is taken up in useless efforts to keep off our end, or provide for a continued existence. Whence, then, is this increased love of life, which grows upon us with our years? Whence comes it that we thus make greater efforts to preserve our existence at a period when it becomes scarce worth the keeping? Is it that Nature, attentive to the preservation of mankind, increases our wishes to live, while she lessens our enjoyments; and, as she robs the senses of every pleasure, equips imagination in the spoil? Life would be insupportable to an old man, who loaded with infirmities, feared death no more than when in the vigor of manhood: the numberless calamities of decaying Nature, and the consciousness of surviving every pleasure would at once induce him with his own hand to terminate the scene of misery: but happily the contempt of death forsakes him at a time when it could only be prejudicial, and life acquires an imaginary value in proportion as its real value is no more.—*Oliver Goldsmith.*

THE PRELUDES—Winter is on my head, but eternal spring is in my heart; I breathe at this hour the fragrance of the lilacs, the violets, and the roses, as at twenty years ago. The nearer I approach to the end, the plainer I hear around me the immortal symphonies of the worlds which invite me.—*Victor Hugo.*

REST

Rest is not quitting
    The busy career;
Rest is the fitting
    Of self to its sphere.
'Tis loving and serving
    The highest and best!
'Tis onwards, unswerving,
    And that is true rest.
                                    —*J. S. Dwight.*

QUIET MINDS can not be perplexed or frightened, but go on in fortune or misfortune at their own private pace, like a clock during a thunderstorm.
                    —*Robert Louis Stevenson.*

"THALATTA"

I stand upon the summit of my years.
Behind, the toil, the camp, the march,
    the strife,
The wandering and the desert; vast,
    afar,
Beyond this weary way, behold! the
    Sea!
The sea o'erswept by clouds and winds
    and wings,
By thoughts and wishes manifold,
    whose breath
Is freshness and whose mighty pulse is
    peace.
Palter no question of the dim Beyond;
Cut lose the bark; such voyage itself
    is rest;
Majestic motion, unimpeded scope,
A widening heaven, a current without
    care.
Eternity!   Deliverance,   Promise,
    Course!
Time-tired souls salute thee from the
    shore.

                        —J. B. BROWN.

FOOTFALLS—Yes, we are all growing old, though unconsciously, and the foot of time falls as softly as ever, and the current of life flows on as smoothly as ever —indeed, the fuller the current, the more noiseless its flow. And months and years are, after all, so very much alike that they pass away without special observation, and we begin to get old before we think of it. And when we sit down to a simple sum in arithmetic—the subtraction of the year of our birth from the current year— we are astonished at the answer, and are so doubtful of its correctness that we go over it a second time, but always with the same result. Children grow up around us, but we get used to that, and are so busy that we seldom stop to compute their ages and realize the swift flight of the years. In fact, our children never get old to us. The wife who has stood lovingly and faithfully at our side so long, never changes, and is always the fair young bride of the old and happy days. Though his hair may have grown grey in some way which we do not exactly understand, and his step may seem a little less elastic, and firm than it was, the husband does not seem to have changed much, after all—*Balfern.*

BETTER THAN SERMONS — I think that to have known one good, old man—one man, who, through the chances and mischances of a long life, has carried his heart in his hand, like a palm-branch, waving all discords into peace—helps our faith in God, in ourselves, and in each other more than many sermons.
—*G. W. Curtis.*

THE GREATEST SIN—Stanley Hall once called the great sin of maturity losing one's zest for life.

TRUTH—Did you ever see a man sitting in his own orchard with the trees (which he planted with his own hand) pouring down their ripened fruit upon him, and he and his children and his grandchildren rejoicing in its beauty? That is the picture of a man who took the truth and planted it, and now he is sitting under the boughs that overarch him. His days are happy and his life is full of joy and usefulness.

EVENTIDE

God loves the Aged.
He gives them greater visions than the
    young;
He puts the words of wisdom on their
    tongue;
And keeps His presence ever by their side,
From dawn to dusk, and on through even-
    tide.

God helps the Aged.
Within their home His Spirit ever dwells;
Their mellow hearts are touched like
    chiming bells;
He calms their fears, then worries dis-
    appear,
Because they know His help is always
    near.

God keeps the Aged.
With hearts of gold, and silver-tinted
    hair,
And earnestness, and greater faith in
    prayer;
He keeps them as a shepherd guards his
    sheep,
'Til in His fold they gently fall asleep.
    —*Charles W. H. Bancroft.*

BIRTHDAYS—Forty is the old age of youth; fifty is the youth of old age.
    —*Victor Hugo.*

SUCCESS—That you may find success, let me tell you how to proceed. Tonight begin your great plan of life. You have but one life to live; yet it is most important that you should not make a mistake. Tonight begin carefully. Fix your eye on the fortieth year of your age, and then say to yourself, "At the age of forty, I will be an industrious man, a benevolent man, a well-read man, a religious man, and a useful man; I resolve and will stand to it."

—C. Brooks.

When You Are Old

When you are old and gray and full of
　　sleep,
And nodding by the fire, take down this
　　book,
And slowly read and dream of the soft
　　look
Your eyes had once, and of their shadows
　　deep;

How many loved your moments of glad
　　grace,
And loved your beauty with love false or
　　true;
But one man loved the pilgrim soul in you,
And loved the sorrows of your changing
　　face.

And bending down beside the glowing
　　bars
Murmur, a little sadly, how love fled
And paced upon the mountains overhead
And hid his face amid a crowd of stars.

—William Butler Yeats.

From COLLECTED POEMS of William Butler Yeats. By permission of The Macmillan Company, publishers; The Macmillan Company of Canada; and A. P. Watts & Co., London.

PERSPECTIVE—To be seventy years young is sometimes far more cheerful and hopeful than to be forty years old.

—Oliver Wendell Holmes.

DIVINE DISCONTENT—Growth is gladdening. He who grows in holiness grows in joy. Spiritual strength brings gladness. It is a poor, half-hearted religion—not spiritual power, but the want of it—that breeds gloom. The consciousness that a man is becoming stronger in his faith, clearer in his convictions, warmer in his love, must, from its very nature, be a glad consciousness. And the hope of greater strength yet to be attained, of loftier heights yet to be reached, is more joyous still. A story is told of Torwaldsen, the sculptor, that on one occasion, when he was adding a few finishing touches to one of his masterpieces—a statue of Christ—a friend called upon him at his studio, and found him in a very depressed and despondent mood. On inquiring the cause of this unusual and apparently untimely depression, the sculptor gave this singular answer—pointing to his work, he said, "I can see no fault in it; my genius is decaying; it is the first of my works that I have felt satisfied with."—Messenger.

HEALTH—It is a sum of money in the bank, which will support you, economically spent. But you spend foolishly and draw on the principal. This diminishes the income, and you draw larger and larger drafts until you become bankrupt. Overeating, overworking, every imprudence is a draft on life which health cashes and charges at a thousand per cent interest. Every abuse of health hastens death!—F. G. Welch.

Serenity

And so, beside the silent sea,
　　I wait the muffled oar;
No harm from Him can come to me
　　On ocean or on shore.

—John Greenleaf Whittier.

GOODNESS — If you would keep young and happy, be good; live a high moral life; practice the principles of the brotherhood of man; send out good thoughts to all, and think evil of no man. This is in obedience to the great natural law; to live otherwise is to break this great Divine law. Other things being equal, it is the cleanest, purest minds that live long and are happy. The man who is growing and developing intellectually does not grow old like the man who has stopped advancing, but when ambition, aspirations and ideals halt, old age begins.—*Public Speakers Library.*

YOUTH — It is refreshing to find a clergyman willing to defend the youth of today. Unfortunately the defense of the youth of today is too frequently made by lawyers.—*Crane.*

The Threshold

The seas are quiet when the winds give
    o'er;
So calm are we when passions are no
    more.
For then we know how vain it was to
    boast
Of fleeting things, so certain to be lost.
Clouds of affection from our younger eyes
Conceal that emptiness which age des-
    cries.

The soul's dark cottage, batter'd and
    decay'd,
Lets in new light through chinks that
    Time hath made:
Stronger by weakness, wiser men become
As they draw near to their eternal home.
Loving the old, both worlds at once they
    view
That stand upon the threshold of the new.
    —*Edmund Waller.*

TIME—The days of the years of our pilgrimage are threescore years and ten. The generations crowd each other off the stage of time in swift succession. The sand runs out in the hour glass. Time is only the tick of the second hand in the clock of the ages. Some morning the senses will fail to resume business. Every door will be locked, every shutter drawn. Eye, ear, and hand will fail to respond. There will no longer be any medium by which to enter the temporal. An invisible hand has written "finis" across another human career, and people say "the man is dead." He has not ceased to be; he has merely finished with time.
    —*Anonymous.*

NEARER HOME—An aged Christian, with the snow of time on his head, may remind us that those points of earth are whitest which are nearest Heaven.
    —*Chapin.*

ASHES AND FLAMES—Oftentimes we look with forebodings to the time of old age, forgetful that at eventide it shall be light. To many saints of old age it is the choicest season in their lives. A balmier air fans the mariner's cheek as he nears the shore of immortality; fewer waves ruffle his sea, quiet reigns, deep, still, and solemn. From the altar of age the ashes of the fire of youth are gone, but the flame of more earnest feeling remains.
    —*Selected.*

BRINGING UP FATHER—When I was a boy of 14, my father was so ignorant I could hardly stand to have the old man around. But when I got to be 21, I was astonished at how much the old man had learned in seven years.
    —*Mark Twain.*

IV. ANALOGIES

LIKE FLAKES of snow that fall imperceptibly upon the earth, the seeming unimportant events of life succeed one another.—As the snowflakes gather, so our *habits* are formed.—No single flake that is added to the pile produces a sensible change—No single action creates, however it may exhibit, a man's character.—But as the tempest hurls the avalanche down the mountain and overwhelms the inhabitant and his habitation, so *passion*, acting on the elements of mischief which pernicious habits have brought together, may overthrow the edifice of truth and virtue.—*Bentham.*

GRAY HAIRS—seem to my fancy like the soft light of the moon, silvering over the evening of life.—*Richter.*

Enthusiasm is reason gone mad to achieve a definite, rational objective.

Enthusiasm is inflamed by opposition, but never converted; it is the leaping lighting that blasts obstacles from its path.

Enthusiasm is the X-ray of the soul, that penetrates and reveals the invisible.

Enthusiasm is a contagion that laughs at quarantine and inoculates all who come in contact with it.

Enthusiasm is the vibrant thrill in your voice that sways the wills of others into harmony with your own.

Enthusiasm is the "philosopher's stone" that transmutes dull tasks into delightful deeds.

Enthusiasm is a magnet that draws kindred souls with irresistible force and electrifies them with the magnetism of its own resolves.

—PRESBYTERIAN OF THE SOUTH.

DIFFICULTY is the nurse of *greatness* —a harsh nurse, who rocks her foster children roughly, but rocks them into strength and athletic proportions.—The mind, grappling with great aims and wrestling with mighty impediments, grows by a certain necessity to the stature of greatness—*Bryant.*

THE LOSS OF A FRIEND is like that of a limb; time may heal the anguish of the wound, but the loss cannot be repaired.—*Southey.*

THE SERMON OF LIFE—Our birth is the text. Youth the introduction. During manhood we lay down a few propositions and prove them. Some passages are dull and some sprightly. Then come Inferences and Application. At seventy we say, "Fifthly and lastly." The Doxology is sung. The Benediction is pronounced. The book is closed. It is getting cold. Frost on the window pane. Audience gone. Shut up the church. Sexton goes home with the key on his shoulder—*Talmage.*

HAPPINESS is like manna; it is to be gathered in grains, and enjoyed every day. It will not keep; it cannot be accumulated; nor have we got to go out of ourselves or into remote places to gather it, since it is rained down from Heaven, at our very doors.—*Tryon Edwards.*

FALSE HAPPINESS is like false money; it passes for a time as well as the true, and serves some ordinary occasions; but when it is brought to the touch, we find the lightness and alloy, and feel the loss.—*Pope.*

LIFE is like a beautiful and winding lane, on either side bright flowers, beautiful butterflies, and tempting fruits, which we scarcely pause to admire and taste, so eager are we to hasten to an opening which we imagine will be more beautiful still. But by degrees, as we advance, the trees grow bleak, the flowers and butterflies fail, the fruits disappear, and we find that we have arrived—to reach a desert waste.—*Sala.*

TROUBLES—I think that human life is much like road life. You stand on a hill, and look down and across the valley, and another prodigious hill lifts itself upon the other side. The day is hot, your horse is weary, and you are tired; and it seems to you that you cannot climb that long hill. But you had better trot down the hill you are on, and not trouble yourself about the other one. You find the valley pleasant and inspiring. When you get across it, you meet only a slight ascent, and begin to wonder where the steep hill is which your saw. You drive along briskly, and when you reach the highest point, you find that there has not been an inch of the hill over which you have not trotted. You see that it was illusory. The slight ascent looked almost like a perpendicular steep; but when you come to pass over it, step by step, you find it to be a good traveling road.

So it is with your troubles. Just in that way your anticipations of mischief hang before you; and when you come to where they are, you find them to be all smooth turnpikes. Men ought to be ashamed, after they have done that two or three times, not to take the hint, and profit by it; yet they will not. They will suffer from anticipated troubles just as much as though they had no such experience. They have not wit enough to make use of the lesson which their life is continually teaching them;

namely, that a large majority of the troubles which they worry themselves about beforehand either never come or are easily borne. They form a habit of fretting about future troubles. It was not the old monks alone who wore sackcloth and hair shirts; you wear them as much as they did; only you wear them inside, while they wore them outside—you wear them in your heart, they wore them on their skins. They were wiser than you are.—*Beecher.*

DESPAIR is like forward children, who, when you take away one of their playthings, throw the rest into the fire for madness. It grows angry with itself, turns its own executioner, and revenges its misfortunes on its own head—*Charron.*

HAPPINESS is as a butterfly, which, when pursued, is always beyond our grasp, but which, if you will sit down quietly, may alight upon you.

—*Hawthorne.*

OUR DEEDS are seeds of fate, sown here on earth, but bringing forth their harvest in eternity.—*Boardman.*

REVERENCE—It is with men as with wheat; the light heads are erect even in the presence of Omnipotence, but the full heads bow in reverence before Him.

—*Cooke.*

GENIUS is the gold in the mine; talent is the miner who works and brings it out.

—*Lady Blessington.*

GOSSIP, pretending to have the eyes of Argus, has all the blindness of a bat.

—*Ouida.*

PALM TREE—The Scripture says: "The righteous shall flourish like the palm tree." Let us see what this comparison means: "The palm grows not in the depths of the forest or in a fertile loam, but in the desert. Its verdure often springs apparently from the scorching dust. 'It is a friendly lighthouse, guiding the traveler to the spot where water is to be found.'" The tree is remarkable for its beauty, its erect aspiring growth, its leafy canopy, its waving plumes, the emblem of praise in all ages. Its very foliage is the symbol of joy and exultation. It never fades, and the dust never settles upon it. It was, therefore, twisted into the booths of the feasts of tabernacles, was borne aloft by the multitude that accompanied the Messiah to Jerusalem, and it is represented as in the hands of the redeemed in Heaven. For usefulness, the tree is unrivalled. Gibbon says that the natives of Syria speak of 360 uses to which the palm is applied. Its shade refreshes the traveler. Its fruit restores his strength. When his soul fails for thirst, it announces water. Its stones are ground for his camels. Its leaves are made into couches, its boughs into fences and walls, and its fibres into ropes or rigging. Its best fruit, moreover, is borne in old age; the finest dates being often gathered when the tree has reached a hundred years. It sends, too, from the same root a large number of suckers, which in time, form a forest by their growth. What an emblem of the righteous in the desert of a guilty world!—*Joseph Angus.*

THE ACTIONS of men are like the index of a book; they point out what is most remarkable in them.—*Heine.*

BEAUTY is like an almanac: if it lasts a year it is well.—*T. Adams.*

HAPPINESS is a sunbeam which may pass through a thousand bosoms without losing a particle of its original ray; nay, when it strikes a kindred heart, like the converged light upon a mirror, it reflects itself with redoubled brightness.—It is not perfected till it is shared.—*Jane Porter.*

WISE ANGER is like the fire from the flint; there is a great ado to bring it out; and when it does come, it is out again immediately.—*M. Henry.*

LIFE, like war, is a series of mistakes, and he is not the best Christian nor the best general who makes the fewest mistakes. Poor mediocrity may secure that, but he is best who wins the most splendid victories by the retrieval of mistakes.
—*Robertson.*

HOPE is like the sun, which, as we journey toward it, casts the shadow of our burden behind us.—*S. Smiles.*

THE LIGHT of *friendship* is like the light of phosphorus, seen plainest when all around it is dark.—*Crowell.*

DEATH is the golden key that opens the palace of eternity.—*Milton.*

MARRIAGE resembles a pair of shears, so joined that they cannot be separated, often moving in opposite directions, yet always punishing anyone who comes between them.—*Sydney Smith.*

REASON clears and plants the wilderness of the imagination to harvest the wheat of art.—*Austin O'Malley.*

THE EVERYDAY CARES and duties, which men call drudgery, are the weights and counterpoises of the clock of time, giving its pendulum a true vibration, and its hands a regular motion; and when they cease to hang upon the wheels, the pendulum no longer swings, the hands no longer move, and the clock stands still.
—*Longfellow.*

NATURE is the glass reflecting God, as by the sea reflected is the sun, too glorious to be gazed on in his sphere.
—*Young.*

MARRIAGE is the Keeley cure for love's intoxication.—*Helen Rowland.*

HOPE is like the cork to a net, which keeps the soul from sinking in despair; and *fear*, like the lead in the net, which keeps it from floating in presumption.
—*Watson.*

A BOOK may be compared to your neighbor: if it be good, it cannot last too long; if bad, you cannot get rid of it too early.—*Brooke.*

NATURE is an Aeolian harp, a musical instrument, whose tones are the re-echo of the higher strings within us.—*Novalis.*

FALSE FRIENDSHIP, like the ivy, decays and ruins the wall it embraces; but *true friendship* gives new life and animation to the object it supports.—*Burton.*

MEN'S FAME is like their hair, which grows after they are dead, and with just as little use to them.—*Villiers.*

SPIRIT—The new position of the Christian is like that of a bankrupt, for whom his liabilities have been met, and who is set up with a new capital, in a new partnership, to make a new start in a new world. God interests Himself for His client's future righteousness. God frees him from the obligations of the past that he may henceforth labor, unencumbered with any liabilities, at this righteousness. God supplies power for this righteousness by a special grant of His own spirit from Himself.—*T. Griffith.*

OVID FINELY compares a broken *fortune* to a falling column; the lower it sinks, the greater the weight it is obliged to sustain.—*Goldsmith.*

THE MARRIED MAN is like the bee that fixes his hive, augments the world, benefits the republic, and by daily diligence, without wronging any, profits all; but he who contemns wedlock, like a wasp, wanders an offense in the world, lives upon spoil, disturbs peace, steals sweets that are none of his own, and meets misery as his just reward.—*Feltham.*

THE AVARICIOUS man is like the barren sandy ground of the desert which sucks in all the rain and dew with greediness, but yields no fruitful herbs or plants for the benefit of others.—*Zeno.*

DEATH is like thunder in two particulars: we are alarmed at the sound of it, and it is formidable only from that which has preceded it.—*Colton.*

A NOBLE DEED is a step toward God.—*Holland.*

DIVINE FIRE—Look at a coal covered with ashes; there is nothing appearing in the hearth but only dead ashes; there is neither light, nor smoke, nor heat; and yet when these embers are stirred to the bottom, there are found some living gleams, which do but contain fire, and are apt to propagate it. Many a Christian breast is like this hearth, no life of grace appearing there for the time, either to his own sense or to the apprehension of others. Whilst the season of temptation lasteth, all seems cold and dead; yet still at the worst there is a secret coal in his bosom, which, upon the gracious motion of the Almighty, doth manifest some remainders of that Divine fire, as is easily raised to a perfect flame. Let no man, therefore, deject himself, or censure others, for the utter extinction of that spirit which doth but hide itself in the soul for a glorious advantage.—*Spencer.*

LEARNING is like mercury, one of the most powerful and excellent things in the world in skillful hands; in the unskillful, the most mischievous.—*Pope.*

LIFE, like a dome of many-colored glass, stains the white radiance of eternity.—*Shelley.*

CLEAR WRITERS, like clear fountains, do not seem so deep as they are; the turbid look the most profound.
—*Landor.*

PITHY SENTENCES are like sharp nails which force truth upon our memory.
—*Diderot.*

JOYS are our wings; sorrows our spurs.
—*Richter.*

MINISTERS should not be merely like dials on watches, or milestones on the road, but like clocks and sirens, to sound the alarm to sinners. Aaron wore bells as well as pomegranates, and the prophets were commanded to lift up their voices like a trumpet. A sleeping sentinel may be the loss of the city.—*Joseph Hall.*

AS WINTER strips the leaves from around us, so that we may see the distant regions they formerly concealed, so *old age* takes away our enjoyments only to enlarge the prospect of the coming eternity.—*Richter.*

DOUBT is the vestibule which all must pass before they can enter the temple of wisdom.—*Colton.*

IT IS of *eloquence* as of a flame; it requires matter to feed it, and motion to excite it; and it brightens as it burns.
—*Tacitus.*

HUMILITY—Trees that, like the poplar, lift upward all their boughs, give no shade and shelter whatever their height. Trees the most lovingly shelter and shade us when, like the willow, the higher soar their summits, the lowlier droop their boughs.—*Bulwer.*

AN UNGRATEFUL MAN is like a hog under a tree eating acorns, but never looking up to see where they come from.
—*Timothy Dexter.*

FALSE FRIENDS are like our shadow, keeping close to us when we walk in the sunshine, but leaving us the instant we cross into the shade.—*Bovee.*

HE WHO does a kindness to an *ungrateful* person, sets his seal to a flint and sows his seed upon sand; on the former he makes no impression, and from the latter finds no product.—*South.*

TEARS are the safety valve of the heart when too much pressure is laid on it.—*Albert Smith.*

LIKE the bee, we should make our *industry* our amusement.—*Goldsmith.*

AN UNJUST ACCUSATION is like a barbed arrow, which must be drawn backward with horrible anguish, or else it will be your destruction.

—*Jeremy Taylor.*

LEISURE is a beautiful garment, but it will not do for constant wear.—*Anon.*

LEARNING, like money, may be so base a coin as to be utterly void of use; or, if sterling, may require good management to make it serve the purposes of sense or happiness.—*Shenstone.*

LIFE is like music; it must be composed by ear, feeling, and instinct, not by rule.—*Samuel Butler.*

JEALOUSY is like a polished glass held to the lips when life is in doubt; if there be breath it will catch the damp and show it.—*Dryden.*

THE SORROWS of a noble soul are as May frosts, which precede the milder season; but the sorrows of a hardened, lost soul are as autumn frosts, which foretell but the coming of winter.—*Richter.*

SORROW is our John the Baptist, clad in grim garments, with rough arms, a son of the wilderness, baptizing us with bitter tears, preaching repentance; and behind him comes the gracious, affectionate, healing Lord, speaking peace and joy to the soul.—*Huntington.*

A PRINTED SPEECH is like a dried flower: the substance indeed is there, but the color is faded and the perfume gone.

—*Lorain.*

UNITY—In a mighty auditorium are four men. They really desire to come together, but neither will come to another's corner. In the center of the room is a beautiful fountain. Finally someone proposes that they all meet at the fountain. They start for the common center. They come on —forty—fifty—one hundred feet. The nearer they come to the fountain, the nearer they come to each other, each making concessions of location and space. At last they reach their destination, and clasp hands around the sparkling waters of the fountain. Jesus Christ, the great fountain of life, liberty and love, is set up in the center of the world. The nearer God's children come to Christ, the nearer they will come to each other. Let us help hasten the day when we can all clasp hands and sing, "Blest be the tie that binds our hearts in Christian love." Let the Christian world strike hands in the spirit of those of old, who said, "We are brethren."—*Hall.*

STYLE is the gossamer on which the seeds of truth float through the world.

—*Bancroft.*

TIME is the chrysalis of eternity.

—*Richter.*

COMPARISONS—Robert Hall once told a minister that the chief fault he found with his sermons was that there were no "likes" in them. He didn't like them on that account. I must say I shouldn't care to live in a house that was all windows, yet I fancy it would be rather dull and dingy in a house that hadn't any. An occasional opening relieves the deadness of the brick wall. So Christ's utterances were lit up with frequent "likes" of all kinds, and the "common people" were charmed with them, and liked them uncommonly.

Benjamin Franklin, the distinguished natural philosopher, made known to the world some of his important discoveries in regard to lightning and electricity by means of such a paltry instrument as a child's kite. So the Great Teacher that came from God brought the most exalted truths down to the level of the humblest understanding, and that through the use of comparisons and illustrations the most simple and plain possible. He took them all from every-day life. He used to talk to farmers about corn and mustard, wheat and tares, sheep and goats, and such like matters, all purely agricultural, and which they thoroughly understood. He used to talk to fishermen about matters widely different, and such as belonged to their craft—nets and fishes; to gardeners about vines and fig-trees; to women about domestic matters, such as come within their province—kneading dough and sweeping houses. By means of these familiar figures He teaches lessons unheard-of before—lessons of Divine wisdom, of supreme value, of sweet interest, of infinite love, and of eternal importance.—*Thomas.*

TEMPTATION is the fire that brings up the scum of the heart.—*Boston.*

PRIDE, like laudanum and other poisonous medicines, is beneficial in small, though injurious in large, quantities. No man who is not pleased with himself, even in a personal sense, can please others.
—*Frederick Saunders*

KNOWLEDGE is not a couch whereon to rest a searching and restless spirit; nor a terrace for a wandering mind to walk upon with a fair prospect; nor a tower of state for a proud mind to raise itself upon; nor a sort of commanding ground for strife and contention; nor a shop for profit and sale; but a rich storehouse for the glory of the Creator, and the relief of man's estate.—*Bacon.*

PRAISE—No ashes burn lighter than those of incense, and few things burn out sooner.—*Landor.*

OH! TO BE CLEAN as a mountain river! Clean as the air above the clouds, or on the middle seas! As the throbbing ether that fills the gulf between star and star! Nay, as the thought of the Son of Man Himself.—*George Macdonald.*

SUNDAY is the golden clasp that binds together the volume of the week.
—*Longfellow.*

PRIDE, like a magnet, constantly points to one object, self; unlike the magnet, it has no attractive pole, but at all points repels.—*Colton.*

CHURCH—The church is not a dormitory for sleepers, it is an institution for workers; it is not a rest camp, it is a front line trench.—*Sunday.*

CHRISTIANS are like the several flowers in a garden that have each of them the dew of Heaven, which, being shaken with the wind, they let fall at each other's roots, whereby they are jointly nourished, and become nourishers of each other.—*John Bunyan.*

PRIDE is to character, like the attic to the house—the highest part, and generally the most empty.—*Gay.*

Life is a web, time is a shuttle, and man is a weaver. The principle of action is a thread in the web of life. Of that web, two things are true, that which enters therein will reappear, and nothing will reappear which was not put therein.
—*J. H. Newman.*

THE VIRTUES, like the Muses, are always seen in groups. A good principle was never found solitary in any breast.
—*Jane Porter.*

WORLDLY RICHES are like nuts: many clothes are torn in getting them, many a tooth broken in cracking them, but never a belly filled with eating them.
—*Venning.*

AS THE IVY twines around the oak, so *misery* and *misfortune* encompass the happiness of man. Felicity, pure and unalloyed, is not a plant of earthly growth; her gardens are in the skies.—*Burton.*

A WORLD without a *Sabbath* would be like a man without a smile, like a summer without flowers, and like a homestead without a garden. It is the joyous day of the whole week.—*Beecher.*

THE MAN without *purpose* is like a ship without a rudder—a waif, a nothing, a no man. Have a purpose in life, and, having it, throw such strength of mind and muscle into your work as God has given you.—*Carlyle.*

TEMPTATIONS are a file which rub off much of the rust of our self-confidence.
—*Fenelon.*

ARCHITECTS—Many men build as cathedrals were built—the part nearest the ground finished, but that part which soars toward heaven, the turrets and the spires, forever incomplete. A kitchen, a cellar, a bar and a bedroom, these are the whole of some men, the only apartments in their soul-house. Many men are mere warehouses full of merchandise, the head, the heart stuffed with goods. Like those houses in the lower streets of the city which were once family dwellings, but are now used for commercial purposes, there are apartments in their souls which were once tenanted by taste and love and joy and worship; but they are all deserted now, and the rooms are filled with earthly and material things.
—*Beecher.*

TEARS are often the telescope through which men see far into heaven.
—*Beecher.*

CONSCIENCE—When it has lost its delicate sensibility, and its power of direction, there seems to be only one method of restoration, and that is by placing it alongside of a pure standard of right and wrong, as the magnetized iron which has lost its virtue is restored by being bound up for a time with a correctly pointing magnet.—*McCosh.*

A MAN who hoards up *riches* and enjoys them not is like an ass that carries gold and eats thistles.—*Burton.*

SORROW is only one of the lower notes in the oratorio of our blessedness.
—*Armistead Gordon.*

HOPE may be described as the flower of desire. It expects that the object shall be attained. It bars despondence and anticipates good. It shakes the mind from stagnations, and animates to encounter danger, and is the balm of life. Though at times it may be associated with doubt and solicitude, yet when hesitance is displaced, it swells into joy and ecstacy. Hope may be held to be universal and permanent. It is entwined with every other affection and passion. It always originates beneficial effects. It animates desire, and is a secret source of pleasure in the transports of joy. Joy triumphs in the success which hope presages will be permanent. It administers consolation in distress—quickens all our pursuits, and communicates to the mind the pleasure of anticipation. This influence, though mild, is nevertheless exhilarating and salutary. There is no happiness which hope cannot promise, no difficulty which it cannot surmount, no grief which it cannot mitigate. It is the wealth of the indigent, the health of the sick, the freedom of the captive, the rest of the toiler.—*Cuyler.*

OUR PRAYER and God's mercy are like two buckets in a well; while one ascends, the other descends.—*Hopkins.*

IT IS with a *word* as with an arrow—once let it loose and it does not return.
—*Abd-el-Kader.*

VIRTUE is like an angel; but she is a blind one and must ask knowledge to show her the pathway that leads to her goal. Mere knowledge, on the other hand, like a Swiss mercenary, is ready to combat either in the ranks of sin or under the banners of righteousness.—*Horace Mann.*

TRIALS are medicines which our gracious and wise physician prescribes, because we need them; and he proportions the frequency and weight of them to what the case requires. Let us trust his skill and thank him for his prescription.
—*Newton.*

WORDS are like leaves; and where they most abound, much fruit of sense beneath is seldom found.—*Pope.*

REASON is like the sun, of which the light is constant, uniform, and lasting; fancy, a meteor of bright but transitory lustre; irregular in its motion and delusive in its direction.—*Johnson.*

FRAGMENTS

What is poetry? Is it a mosaic
   Of colored stones which curiously are
      wrought
   Into a pattern? Rather glass that's
      taught
By patient labor any hue to take
And glowing with a sumptuous splendor,
   make
   Beauty a thing of awe where sunbeams caught,
   Transmitted fall in sheafs of rainbows
      fraught
With storied meaning for religion's sake.
—*Amy Lowell.*

V. APPRECIATION

SPIRITUAL DISCERNMENT.— When a man stood before one of Turner's unrivalled paintings and said, "I can see nothing in it," the great artist replied, "Don't you wish you could?" A tourist upon his return home was asked what he thought of Notre Dame, and the Sistine Madonna, and some other of the world's remarkable productions. He said he did not see them, and went on to say that while his wife did the Cathedrals and his daughter did the art galleries, he did the cafes. There are some things that must be spiritually discerned and appreciated, and if eyes are blind, and heart is dull, and the soul desensitized, no wonder it is difficult to appreciate the higher things of God.—*Swift.*

RECOMPENSE — Do right, and God's recompense to you will be the power of doing more right. Give, and God's reward to you will be the spirit of giving more; a blessed spirit, for it is the Spirit of God Himself, whose Life is the blessedness of giving. Love, and God will pay you with the capacity of more love; for love is Heaven—love is God within you.—*F. W. Robertson.*

LOVE AND UNDERSTANDING —I am happy in having learned to distinguish between ownership and possession. Books, pictures, and all the beauty of the world belong to those who love and understand them—not usually to those who possess them. All of these things that I am entitled to I have—I own them by divine right. So I care not a bit who possesses them. I used to care very much and consequently was very unhappy.
—*James Howard Kehler.*

PRAISE—A noted editor once noticed a particularly fine achievement by a friend, also an editor. He thought he would write immediately a letter of congratulation to his friend. But he didn't. There was a day or two of delay, and then he said to himself, "Oh, pshaw! he will get hundreds of other notes about it, so I shall not bother him with mine." Then he met his friend and told him how it happened he had failed to send his letter of commendation. "How many do you think I did receive?" asked the friend. The editor guessed many scores. But the real answer was, "Not one."
—*John T. Faris.*

IF I HAD THE TIME

*If I had the time to find a place
And sit me down full face to face
　With my better self, that stands no
　　show
In my daily life that rushes so,
It might be then I would see my soul
Was stumbling still toward the shin-
　ing goal—
　I might be nerved by the thought
　　sublime,
　　If I had the time!*

*If I had the time to learn from you
How much for comfort my word would
　do;
　And I told you then of my sudden
　　will
　To kiss your feet when I did you ill—
If the tears aback of the bravado
Could force their way and let you
　know—
　Brothers, the souls of us all would
　　chime,
　　If we had the time!*
—RICHARD BURTON.

ASK Him to increase your powers of sympathy: to give you more quickness and depth of sympathy, in little things as well as great. Opportunities of doing a kindness are often lost from mere want of thought. Half a dozen lines of kindness may bring sunshine into the whole day of some sick person. Think of the pleasure you might give to some one who is much shut up, and who has fewer pleasures than you have, by sharing with her some little comfort or enjoyment that you have learned to look upon as a necessary of life,—the pleasant drive, the new book, flowers from the country, etc. Try to put yourself in another's place. Ask "What should I like myself, if I were hard-worked, or sick, or lonely?" Cultivate the habit of sympathy.

—*G. H. Wilkinson.*

UNKINDNESS—Go to the grave of buried love, and meditate. There settle thy account with thy conscience for every past benefit unrequited, every past endearment unregarded, of that departed being, who can never, never return to be soothed by thy contrition. If thou art a husband, and hast ever caused that fond bosom that ventured its whole happiness in thy arms to doubt one moment of thy kindness or thy truth; if thou hast ever wronged in thought, in word, or deed, the spirit that generously confided in thee; if thou hast ever given one unremitted pang to that true heart which now lies cold and still beneath thy feet, then be sure that every unkind look, every ungracious word, every ungentle action will come thronging back upon thy memory, and knocking dolefully at thy soul. Then be sure that thou wilt lie down sorrowing and repentant at the grave, and utter the unheard groan, and pour the unavailing tear, more deep, more bitter because

unavailing. Then weave thy chaplet of flowers, and strew the beauties of nature about the grave; console thy broken spirit, if thou canst, with those tender but futile tributes of regret; but take warning by the bitterness of this thy contrite affliction over the dead, and be more faithful and affectionate in the duties to the living.

—*Irving.*

Give Them the Flowers Now

Closed eyes can't see the white roses,
   Cold hands can't hold them, you know,
Breath that is stilled can not gather
   The odors that sweet from them blow
Death, with a peace beyond dreaming,
   Its children of earth doth endow;
Life is the time we can help them,
   So give them the flowers now!

Here are the struggles and striving,
   Here are the cares and the tears;
Now is the time to be smoothing
   The frowns and the furrows and fear,
What to closed eyes are kind sayings?
   What to hushed heart is deep vow?
Naught can avail after parting,
   So give them the flowers now!

Just a kind word or a greeting;
   Just a warm grasp or a smile—
There are the flowers that will lighten
   The burdens for many a mile.
After the journey is over
   What is the use of them; how
Can they carry them who must be carried?
   Oh, give them the flowers now!

Blooms from the happy heart's garden
   Plucked in the spirit of love;
Blooms that are earthly reflections
   Of flowers that blossom above.
Words cannot tell what a measure
   Of blessing such gifts will allow
To dwell in the lives of many,
   So give them the flowers now!

—*Leigh M. Hodges.*

DEBTORS—When Paul said, "I am a debtor to both the Greeks and to the barbarians, both to the wise and to the unwise," he did not mean that he had received anything from them for which he was bound to pay them. He had never bought anything in their markets without giving its price; neither had they lent him any sums on interest. No human being had any pecuniary claim against him. Neither did he owe to Greek or barbarian any gratitude for favors which he had received at their hands, for in almost every city in which he labored he had encountered persecution and suffered wrong.

Not, therefore, on the ground of anything which he had obtained from them, but solely on the ground of that which he had received from another for them, does he acknowledge himself the debtor. "The glorious Gospel of the blessed God" had been "committed" to his "trust;" he had been "allowed of God to be put in trust with the Gospel" for their benefit, and therefore, that he might be a faithful steward of the mysteries of God, he was exceedingly desirous of preaching the truth, as it is in Jesus, to men of every nation and of every degree. He could not honestly hold it back. It had not been given to him for himself alone; and if he had attempted to keep it from his fellowmen, he would have been guilty of the greatest defalcation, and could not have vindicated himself either at the bar of conscience, or at the bar of God.

This explains the earnestness, the perseverance, and the self-sacrifice of his missionary life.—*Cuyler.*

INDIFFERENCE—It is a sad thing to reflect that in a world so overflowing with goodness of smell, of fine sights and sweet sounds, we pass by hastily and take so little note of them.—*David Grayson.*

KIND—The Christian surely means to be considerate and kind in Heaven! But why not here on earth and in these trying circumstances where perhaps his friends and neighbors need it most?
—*Bolton Jones.*

WORKING WITH GOD—If I can put one touch of rosy sunset into the life of any man or woman, I shall feel that I have worked with God.
—*George Macdonald.*

ONE IN TEN—There were ten lepers healed, and only one turned back to give thanks, but it is to be noticed that our Lord did not recall His gift from the other nine because of their lack of gratitude. When we begin to lessen our acts of kindness and helpfulness because we think those who receive do not properly appreciate what is done for them, it is time to question our own motives.

TOO LATE—There is a wealth of unexpressed love in the world. It is one of the chief causes of sorrow evoked by death: what might have been said or might have been done that never can be said or done.—*Arthur Hopkins.*

A ROSE TO THE LIVING

A rose to the living is more
    Than sumptuous wreaths to the
        dead;
In filling love's infinite store,
    A rose to the living is more
If graciously given before
    The hungering spirit is fled—
A rose to the living is more,
    Than sumptuous wreaths to the
        dead.
—*Nixon Waterman.*

33

THE ALABASTER BOX—Do not keep the alabaster box of your love and friendship sealed up until your friends are dead. Fill their lives with sweetness. Speak approving, cheering words while their ears can hear them, and while their hearts can be thrilled and made happier. The kind things you mean to say when they are gone, say before they go.
—*George W. Childs.*

THANKFULNESS—First among the things to be thankful for is a thankful spirit. Some people would grumble at the accommodations in Heaven if they ever got there. They take their blessings here so much as a matter of course, that even a day of general thanksgiving once in a year is more than they feel any need of. And if their personal blessings in any measure fail, gratitude for what they have had or still enjoy is the last thing they think of. Another class really desire to be thankful, but they are naturally despondent. Their sky is as dark with clouds as though a special Old Probabilities were employed to keep it full. They go through the world in a deprecating spirit, hoping things may turn out well yet fearing for the worst. We always feel glad for this class when Thanksgiving Day comes around. They then have an official warrant for gratitude. If their own hearts do not formulate blessings, they can listen to the sermon, or look to the President's proclamation.

How different with the thankful heart! What a gift it is to be born with an outlook toward the bright side of things! And if not so by nature, what a triumph of grace to be made thankful through a renewed heart! It is so much more comfortable and rational to see what we have to be thankful for and to rejoice accordingly, than to have our vision for ever filled with our lacks and our needs. Happy are they who possess this gift! Blessings may fail and fortunes vary, but the thankful heart remains. The happy past, at least, is secure—and Heaven is ahead.
—*Golden Rule.*

Gratitude

O Thou, whose bounty fills my cup
  With every blessing meet!
I give Thee thanks for every drop—
  The bitter and the sweet.
I praise Thee for the desert road,
  And for the riverside;
For all Thy goodness hath bestowed,
  And all Thy grace denied.
—*Jane Crewdson.*

WASTED OPPORTUNITY—Ruskin once said that when we fail to praise a man who deserves praise, two sad things happen; we run a chance of driving him from the right road for want of encouragement, and we deprive ourselves of one of the very happiest of our privileges, the privilege of rewarding labor that deserves a reward.

High thoughts and noble in all lands
  Help me; my soul is fed by such.
But ah, the touch of lips and hands—
  The human touch!
Warm, vital, close, life's symbols dear,—
These need I most, and now, and here.
—*Richard Burton.*

"Shut in with God! O wondrous thought:
Shut in with the peace his sufferings
  brought;
Shut in with the love that wields the rod:
O company blest! Shut in with God!"

VI. ASPIRATION

BUILDING TEMPLES — The Bible tells of dreamers, and among the most conspicuous was Joseph. He told his dreams to his brothers, and his brothers hated him because of his dreams. One day when his father sent him out where his brothers were keeping their flocks in Dothan, they saw him coming afar off and said: "Behold, the dreamer cometh." They plotted to kill him—and he is not the only dreamer who has been plotted against in this old world. But finally they decided that instead of killing him they would put him down in a pit; but some merchants passing that way, the brothers decided to sell him to the merchants, and the merchants carried Joseph down into Egypt.

Time went on and the brothers had almost forgotten the dreamer Joseph. But a famine came,—yes a famine,—and then they had to go down into Egypt, and buy corn, and when they got there, they found the dreamer—and he had the corn. So I decided that it was not so bad after all for one to be a dreamer—if one has the corn.

But the more I thought of the dreamer's place in history, the less I felt entitled to the distinction. John Boyle O'Reilly says that: "The dreamer lives forever, while the toiler dies in a day."

In traveling through Europe you find great cathedrals. An architect had a vision of a temple of worship and he put that vision upon paper. Then the builders began, and they laid stone upon stone and brick upon brick, until finally the temple was completed—completed sometimes centuries after the dreamer's death. And people now travel from all corners of the world to look upon the temple, and the name of the dreamer is known while the names of the toilers are forgotten.

No, I cannot claim a place among the dreamers, but there has been a great dreamer in the realm of statesmanship— Thomas Jefferson. He saw a people bowed beneath oppression and he had a vision of a self-governing nation, in which every citizen would be a sovereign. He put his vision upon paper, and for more than a century multitudes have been building. They are building at this temple in every nation; some day it will be completed and then the people of all the world will find protection beneath its roof and security within its walls. I shall be content if, when my days are numbered, it can be truthfully said of me that with such ability as I possessed, and whenever opportunity offered, I labored faithfully with the multitude to build this building higher in my time.

—*William Jennings Bryan.*

GOD THE ARCHITECT

Who Thou art I know not
But this much I know;
Thou hast set the Pleiades
In a silver row;

Thou hast sent the trackless winds
Loose upon their way;
Thou hast reared a colored wall
Twixt the night and day;

Thou hast made the flowers to bloom
And the stars to shine;
Hid rare gems of richest ore
In the tunneled mine;

But chief of all Thy wondrous works,
Supreme of all Thy plan,
Thou hast put an upward reach
Into the heart of man.

—HARRY KEMP.

VISION—It was sagacious Thomas Carlyle who said that the man who cannot wonder, who does not habitually wonder and worship, though he were president of innumerable royal societies, and carried the whole *Mechanique Celeste* and Hegel's philosophy and the epitome of all laboratories and observatories, with their results, in his single head, is but *a pair of spectacles behind which there is no eye.*

PRAYER

God, though this life is but a wraith,
    Although we know not what we use;
Although we grope with little faith,
    Give me the heart to fight—and lose.

Ever insurgent let me be,
    Make me more daring than devout;
From sleek contentment keep me free,
    And fill me with a buoyant doubt.

Open my eyes to visions girt
    With beauty, and with wonder lit—
But let me always see the dirt,
    And all that spawn and die in it.

Open my ears to music, let
    Me thrill with Spring's first flutes and
        drums—
But never let me dare forget
    The bitter ballads of the slums.

From compromise and things half-done,
    Keep me, with stern and stubborn pride;
And when, at last, the fight is won,
    God, keep me still unsatisfied.
                                    —*Louis Untermeyer.*

From CHALLENGE by Louis Untermeyer, copyright, 1914, by Harcourt, Brace and Company, Inc. Reprinted by permission.

FAILURE—The men who try to do something and fail are infinitely better than those who try to do nothing and succeed.—*Lloyd Jones.*

THE DREAMERS—They are the architects of greatness. Their vision lies within their souls. They never see the mirages of Fact, but peer beyond the veils and mists of doubt and pierce the walls of unborn Time.

Makers of empire, they have fought for bigger things than crowns and higher seats than thrones.

They are the Argonauts, the seekers of the priceless fleece—the Truth.

Through all the ages they have heard the voice of destiny call to them from the unknown vasts.

Their brains have wrought all human miracles. In lace of stone their spires stab the Old World's skies and with their golden crosses kiss the sun.

They are a chosen few—the blazers of the way—who never wear doubt's bandage on their eyes—who starve and chill and hurt, but hold to courage and to hope, because they know that there is always proof of truth for them who try—that only cowardice and lack of faith can keep the seeker from his chosen goal, but if his heart be strong and if he dream enough and dream it hard enough, he can attain, no matter where men failed before.

Walls crumble and the empires fall. The tidal wave sweeps from the sea and tears a fortress from its rocks. The rotting nations drop from off Time's bough, and only things the dreamers make live on.

They are the Eternal Conquerors—their vassals are the years.
                                    —*Herbert Kaufman.*

STAR GAZERS—Ideals are like stars, you will not succeed in touching them with your hands, but like the seafaring man on the desert of waters, you choose them as your guides, and, following them, you reach your destiny.—*Carl Schurz.*

CONSIDER FUNDAMENTALS— Utopia has long been another name for the unreal and the impossible. . . . As a matter of fact, it is our Utopias that make the world tolerable to us: the cities and mansions that people dream of are those in which they finally live . . . What makes human history such an uncertain and fascinating story is that man lives in two worlds—the world within and the world without . . . In the midst of the tepid and half-hearted discussions that continue to arise . . . let us break in with the injunction to talk about fundamentals—consider Utopia!

—Lewis Mumford.

UPWARD — Nothwithstanding the sight of all our miseries, which press upon us and take us by the throat, we have an instinct which we cannot repress, and which lifts us up.—*Pascal.*

HERE OR NOWHERE—Here in this poor, miserable, hampered, despicable Actual, wherein thou now standest, here or nowhere is thy Ideal; work it out therefrom, and working, believe, live, be free.— O thou that pinest in the imprisonment of the Actual, and criest bitterly to the gods for a kingdom wherein to rule and create, know this for a truth: the thing thou seekest is already here, "here or nowhere," couldst thou only see.—*Thomas Carlyle.*

THE IDEAL LIFE is in our blood and never will be still. Sad will be the day for any man when he becomes contented with the thoughts he is thinking and the deeds he is doing,—where there is not forever beating at the doors of his soul some great desire to do something larger, which he knows that he was meant and made to do.—*Phillips Brooks.*

AIM HIGH — Success lies, not in achieving what you aim at, but in aiming at what you ought to achieve, and pressing forward, sure of achievement here, or if not here, hereafter.—*R. F. Horton.*

Hills

I never loved your plains!—
    Your gentle valleys,
Your drowsy country lanes
    And pleached alleys.

I want my hills!—the trail
    That scorns the hollow.
Up, up the ragged shale
    Where few will follow.

Up, over wooded crest
    And mossy bowlder
With strong thigh, heaving chest,
    And swinging shoulder,

So let me hold my way,
    By nothing halted,
Until, at close of day,
    I stand, exalted,

High on my hills of dream—
    Dear hills that know me!
And then, how fair will seem
    The lands below me.

How pure, at vesper-time,
    The far bells chiming!
God, give me hills to climb,
    And strength for climbing!

—Arthur Guiterman.

Taken from DEATH AND GENERAL PUTNAM, by Arthur Guiterman, published and copyright by E. P. Dutton & Co., Inc., New York, 1935.

PURSUIT OF THE IDEAL — Our duty to God is to make of ourselves the most perfect product of divine incarnation that we can become. This is possible only through the pursuit of worthy ideals.

—Edgar White Burrill.

DARE GREATLY—It is not the critic who counts; not the man who points out how the strong man stumbled, or where the doer of deeds could have done better. The credit belongs to the man who is actually in the arena; whose face is marred by dust and sweat and blood; who strives valiantly; who errs and comes short again and again; who knows the great enthusiasms, the great devotions, and spends himself in a worthy cause; who at the best knows in the end the triumph of high achievement; and who at the worst, if he fails, at least fails while daring greatly; so that his place shall never be with those cold and timid souls who know neither victory nor defeat.—*Theodore Roosevelt.*

VICTORY

Attempt the end, and never stand to doubt,
Nothing's so hard but search will find it out.

—*Herrick.*

EMERSON SAID: "Hitch your wagon to a star." One can see in those six little words the summary of human achievement, and an everlasting inspiration to the future races of men. From Socrates to Edison, every forward step taken by mankind through revolving centuries, every advance by humanity towards the ultimate goal, has been led by some valiant dreamer whose eyes were fixed upon the dawn. Moses, with dying eyes, saw a star that blazed in the Promised Land; the radiance of an eternal star led Three Wise Men to the manger in Bethlehem; Columbus pinned his faith in the dawn of a new day; Kepler, announcing the laws of the unchanging spheres; Newton, watching the apple fall, each looked beyond, and into the future.

—*J. E. Dinger.*

WHAT MEN LIVE BY—Not long before his death Renan said that one could not do a finer service to mankind than to preach constantly that man doth not live by bread alone. We cannot too soon learn that the saving power in civilization is not coal or wheat or wool, but elements more ideal.—*Clarke.*

CREEDS—We find in our study of social development three human creeds: First, might makes right; second, knowledge is power; third, goodness is greatness. Humanity has outgrown its first creed, is distrusting the second, and is apprehending the third. Under the first, monarchy was the form of government. Under the second, aristocracy. Under the third, democracy will appear. Under the first the warrior was king, under the second the philosopher. Under the third, the servant will be master. In the light of eternity past I read that a man's greatness was measured by his ability to make the world serve him, but in the light of eternity to come a man's greatness will be measured by his ability to serve his fellowmen. Under the monarchy there were slaves. Under the aristocracy, there were wage earners. Under the democracy all will be fellow-workers. You may call this a Utopian dream, but it is the logic of events. It is the program of the inevitable. It is the march of the centuries. Caesar and Plato must pass on, and Christ will be supreme.

—*Christian Evangelist.*

DREAMS do come true, if we only wish hard enough. You can have anything in life if you will sacrifice everything else for it. "What will you have?" says God. "Pay for it and take it."

—*James Barrie.*

IDEALS — Now, believe me, God hides some ideal in every human soul. At some time in our life we feel a trembling, fearful longing to do some good thing. Life finds its noblest spring of excellence in this hidden impulse to do our best. There is a time when we are not content to be such merchants or doctors or lawyers as we see on the dead level or below it. The woman longs to glorify her womanhood as sister, wife, or mother. Here is God,—God standing silently at the door all day long.—*Robert Collyer.*

THE WAY TO UTOPIA—Before men can come to Utopia, they must learn the way there. Utopia, I see, is only a home for those who have learnt the way . . . it is not the place for men who grow wealthy by intercepting but by serving.
—*H. G. Wells.*

Upward

Glad that I live am I;
   That the sky is blue;
Glad for the country lanes,
   And the fall of dew.

After the sun, the rain.
   After the rain, the sun,
This is the way of life
   Till the work is done.

All that we need to do,
   Be we low or high
Is to see that we grow
   Nearer the sky.

From THE SELECTED POEMS OF LIZETTE WOODWORTH REESE, copyright, 1926, by Lizette Woodworth Reese, and reprinted by permission of Rinehart & Company, Inc., Publishers.

SOWERS—A handful of pine-seed will cover mountains with the green majesty of forests. I too will set my face to the wind and throw my handful of seed on high.—*Fiona Macleod.*

The Truer Life

No star is ever lost we once have seen,
We always may be what we might have
   been.
Since Good, though only thought, has
   life and breath,
God's life—can always be redeemed from
   death;
And evil, in its nature, is decay,
And any hour can blot it all away;
The hopes that lost in some far distance
   seen,
May be the truer life, and this the dream.
   —*Adelaide Ann Procter.*

FOUNDATIONS—If you have built castles in the air, your work need not be lost; that is where they should be. Now put the foundations under them.
   —*Thoreau.*

CASTLES IN THE AIR—I find the gayest castles in the air that were ever piled far better for comfort and for use than the dungeons in the air that are daily dug and caverned out by grumbling, discontented people. A man should make life and nature happier to us, or he had better never been born.—*Emerson.*

He . . . loved to weave
Dream warp and woof more fair than
   things that are.
He made believe . . . that far beyond the
   goal
That lures our eyes, to nobler ports we
   steer;
That grief was meant to forge the living
   soul,
And death itself is not for men to fear . . .
So well he made believe, he really made
The world believe his make-believes
   were true.

Taken from DEATH AND GENERAL PUTNAM, by Arthur Guiterman, published and copyright by E. P. Dutton & Co., Inc., New York, 1935.

VII. BEAUTY

THE FOUNTAIN—All beauty is a gleam from the fountain of beauty. No work of beauty can be more beautiful than the mind which designed it. I do not think a sculptor can possibly chisel a marble so as to make it more beautiful than his own ideal conception. I do not think a painter can produce a painting more beautiful than the thought of his mind which led up to it; I do not think a musician can express in sound, or a poet on paper, anything beyond the thought within him. I know, indeed, that the conception of either may grow with the process by which it is presented to others, and that the man may, as he proceeds, have a fairer and nobler view of what he is trying to express; but, after all, the mind of the sculptor is more beautiful than the marble which he has sculptured; and the mind of the painter is a more beautiful thing than the work of art which he has painted; and the mind of the musician is better and higher and nobler than the most exquisite symphony which he has composed and reduced to writing; and the mind of the poet is better than his most beautiful piece of poetry. And so we must rise from all the fragments of beauty which God has scattered so widely over His world to say with Milton—

"Thine this universal frame
Thus wondrous fair; Thyself how wondrous then!"

—*E. H. Bickersteth.*

EXPRESSION—Beauty does not lie in the face. It lies in the harmony between man and his industry. Beauty is expression. When I paint a mother I try to render her beautiful by the mere look she gives her child.—*Jean Francois Millet.*

THE MIRROR OF THE SOUL— Goodness and love mould the form into their own image, and cause the joy and beauty of love to shine forth from every part of the face. When this form of love is seen, it appears ineffably beautiful, and affects with delight the inmost life of the soul.—*E. Swedenborg.*

COMPLEXION HINT—There is no beautifier of complexion, or form, or behavior, like the wish to scatter joy and not pain around us.—*Ralph Waldo Emerson.*

GOOD LOOKS—Cheerfulness and content are great beautifiers and are famous preservers of youthful looks.
—*Charles Dickens.*

BARTER

Life has loveliness to sell,
  All beautiful and splendid things,
Blue waves whitened on a cliff,
  Soaring fire that sways and sings,
And children's faces looking up
Holding wonder like a cup.

Life has loveliness to sell,
  Music like a curve of gold,
Scent of pine trees in the rain,
  Eyes that love you, arms that hold,
And for your spirit's still delight,
Holy thoughts that star the night.

Spend all you have for loveliness,
  Buy it and never count the cost;
For one white singing hour of peace
  Count many a year of strife well lost,
And for a breath of ectasy
Give all you have been, or could be.
  —SARA TEASDALE.

From THE COLLECTED POEMS of Sara Teasdale. By permission of The Macmillan Company, publishers.

Bible

The Bible is a window
in this prison of hope,
through which we look
into eternity. — *Dwight.*

DAYSTAR AND DAWN—Our fair morning is at hand; the daystar is near the rising, and we are not many miles from home. What matter, then, of ill-entertainment in the smoky inns of this worthless world? We are not to stay here, and we shall be dearly welcome to Him to whom we are going.—*Samuel Rutherford.*

THE TEMPLE OF BEAUTY—Beauty is an all-pervading presence. It unfolds to the numberless flowers of the Spring; it waves in the branches of the trees and in the green blades of grass; it haunts the depths of the earth and the sea, and gleams out in the hues of the shell and the precious stone. And not only these minute objects, but the ocean, the mountains, the clouds, the heavens, the stars, the rising and the setting sun, all overflow with beauty. The universe is its temple; and those men who are alive to it can not lift their eyes without feeling themselves encompassed with it on every side. Now, this beauty is so precious, the enjoyment it gives so refined and pure, so congenial and so akin to worship, that it is pain living in the midst of it, and living almost as blind to it, as if, instead of this fair earth and glorious sky, they were tenants of a dungeon. An infinite joy is lost to the world by the want of culture of this spiritual endowment. The greatest truths are wronged if not linked with beauty, and they win their way most surely and deeply into the soul when arrayed in this their natural and fit attire.
—*W. E. Channing.*

TRIALS

I would not miss one single tear,
    Heart pang, or throbbing brow;
Sweet was the chastisement severe,
    And sweet its memory now.
        —*Amelia E. Barr.*

THE GREATER THING

Great it is to believe the dream
When we stand in youth by the starry
    stream;
But a greater thing is to fight life through
And say at the end, "The dream was
    true."
        —*Edwin Markham.*
        Reprinted by permission.

GOODNESS—Did it ever strike you that goodness is not merely a beautiful thing, but by far the most beautiful thing in the whole world? So that nothing is to be compared for value with goodness; that riches, honor, power, pleasure, learning, the whole world and all in it, are not worth having in comparison with being good; and the utterly best thing for a man is to be good, even though he were never to be rewarded for it.—*Charles Kingsley.*

ETERNITY AFFIRMS THE HOUR

All we have willed or hoped or dreamed
    of good shall exist;
    Not its semblance, but itself; no beauty,
    nor good, nor power
Whose voice has gone forth, but each
    survives for the melodist
    When eternity affirms the conception
    of an hour.
The high that proved too high, the heroic
    for earth too hard,
    The passion that left the ground to love
    itself in the sky,
Are music sent up to God by the lover
    and the bard;
    Enough that he heard it once: we shall
    hear it by and by.
        —*Robert Browning.*

FAR AWAY there in the sunshine are my highest aspirations. I may not reach them, but I can look up and see their beauty, believe in them, and try to follow where they lead.—*Louisa May Alcott.*

TO CULTIVATE the sense of the beautiful, is one of the most effectual ways of cultivating an appreciation of the divine goodness.—*Bovee.*

BEAUTY OF FORM affects the mind, but then it must not be the mere shell that we admire, but the thought that this shell is only the beautiful case adjusted to the shape and value of a still more beautiful pearl within.—The perfection of outward loveliness is the soul shining through its crystalline covering.
—*Jane Porter.*

WALKING WITH GOD—There is only one basis for really enjoying life, and that is, to walk in the way in which God leads you. Then you are prepared to find delight in all sorts of wayside incidents.

For one thing, the ability of the senses to enjoy anything depends as much on the tone of the mind as on any external happening. Some people are like Peter Bell of whom Wordsworth wrote:

"A primrose by a river's brim
A yellow primrose was to him,
And it was nothing more."

When a man is drifting through life, seeking nothing outside of self-gratification, the world must become increasingly a barren and forbidding wilderness.

But it is wonderful how many delights fall to the lot of him who is led by God. For such a one the clasp of a friends' hand, a cool drink in the heat of noon, a merry salutation from a passing traveler, a glimpse of beauty by the road, a quiet resting-place at night, are all full of unspeakable pleasure.

JUST A BIT—If the nose of Cleopatra had been a little shorter, it would have changed the history of the world.—*Pascal.*

ACID TEST—The criterion of true beauty is, that it increases on examination; if false, that it lessens.—There is therefore, something in true beauty that corresponds with right reason, and is not the mere creation of fancy.—*Greville.*

BEAUTY is as summer fruits, which are easy to corrupt and cannot last; and for the most part it makes a dissolute youth, and an age a little out of countenance; but if it light well, it makes virtues shine and vice blush.—*Bacon.*

CHEAP LUXURY—No man receives the full culture of a man in whom the sensibility to the beautiful is not cherished; and there is no condition of life from which it should be excluded.—Of all luxuries this the cheapest, and the most at hand, and most important to those conditions where coarse labor tends to give grossness to the mind.—*Channing.*

EVERY YEAR of my life I grow more convinced that it is wisest and best to fix our attention on the beautiful and the good, and dwell as little as possible on the evil and the false.—*Cecil.*

MENTAL PICTURES—One of the most practical things a man can do with his holidays and leisure time is to store his mind with pictures of beauty and truth. By discriminating thought, conversation, observation, he may lay up hidden sources of strength and grace.

CRITERION—That which is striking and beautiful is not always good; but that which is good is always beautiful.
—*Ninon de l'Enclos.*

MANY CHARMS—Beauty hath so many charms one knows not how to speak against it; and when a graceful figure is the habitation of a virtuous soul—when the beauty of the face speaks out the modesty and humility of the mind, it raises our thoughts up to the great Creator; but after all, beauty, like truth, is never so glorious as when it goes the plainest.

—*Sterne.*

BEAUTY AND TRUTH—The most natural beauty in the world is honesty and moral truth.—For all beauty is truth.— True features make the beauty of the face; true proportions, the beauty of architecture; true measures, the beauty of harmony and music.—*Shaftesbury.*

REMEDY—There is no more potent antidote to low sensuality than the adoration of beauty.—All the higher arts of design are essentially chaste.—They purify the thoughts, as tragedy, according to Aristotle, purifies the passions.—*Schlegel.*

EVERY TRAIT of beauty may be referred to some virtue, as to innocence, candor, generosity, modesty, or heroism.

—*St. Pierre.*

AFTER ALL, it is the divinity within that makes the divinity without; and I have been more fascinated by a woman of talent and intelligence, though deficient in personal charms, than I have been by the most regular beauty.

—*Washington Irving.*

BEAUTY is but the sensible image of the Infinite.—Like truth and justice it lives within us; like virtue and the moral law it is a companion of the soul.—*Bancroft.*

THE MIDDLE WAY — The finest lives, in my opinion, are those who rank in the common model, and with the human race, but without miracle, without extravagance.—*Montaigne.*

THE BEAUTY SEEN is partly in him who sees it.—*Bovee.*

COURSES—To give pain is the tyranny; to make happy, the true empire of beauty.—*Steele.*

HINDSIGHT—What we have, we prize, not to the worth while we enjoy it; but being lacked and lost, why then we reck the value; then we find the virtue that possession would not show us while it was ours.—*Shakespeare.*

DEFINING—Socrates called beauty a short-lived tyranny; Plato, a privilege of nature; Theophrastus, a silent cheat; Theocritus, a delightful prejudice; Carneades, a solitary kingdom; Aristotle, that it was better than all the letters of recommendation in the world; Homer, that it was a glorious gift of nature, and Ovid, that it was a favor bestowed by the gods.

The fountain of beauty is the heart, and every generous thought illustrates the walls of your chamber.

If virtue accompanies beauty it is the heart's paradise; if vice be associate with it, it is the soul's purgatory.—It is the wise man's bonfire, and the fool's furnace.

—*Quarles.*

EVEN VIRTUE is more fair when it appears in a beautiful person.—*Virgil.*

THE BEST PART of beauty is that which no picture can express.—*Bacon.*

VIII. THE BIBLE

ENLIGHTENMENT.—The Bible as a book stands alone. There never was, nor ever will be, another like it. As there is but one sun to enlighten the world naturally, so there is but one Book to enlighten the world spiritually. May that Book become to each of us the man of our counsel, the guide of our journey, the inspiration of our thought, and our support and comfort in life and in death.

—*A. Galloway.*

The Bible contains 3,566,480 letters, 733,746 words, 31,163 verses, 1,189 chapters and 66 books. The longest chapter is the 119th Psalm; shortest, the middle chapter, the 117th Psalm. The middle verse is the 8th of the 118th Psalm. The longest name is in the 8th chapter of Isaiah. The word "and" occurs 46,227 times; the word Jehovah 6,855 times. The thirty-seventh chapter of Isaiah and the 19th chapter of the 2nd book of Kings are alike. The longest verse is the 9th of the 8th chapter of Esther; the shortest verse is the 35th of the 11th chapter of John. In the 21st verse of the 7th chapter of Ezra is the alphabet. The finest piece of reading is the 26th chapter of Acts. The name of God is not mentioned in the book of Esther. The Bible contains two testaments. The Old is Law, The New is Love. The Old is the Bud, The New is the Bloom. In the Old, man is reaching up for God. In the New, God is reaching down for man. In the Old, man is in the valley but can see the sun shining on the mountain tops. In the New he is on the mountain top basking in the sunlight of God's infinite love.

SHEPHERD.—Who is it that is your shepherd? The Lord! Oh, my friends, what a wonderful announcement! The Lord God of Heaven and Earth, the almighty Creator of all things, He who holds the universe in His hand as though it were a very little thing,—He is your shepherd, and has charged Himself with the care and keeping of you, as a shepherd is charged with the care and keeping of his sheep. If your hearts could really take in this thought, you would never have a fear or a care again; for with such a shepherd, how could it be possible for you ever to want any good thing?

—*H. W. Smith.*

DIFFICULTIES.—Believe the Bible and thou shalt be saved. No. There is no such word written. It is "Believe on the Lord Jesus Christ and thou shalt be saved." Do not trouble yourself in the first instance about questions connected with the book of Genesis, or difficulties suggested by the book of Revelation. Let the wars of the Jews alone in the meantime, and dismiss Jonah from your mind. Look to Jesus: get acquainted with Him —listen to His word—believe in Him— trust Him—obey Him. This is all that is asked of you in the first instance. After you have believed on Christ, and taken Him as your Savior, your Master, your Model, you will not be slow to find out that "all Scripture is given by inspiration of God, and is profitable for doctrine, and for reproof, and for correction, and for instruction in godliness." You may never have all your difficulties solved, or all your objections met, but you will be sure of your foundation; you will feel that your feet are planted on the "Rock of Ages."

—*Gibson.*

PREACHERS—Strong preachers have ever been Bible preachers. The old Reformers drew their weapons from the heavenly armory. The sermons of Bunyan, and Baxter, and Flavel, and men of their stamp, were full of God—instinct with living doctrines. Their very garb was after the Scripture pattern. Whitefield, as a custom, read the Bible with Henry's Commentary, day by day, on his knees, praying over every sentence, line, and word. Edward and Davies were mighty in the Scriptures. Of Chalmers, it has been said, that his sermons "held the Bible in solution." Preachers who saturate their sermons with the word of God never wear out. The manna which they bring is pure, and sweet, and freshly gathered. It never cloys. God's word is deep, and he who studies it will ever have something new. He will never be dull, for the words of the Bible are strong, living words, and its images and descriptions are very flowers of elegance. Apt citations clinch the passages of the preacher's discourse, and give sanction, dignity, positiveness, authority to it. And they shed light into his subject, like windows in houses.—*Fish*.

INEXHAUSTIBLE—Some one describes packing his bag for a journey. Just before closing it, he observes a small corner not yet filled. He says, "Into this little corner I put a guide-book, a lamp, a mirror, a microscope, a telescope, a volume of choice poems, several well written biographies, a package of old letters, a book of songs, a sharp sword and a small library of more than sixty volumes; yet, strange enough to say, all these did not occupy a space of more than three inches long by two inches wide." "But how could you do it?" "Well, it was all in the packing, I put in my Bible."—*Selected*.

SCRIPTURES—A bright little boy once took the Bible from the center-table of his father's home and turned its dusty pages and said: "Mother, is this God's Book?" "Certainly," was the good mother's reply. "Well, I think we had better send it back to God, for we don't use it here," said the little fellow. This is a fair picture of many a home and the way the Bible is treated. The center-table Bible is a catch-all. It is a place for relics, letters, poetry and pressed flowers. He has revealed to us words of truth and grace, and like David, we should meditate upon His word by day and by night. The Scriptures are sufficient to make us wise unto salvation. Christ says, we are sanctified by them. Paul says, we are begotten by them. Peter says, we are born again by them.
—*Public Speakers Library*.

HANDBOOK OF CIVILIZATION—The Bible has made an ineffaceable impression upon child life. Upon it poets have fed their genius. Its thoughts lie like threads of gold upon the rich pages of each Macaulay or Burke. Orators have quoted from it so largely that we may say that, in proportion as men are cultured, have they been students of the Bible. Today its moral principles form the very substance and body of modern law and jurisprudence. For centuries it has been the book for patriots and reformers; it has been the slave's book; it has been the book for the common people struggling upward; it has been the book of hope for all prodigals; it has been a medicine book for the heart-broken, while its ideas furnish goals for society's future progress. For the individual it teaches the art of individual worth, and is a guide to conduct and character. For the state it is a handbook of universal civilization.
—*Hillis*.

SHEPHERD—The Shepherd knows what pastures are best for His sheep, and they must not question nor doubt, but trustingly follow Him. Perhaps He sees that the best pastures for some of us are to be found in the midst of opposition or of earthly trials. If He leads you there, you may be sure they are green for you, and you will grow and be made strong by feeding there. Perhaps He sees that the best waters for you to walk beside will be raging waves of trouble and sorrow. If this should be the case, He will make them still waters for you, and you must go and lie down beside them, and let them have all their blessed influences upon you.—*H. W. Smith.*

READ—When in sorrow, read John 14.

When men fail you, Psalm 27.

When you have sinned, Psalm 51.

When you worry, Matthew 6:19-34.

Before church service, Psalm 84.

When you are in danger, Psalm 91.

When you have the blues, Psalm 34.

When God seems far away, Psalm 139.

When you are discouraged, Isaiah 40.

If you desire to be fruitful, John 15.

When doubts come upon you, John 7:17.

When you are lonely or fearful, Psalm 33.

When you forget your blessings, Psalm 103.

For Jesus' idea of a Christian, Matthew 5.

For James' idea of religion, James 1:19-27.

For stirring of faith, Hebrews 11.

When you feel down and out, Romans 8:31-39.

When you lack courage for your task, Joshua 1.

When the world seems bigger than God, Psalm 90.

When you want Christian assurance, Romans 8:1-30.

When you leave home for labor or travel, Psalm 121.

When you grow bitter or critical, I Cor. 13.

For Paul's idea of Christianity, II Cor. 5:15-19.

For Paul's rules on how to get along with men, Romans 12.

—*Selected.*

BE STILL—"Be still, and know that I am God."—Ps. 46:10.

It is not easy to be still in this rough and restless world. Yet God says, "Be still;" and He says also, "In returning and rest shall ye be saved; in quietness and confidence shall be your strength" (Isa. 30:15).

1. Be still, and thou shalt know I can put all enemies to shame. "He that sitteth in the Heavens shall laugh; the Lord shall hold them in derision. Who shall contend with Him who made the Heavens and the earth?" He is still God.

2. Be still, and thou shalt know that I can uphold My own truth in a day of error. Is not My truth precious to Me? and My Book of truth, is it not above all books in Mine eyes? I am God.

3. Be still, and thou shalt know that I can say to the nations, Peace, be still. The waves rise, but I am mightier than all. These tumults do not touch My throne. Take no alarm because of this world-wide resistance to My authority and law. I am still God.

4. Be still, and thou shalt see the glorious issue of all these confusions. This world is My world, and thou shalt see it to be such; this earth shall yet be the abode of the righteous.—*Bonar.*

WANT—"The Lord is my shepherd; I shall not want."

I shall not want rest. "He maketh me to lie down in green pastures."

I shall not want drink. "He leadeth me beside the still waters."

I shall not want forgiveness. "He restoreth my soul."

I shall not want guidance. "He leadeth me in the paths of righteousness for His name's sake."

I shall not want companionship. "Yea, though I walk through the valley of the shadow of death, I will fear no evil; for Thou art with me."

I shall not want comfort. "Thy rod and Thy staff they comfort me."

I shall not want food. "Thou preparest a table before me in the presence of mine enemies."

I shall not want joy. "Thou anointest my head with oil."

I shall not want anything. "My cup runneth over."

I shall not want anything in this life. "Surely goodness and mercy shall follow me all the days of my life."

I shall not want anything in eternity. "And I will dwell in the house of the Lord Forever."—Selected.

WAIT—Many times, this little verse by Harry Chester has fallen on my heart like a benediction:
The Scripture says that in His own sweet way
    If we but wait,
The Lord will take our burdens and set
    Crooked matters straight.
                        —Jowett.

THE STUDY of God's word, for the purpose of discovering God's will, is the secret discipline which has formed the greatest characters.—J. W. Alexander.

TEN COMMANDMENTS — Thou shall not have another God but me.

Thou shalt not to an image bow the knee.

Thou shalt not take the Name of God in vain:

See that the Sabbath thou do not profane.

Honor thy father and thy mother too:

In act, or thought, see thou no murder do,

From fornication keep thy body clean:

Thou shalt not steal, though thou be very mean.

Bear no false witness; keep thee without spot,

What is thy neighbor's, see thou covet not.

                        —John Bunyan.

BETTER THAN GOLD

O for a Booke and a Shadie Nooke
    Eyther in-a-doore or out;
With the greene leaves whispering over-
        hede,
    Or the Streete cries all aboute,
Where I maie reade all at my ease,
    Bothe of the Newe and Olde,
For a jollie goode Booke whereon to
        looke,
    Is better to me than Golde.
                        —John Wilson.

SCHOOL HOURS — The Disciples were not losing time when they sat down beside their Master, and held quiet converse with Him under the olives of Bethany or by the shores of Galilee. Those were their school hours; those were their feeding times. The healthiest Christian, the one who is best fitted for Godly living and Godly labors, is he who feeds most on Christ. Here lies the benefit of Bible reading.—Evangelist.

SPIRIT — In Tremont Temple there were two colored men; one of them was Robert. He was born in slavery, never saw the inside of a school, and learned to read only through great effort of his own. But Black Robert knew more about the Bible than any other man in Tremont Temple. Why? I will tell you why. For years Black Robert never read his Bible except on his knees. For two, three, four hours at a time, he read the Bible on his knees. He never went to bed that he did not put the Bible under his pillow, and when they found him dead in a hospital ward they found the Bible under his curly head. I had the privilege of being under one of the great Hebrew scholars of his day. He thought Hebrew, he was saturated in Hebrew; a gentle, Christian man, a great scholar with a great brain. He would come straight to his desk, open that old Hebrew Bible, drop his face right down between the pages, and say something like this: "Oh, Lord Jesus, may thy Holy Spirit teach us the Word." Do you wonder that he knew his Bible? He knew it by the same process that Black Robert knew his. You can't read your Bible without the Holy Spirit.

—*Cortland Myers.*

PSALM XIX—The nineteenth psalm sets forth most beautifully the true relation which ought to exist between God's world and God's word. In the first six verses of that psalm we have natural religion: "The heavens declare the glory of God, and the firmament showeth His handiwork. Day unto day uttereth speech and night unto night showeth knowledge." We have here one of the finest personifications I know of anywhere. One day is represented as calling to the next day, and the next takes up the cry, and passes it on, thus day unto day in ceaseless procession, shows God's wondrous revelation of Himself. In the seventh verse of this psalm you enter into a new atmosphere. You feel now that you are breathing the air more distinctively of Heaven, and that your feet are standing upon the solid rock, for you read, "The law of the Lord is perfect, restoring the soul." Down to the end of the thirteenth verse you have revealed religion and the effect which it produces on action and character. Then in the last verse you have experimental religion: "Let the words of my mouth and the meditations of my heart be acceptable in thy sight, O Lord, my strength and my redeemer." Observe what progress you have in this psalm. You have first, creation; second, revelation; third, generation; natural religion, revealed religion, experimental religion. This psalm is an epitome of the whole Bible.—*Powell.*

GOD'S CHART—The Bible is God's chart for you to steer by, to keep you from the bottom of the sea, and to show you where the harbor is, and how to reach it without running on rocks or bars. If you have been reading it to gratify curiosity; or to see if you could not catch a universalist; or to find a knife with which to cut up a Unitarian; or for the purpose of setting up or taking down a bishop; or to establish or overthrow any sect—if you have been reading it so, then stop. It is God's medicine-book. You are sick. You are mortally struck through with disease. There is no human remedy for your trouble. But here is God's medicine-book. If you read it for life, for growth in righteousness, then blessed is your reading; but if you read it for disputation and dialectical ingenuities, it is no more to you than Bacon's "Novum Organum" would be.—*Beecher.*

OLD TESTAMENT—The Old Testament is the watershed of the New. These deep springs, which irrigate and fructify the New Testament Church, took their rise from the mountains of Judea, and descended, like the volume of the Nile, to fertilize and fructify the landscape around it.—*Gordon.*

ASPECTS OF FAITH — 1. Strong faith will make the soul resolute in resisting, and happy in conquering the strongest temptations.—*Heb.* 11:38; *Dan.* 6:10.

2. It will make a man own God and cleave to, and hang upon God in the face of the greatest difficulties and dangers.—*Psa.* 44:16-18; *Rom.* 4:18.

3. It will enable men to prefer Christ's cross before the world's crown, to prefer tortures before deliverance.—*Heb.* 11:3.

4. It will make a soul divinely fearless, and divinely careless; it will make a man live as a child lives in the family, without fear or care.—*Psa.* 23:4; *Dan.* 3:16; *Micah.* 7:7-9.

5. It will make a man cleave to the promise when Providence runs cross to the promise. — *Numb.* 10:29; 2 *Chron.* 20:9-11; *Psa.* 60:6-7.

6. It will make men comply with those commands that do most cross them in their desirable comforts.—*Heb.* 11:8-9.
—*T. Brooks.*

DETERMINATION — The Bible makes much of determination. Choose ye this day whom ye will serve. Strive to enter in at the strait gate. See that ye refuse not Him that speaketh. Quench not the Spirit. Escape for thy life. All this style of admonition and direction shows that the sinner has a host of obstacles between him and Heaven; and he must push his way through, or perish.
—*H. Cuyler.*

GARDEN—The Bible resembles an extensive and highly cultivated flower garden, where there is a vast variety and profusion of fruits and flowers, some of which are more essential or more splendid than others; but there is not a blade suffered to grow in it which has not its use and beauty in the system. Salvation for sinners is the grand truth presented everywhere, and in all points of light; but the pure in heart sees a thousand traits of the Divine character, of himself, and of the world: some striking and bold —others cast as it were into the shade, and designed to be searched for and examined; some direct, others by way of intimation or inference.—*Cecil.*

FARMING

Matt. 21:28: Son, go work today.

Matt. 13:38: The field is the world.

Jer. 4:3: Break up your fallow.

Luke 8:11: The seed is the word of God.

Mark 4:14: The sower soweth the word.

Jer. 4:3: Sow not among thorns.

Eccl. 11:6: In the morning sow.

Prov. 11:18: He that soweth in righteousness.

Ps. 126:5: They that sow in tears.

Eccl. 11:4: He that observeth wind shall not sow.

Ps. 126:6: Bearing precious seed.

Is. 32:20: Blessed are ye that sow.

Hos. 10:12: In righteousness.

2 Cor. 9:6: He that soweth sparingly.

Gal. 6:7: Whatsoever a man soweth.

1 Cor. 3:6: Planted, watered, increase.

Gal. 6:8, 9: He that soweth to the Spirit.

Jno. 4:35: White already to harvest.

Jno. 4:36: He that reapeth receiveth wages.
—*Handy Outlines.*

EPISTLES — In the business world great importance is placed upon letters of recommendation. Yet how worthless such a letter would be if it were illegible! Have you ever seen an illegible letter of recommendation in the Christian life? The Holy Spirit tells us 2 Cor. 3, 3, that we are "epistles of Christ. . . written, not with ink, but with the spirit of the living God." A speaker at America's Keswick in New Jersey said: "Some folks are illegible letters. You can't make out whether they are Christians or not. Their names are on the church record, but so much writing of the world is on them that you can't quite be sure of them."—It is a blessed thing in this day, when Christ is disowned by so many in the visible Church, to have those who will let the Lord Jesus Christ cleanse their hearts from every stain and then permit Him to write plainly and clearly upon their lives that they belong to Him and serve Him.—*The Way.*

TABERNACLE—We may compare the Bible to the Tabernacle with its three courts. The outer court is the letter of the Scripture, the inner court, or holy place, is the truth of the Scripture; the holiest place of all is the person of Jesus Christ; and only when we pass the inmost veil do we come to Him.

—*A. T. Pierson.*

GOOD—A party of engineers became lost in a forest in Africa. Their supply of food was exhausted. They found some berries which seemed to perfectly satisfy the appetite. They ate them for several days, but became weaker and weaker, and one after another died, until, when help came, there was only one left to tell the sad story. They still had some of the berries, but when they were analyzed they were found to be absolutely worthless as a food. While their appetites were satisfied they were actually starving to death. Many people are like that—perfectly satisfied to starve their nature on food which is of no value, while they might feast on the "true bread from Heaven."

—*Miller.*

JOHN 3:16

1. God—the greatest lover.
2. So loved—the greatest degree.
3. The world—the greatest company.
4. That He gave—the greatest act.
5. His only begotten Son—the greatest gift.
6. That whosoever—the greatest opportunity.
7. Believeth—the greatest simplicity.
8. In Him—the greatest attraction.
9. Should not perish—the greatest promise.
10. But—the greatest difference.
11. Have—the greatest certainty.
12. Eternal life—the greatest possession.

—*Davies.*

GUIDE—A man, who was about to take a perilous journey through the mountains, was given not a little advice. As is often the case in such situations, the advice was contradictory. One warned him against taking any of the bypaths that led away from the main road, while others declared that many of these paths could be pursued with profit, since they meant shortening the distance toward his destination. So it was with a number of things that left him in doubt. "It seems," he said to himself, "I shall have to guess at what I do not know." Just then one appeared and said: "I am the authorized guide. I am ready to go with you all the way, if you will but follow my teachings."

—*Mattie M. Boteler.*

EYES OF GOD—All seeing eyes: The eyes of the Lord are in every place, beholding the evil and the good.—Prov. 15:3.

Penetrating eyes: All things are naked and opened unto the eyes of Him with whom we have to do.—Heb. 4:13.

Thoughtful eyes: For the ways of man are before the eyes of the Lord, and He pondereth all His goings.—Prov. 5:21.

Remembering eyes: And they consider not in their hearts that I remember all their wickedness; now their own doings have beset them about; they are before My face.—Hosea 7:2.

Judging eyes: Thine eyes are open upon all the ways of the sons of men; to give every one according to the fruit of his doings.—Jer. 32:19.

Providing eyes: A land which the Lord thy God careth for; the eyes of the Lord thy God are always upon it, from the beginning of the year even unto the end of the year.—Deut. 11:12.

IDENTIFIED—The New Testament scene does not lie in some misty, undefined portion of time, the place of which cannot be ascertained, but in a period as historical and as recognizable as that of Queen Elizabeth or Charles the Second. The geography of the New Testament is historical. It includes empires and kingdoms, provinces and cities, mountains and oceans, rivers and valleys, which are all real and correctly indicated. The smallest villages equally with the largest cities are accurately represented and located. The progress of modern discovery has only tended to confirm the book in its minutest details. This is not usual with mythical and purely fabulous writings, with which, indeed, the rule is quite the opposite.
—B. H. Cowper.

THE STREAM—The Scriptures teach us the best way of living, the noblest way of suffering, and the most comfortable way of dying.—Flavel.

A stream where alike the elephant may swim and the lamb may wade.
—Gregory.

AUTHORS—The Bible itself is a standing and an astonishing miracle. Written, fragment by fragment, throughout the course of fifteen centuries, under different states of society, and in different languages, by persons of the most opposite tempers, talents, and conditions, learned and unlearned, prince and peasant, bond and free; cast into every form of instructive composition and good writing, history, prophecy, poetry, allegory, emblematic representation, judicious interpretation, literal statement, precept, example, proverbs, disquisition, epistle, sermon, prayer—in short all rational shapes of human discourse; and treating, moreover, of subjects not obvious, but most difficult;—its authors are not found, like other writers, contradicting one another upon the most ordinary matters of fact and opinion, but are at harmony upon the whole of their sublime and momentous scheme.—Maclagan.

CONSOLATION — Never on earth calamity so great, as not to leave to us, if rightly weighed, what would console us 'mid what we sorrow for.—Shakespeare.

THE SAVOR LOST — Possession, why more tasteless than pursuit? Why is a wish far dearer than a crown? That wish accomplished, why the grave of bliss? Because, in the great future buried deep, beyond our plans, lies all that man with ardor should pursue.—Young.

IX. COURAGE

SUNSHINE—A Boston daily spoke one day, thus: "The day opened cloudy and cheerless, but about noon Phillips Brooks came down town and then everything brightened up."

Many Christians are just like Phillips Brooks in this respect, and one such Christian is the author of "In the Service of the King." Always he radiated joy and gladness. Early in the first chapter he told how he deliberately made up his mind to do this. One day he was reading Gulliver's tale of the great inventor who had hit upon a device for extracting from cucumbers sunshine which he then "stored away in bottles to be used in the home on dark days to light the house." As he thought on this story "the deacon's mission became clear: he would be the agent of the great inventor, a dispenser of bottled sunshine." So he set out to make his people laugh. "Counting the cost, he deliberately donned the motley . . . With a persistency that even now he feels a pride in, he determined never to desist till he could say that he had had a laugh from every one of his people . . . Whatever else he may have left undone, the deacon knows that in those first days he taught to many a sad heart the long-forgotten trick of laughter. . . Experience gives him courage to insist that when the sunshine is unbottled in the home of desolation, it discovers a heart of gold that was near to perishing in the shadow."

—*John T. Faris.*

OPPORTUNITY

*They do me wrong who say I come no
    more
When once I knock and fail to find
    you in;
For every day I stand outside your door,
And bid you wake, and rise to fight
    and win.*

*Wail not for precious chances passed
    away!
Weep not for golden ages on the wane.
Each night I burn the records of the
    day,
At sunrise every soul is born again.*

*Though deep in mire, wring not your
    hands and weep:
I lend my arm to all who say, "I can!"
No shamefaced outcast ever sank so
    deep,
But yet might rise and be again a man!*

—WALTER MALONE.

FORTITUDE—True fortitude I take to be the quiet possession of a man's self, and an undisturbed doing his duty, whatever evil besets or danger lies in his way.

—*Locke.*

The fortitude of a Christian consists in patience, not in enterprises which the poets call heroic, and which are commonly the effects of interest, pride, and worldly honor.—*Dryden.*

Fortitude implies a firmness and strength of mind, that enables us to do and suffer as we ought. It rises upon an opposition, and, like a river, swells the higher for having its course stopped.

—*Jeremy Collier.*

THE CONQUEST OF FEAR — Courage consists not in hazarding without fear, but being resolutely minded in a just cause. The brave man is not he who feels no fear, for that were stupid and irrational, but he whose noble soul subdues its fear, and bravely dares the danger nature shrinks from.—*Ferrold.*

FAILURE—There are always reasons for giving up. Arguments for self-pity are thick as blackberries. The world is crowded with thorns and cruelties, causes for tears. Courage is the divine unreason against which, as against a rock, the waves of disaster beat in vain. Say to yourself: I am unconquerable. I shall arrive. In the center of creation sits not an enemy, but my Friend. I shall arrive—what time, what circuit first, I ask not. In some time, His good time, I shall arrive. Let come what will, I shall never say I am beaten. I am not a negligible molecule, a mote in the sunbeam, a worm! I am a man, and, so help me God! I shall play the man. Failure! There is no such word in all the bright lexicon of speech, unless you yourself have written it there! There is no such thing as failure except to those who accept and believe in failure.—*Marden.*

MOTIVE POWER—It is only through labor and prayerful effort, by grim energy and resolute courage, that we move on to better things.—*Theodore Roosevelt.*

IGNORANCE—Fear is lack of faith. Lack of faith is ignorance. Fear can only be cured by vision. Give the world eyes. It will see. Give it ears. It will hear. Give it a right arm. It will act. Man needs time and room. Man needs soil, rain and sunshine. Needs a chance. Open all your doors and windows. Let everything pass freely in and out, out and in. Even the evil. Let it pass out and in, in and out. No man hates the truth. But most men are afraid of the truth. Make the truth easier than a lie. Make the truth welcomer than its counterfeits. Then man will no longer be afraid; being afraid is being ignorant. Being ignorant is being without faith.—*Horace Traubel.*

REJOICE—Religion is not a funeral announcement. There are religious leaders who seem to be always saying—"Let us cry." They have gotten the wrong phrase. "Let us rejoice!" When you begin to talk about faith and God, do not turn the corners of your mouth down. Face these matters as naturally, as joyously, as genuinely, as you would face any other interest in life.—*Mills.*

Changed

Time was, I shrank from what was right,
   From fear of what was wrong;
I would not brave the sacred fight,
   Because the foe was strong.
But now I cast that finer sense
   And sorer shame aside;
Such dread of sin was indolence,
   Such aim at Heaven was pride.
        —J. H. Newman.

LETTING OUT THE REINS—Every year I live I am more convinced that the waste of life lies in the love we have not given, the powers we have not used, the selfish prudence that will risk nothing, and which, shirking pain, misses happiness as well. No one ever yet was the poorer in the long run for having once in a lifetime "let out all the length of all the reins."
        —Mary Cholmondeley.

TAKING CHANCES — No man is worth his salt who is not ready at all times to risk his body, to risk his well-being, to risk his life, in a great cause.
        —Theodore Roosevelt.

WHAT COUNTS—'Tisn't life that matters! It's the courage you bring to it.
        —Hugh Walpole.

IMPREGNABLE—Courage does not consist in feeling no fear, but in conquering fear. He is the hero who seeing the lions on either side goes straight on, because there his duty lies.

—*Saturday Magazine.*

I hate to see things done by halves. If it be right, do it boldly, if it be wrong, leave it undone.—*Gilpin.*

Courage consists not in hazarding without fear, but being resolutely minded in a just cause.—*Plutarch.*

True courage is the result of reasoning. A brave mind is always impregnable. Resolution lies more in the head than in the veins; and a just sense of honor and of infamy, of duty and of religion, will carry us farther than all the force of mechanism.

—*Jeremy Collier.*

ENVIRONMENT—It is possible to live very near to God under every conceivable environment, and what is possible is our highest duty.

—*William E. McLaren.*

Risky Business

It's a risk to have a husband, a risk to have
    a son;
A risk to pour your confidences out to
    anyone;
A risk to pick a daisy, for there's sure to
    be a cop;
A risk to go on living, but a greater risk
    to stop.

—*Ruth Mason Rice.*

DISCOURAGEMENTS — Pay as little attention to discouragements as possible! Plough ahead as a steamer does, rough or smooth, rain or shine! To carry your cargo and make your port is the point.—*Maltbie Babcock.*

KEEPERS OF THE LIGHT—The keeper of the lighthouse does not launch any ships, it is true, but he keeps many a good ship from going to wreck. The light shines farther than the keeper can see, and brightest when he cannot see at all. Two things he has got to remember—to keep the light burning, and never to get in between the light and the darkness he is set to lighten.—*John T. Faris.*

Steadfast Hearts

Darkness enwrapped him, yet with stead-
    fast heart
    He sought, unfaltering, the highest
    light.
    His keen-eyed spirit failed not in the
    sight
Which sees, and seeing, loves the better
    part.

UNWITNESSED—Perfect valor is to do unwitnessed what we should be capable of doing before all the world.

—*La Rochefoucauld.*

PROTECTION—Though no friend, no man, be with thee, fear nothing! Thy God is here.—*Dinger.*

"Underneath are the everlasting arms." What child of God was ever permitted to fall lower than God's "underneath"?

—*H. Gill.*

Be not faint-hearted in misfortune. When God causes a tree to be hewn down He takes care that His birds can nestle on another.—*Anonymous.*

God accompanies thee, His child—fear not! On each spot that thou standest is an angel of protection; where thou art is thy God; where thy God is there is thy Savior.

THE BRAVEST THING—The Courage we desire and prize is not the Courage to die decently, but to live manfully.
—*Carlyle.*

RESISTANCE — Courage is resistance to fear, mastery of fear—not absence of fear.—*Mark Twain.*

LOST TALENT — A great deal of talent is lost in the world for want of a little courage. Every day sends to their graves obscure men whom timidity prevented from making a first effort; who, if they could have been induced to begin, would in all probability have gone great lengths in the career of fame. The fact is, that to do anything in the world worth doing, we must not stand back shivering and thinking of the cold and danger, but jump in and scramble through as well as we can. It will not do to be perpetually calculating risks and adjusting nice chances; it did very well before the Flood, when a man would consult his friends upon an intended publication for a hundred and fifty years, and live to see his success afterwards; but at present, a man waits, and doubts, and consults his brother, and his particular friends, till one day he finds he is sixty years old and that he has lost so much time in consulting cousins and friends that he has no more time to follow their advice.—*Sydney Smith.*

THE DEBT SIDE—The worst sorrows in life are not in its losses and misfortunes, but its fears.—*A. C. Benson.*

WHAT TO FEAR—Fear not that thy life shall come to an end, but rather fear that it shall never have a beginning.
—*J. H. Newman.*

FREEDOM — Many a boy has discovered that real freedom is never gained by breaking legitimate laws. "Obedience to Law is Liberty" is the appropriate inscription over the massive entrance of a great courthouse in Cleveland, and it is wonderfully true. There is no real liberty in any other course. Just doing what you please, and following that impulse, is not true freedom. Obeying a sudden impulse to follow the primrose path usually starts or strengthens some bad habit which forges shackles on our characters and destroys by just so much our freedom. A lawless person is never free. He is a victim of his own unaccountable impulses and soon a slave to his bad habits.
—*George Walter Fiske.*

THE DIVINE SPARK
Courage—an independent spark from heaven's bright throne,
By which the soul stands raised, triumphant, high, alone.
—*George Farquhar.*

HARDSHIP — Dr. Cane, finding a flower under the Humboldt glacier, was more affected by it because it grew beneath the lip and cold bosom of the ice, than he would have been by the most gorgeous garden bloom. So some single struggling grace in the heart of one far removed from Divine influences may be dearer to God than a whole catalog of virtues in the life of one more favored of Heaven.

As in nature, as in art, so in grace; it is rough treatment that gives souls, as well as stones, their lustre. The more the diamond is cut the brighter it sparkles; and in what seems hard dealing, there God has no end in view but to perfect His people.
—*Guthrie.*

X. DEFINITIONS

ADORATION is a universal sentiment: it differs in degree in different natures; it takes the most varied forms—often ignores its own existence; sometimes it betrays itself by an exclamation uttered from the heart in the midst of the grand scenes of nature and life; sometimes it rises silently in the mute and penetrated soul; it may wander in its mode of expression, and err as to its object.—*V. Cousin.*

THE GREATEST MAN is he who chooses the right with invincible resolution; who resists the sorest temptations from within and without; who bears the heaviest burdens cheerfully; who is calmest in storms, and most fearless under menace and frowns; and whose reliance on truth, on virtue, and on God, is most unfaltering.—*Channing.*

> ### EACH IN HIS OWN TONGUE
>
> A fire-mist and a planet,—
>   A crystal and a cell,—
> A jellyfish and a saurian,
>   And caves where the cavemen dwell;
> Then a sense of law and beauty,
>   And a face turned from the clod,—
> Some call it Evolution,
>   And others call it God.
>
> A picket frozen on duty,—
>   A mother starved for her brood,—
> Socrates drinking the hemlock,
>   And Jesus on the rood;
> And millions who humble and nameless,
>   The straight hard pathway plod,—
> Some call it Consecration,
>   And others call it God.
>
> —WILLIAM HERBERT CARRUTH.

THE CYNIC is one who never sees a good quality in a man, and never fails to see a bad one.

The *cynic* is one who knows the price of everything and the value of nothing.
—*Oscar Wilde.*

DIFFICULTIES are God's errands; and when we are sent upon them, we should esteem it a proof of God's confidence.—*Beecher.*

GIFTS are what a man has, but graces are what a man is.—*F. W. Robertson.*

SYMPATHY

What is sympathy? It is thinking
More of others than yourself,
Counting hearts of fellow mortals
Of more worth than paltry self,
Acting for your comrade's pleasure,
Giving without stint or art;
It is blessing every creature
With your hand and voice and heart.

ENTHUSIASM is a telescope that yanks the misty, distant future into the radiant, tangible present.

DUTY is a power which rises with us in the morning, and goes to rest with us at night. It is co-extensive with the action of our intelligence. It is the shadow which cleaves to us, go where we will, and which only leaves us when we leave the light of life.—*Gladstone.*

FORTITUDE is the marshal of thought, the armor of the will and the fort of reason.—*Bacon.*

MAN—Every man is a volume, if you know how to read him.—*Channing.*

Flower in the crannied wall,
I pluck you out of the crannies;—
Hold you here, root and all, in my hand,
Little flower—but if I could understand
What you are, root and all, and all in all,
I should know what God and man is.
                              —*Tennyson.*

PRAYER is a shield to the soul, a sacrifice to God, and a scourge for Satan.
                              —*Bunyan.*

What Is Good

"What is the real good?"
   I asked in musing mood,
"Order," said the law court;
   "Knowledge," said the school;
"Truth," said the wise man;
   "Pleasure," said the fool;
"Love," said the maiden;
   "Beauty," said the page;
"Freedom," said the dreamer;
   "Home," said the sage;
"Fame," said the soldier;
   "Equity," the seer.
Spake my heart full sadly
   "The answer is not here."
Then within my bosom
   Softly this I heard:
"Each heart holds the secret,
   Kindness is the word."
                —*John Boyle O'Reilly.*

FRIENDSHIP is, strictly speaking, reciprocal benevolence, which inclines each party to be solicitous for the welfare of the other as for his own. This equality of affection is created and preserved by a similarity of disposition and manners.—*Plato.*

HELL is truth seen too late.—*Adam.*

FAITH is the soul riding at anchor.
                              —*H. W. Shaw.*

PERSEVERENCE is failing nineteen times and succeeding the twentieth.
                              —*J. Andrews.*

RICHES—To have what we want is riches, but to be able to do without is power.—*Donald Grant.*

STATEMANSHIP — True statesmanship consists of discovering which way God is going and getting the obstacles out of the way.—*Gunsaulus.*

ADVERSITY is the path of truth.
                              —*Byron.*

CHRISTIANITY is a battle, not a dream.—*Wendell Phillips.*

SAINT—"A little child on a summer morning stood in a great Cathedral Church. The sunlight streamed through the beautiful stained glass windows and the figures in them of the servants of God were bright with brilliant color. A little later the question was asked, 'What is a saint?' and the child replied, A saint is a person who lets the light shine through'."—*Anonymous.*

GOD—That unity of bests.
                              —*Mrs. Browning.*

PREACHERS—"The poorest of trades and the noblest of callings," is what Dr. Cuyler calls the ministry of the Gospel.

PRUDENCE is the footprint of wisdom.—*A. Bronson Alcott.*

XI. EDUCATION

INFLUENCE — James A. Garfield said that a log with a student on one end and Mark Hopkins, his old teacher, on the other end was his ideal college. The point in it all is that personal contact and direct interest in the individual student by an instructor of lofty character is the main thing in any institution of learning.—*F. S. Groner.*

TRUTH — Nobody wants mathematics from a Methodist viewpoint, nor physics as a Presbyterian doctrine, nor chemistry as a Congregational subject, nor ethics from an Episcopalian angle, nor dogma mixed with science, nor denominationalism taught. But with its chief and eternal concern with truth, the Church is becoming free intellectually and spiritually through truth wherever discovered.
—*Winifred Willard.*

THE THINKER

Back of the beating hammer
  By which the steel is wrought,
Back of the workshop's clamor
  The seeker may find the thought;
The thought that is ever master
  Of iron and steam and steel,
That rises above disaster
  And tramples it under heel!

Might of the roaring boiler,
  Force of the engine's thrust,
Strength of the sweating toiler,
  Greatly in these we trust.
But back of them stands the schemer,
  The thinker who drives things
    through;
Back of the job—the dreamer,
  Who's making the dream come true!
      —BERTON BRALEY.
Copyright by Berton Braley, all rights reserved.

INSPIRATION — I read in Shakespeare of the majesty of the moral law, in Victor Hugo the sacredness of childhood, in Tennyson, the ugliness of hypocrisy, in George Elliot the supremacy of duty, in Dickens the divinity of kindness, and in Ruskin the dignity of service. Irving teaches me the lesson of cheerfulness. Hawthorne shows me the hatefulness of sin, Longfellow gives me the soft, tranquil music of hope. Lowell makes us feel that we must give ourselves to our fellow men. Whittier sings to me of divine Fatherhood and human brotherhood. These are Christian lessons. Who inspired them?

Who put it into the heart of Martin Luther to nail those theses on the church door of Wittenberg? Who stirred and fired the soul of Savonarola? Who thrilled and electrified the soul of John Wesley? Jesus Christ is back of these all.
—*Powell.*

SCIENCE—The goal of science is to describe the universe; the goal of religion is to find the most abundant life which man may possess in such a universe.
—*Kirtley F. Mather.*

RELIGION as regards its general influence over the mind of a nation, apart from and independent of religious education, forms a separate and very important element in the promotion of civilization. The Christian religion is in its nature highly favorable to the civilization alike of individuals and of states, and both intellectually and morally. The knowledge that it teaches is the highest and most elevating; and the principles that it enforces are the purest and most comprehensive.—*George Harris.*

THE WAY TO FREEDOM — We are accustomed to say that the truth makes men free. It does nothing of the kind. It is the knowledge of the truth that creates freedom. "Ye shall know the truth, and the truth shall make you free." We are now at the stage where the main emphasis must be laid on the dissemination of the truth. We need as we have never needed a campaign of education, with men and women going hither and thither in a great lecture campaign, weaving itself across this nation like a weaver's shuttle. We need a baptism of the right kind of literature, periodicals, and truth-carrying messages that will make the people of the nations and the rest of the world sit up and take notice. We have reached the place where we can no longer take the defensive: we must once again resume the offensive. The colleges, universities, and high schools, with the three millions of young men and women in those institutions, who are to take their place in the life of the nation just a few years hence, are the laboratory where truth must be demonstrated.

—*Ernest H. Cherrington.*

STAGNANT TRUTH—Do not mistake acquirement of mere knowledge for power. Like food, these things must be digested and assimilated to become life or force. Learning is not wisdom; knowledge is not necessarily vital energy. The student who has to cram through a school or a college course, who has made himself merely a receptacle for the teacher's thoughts and ideas, is not educated; he has not gained much. He is a reservoir, not a fountain. One retains, the other gives forth. Unless his knowledge is converted into wisdom, into faculty, it will become stagnant like still water.

—*J. E. Dinger.*

HEAD VS. HEART—What I am concerned about in this fast-moving world in a time of crisis, both in foreign and domestic affairs, is not so much a program as a spirit of approach, not so much a mind as a heart. A program lives today and dies tomorrow. A mind, if it be open, may change with each day, but the spirit and the heart are as unchanging as the tides.

—*Owen D. Young.*

A builder builded a temple;
  He wrought with care and skill;—
Pillars and groins and arches
  Were fashioned to meet his will;
And men said when they saw its beauty:
  "It shall never know decay.
Great is thy skill, O Builder,
  Thy fame shall endure for aye."

A teacher builded a temple;
  She wrought with skill and care;—
Forming each pillar with patience,
  Laying each stone with prayer.
None saw the unceasing effort;
  None knew of the marvelous plan;
For the temple the teacher builded
  Was unseen by the eyes of man.

Gone is the builder's temple;—
  Crumbled into the dust,—
Pillar and groin and arches
  Food for consuming rust;
But the temple the teacher builded
  Shall endure while the ages roll;—
For that beautiful, unseen temple
  Was a child's immortal soul.

REFLECTION — The man who thinks, reads, studies, and meditates has intelligence cut in his features, stamped on his brow, gleaming in his eyes, and sooner or later the face tells the status or the condition of the soul—a reflection of the divinity within the man.—*Record.*

STUDY—A beginning of days to many preachers would be to take possession of some new province of literature, as Robert Hall did when, after sixty, he studied Italian to read Dante; as Arnold did when, two years before his death, he began Sanskrit, pleading that he "was not so old as Cato when he learned Greek." How many weary and starved congregations listen hopelessly to a dejected preacher who will never give them a word, a phrase, or a thought they have not heard hundreds of times.—*Beecher.*

DEDICATION—Let us now with earnest hearts and with exalted faith and hope solemnly consecrate this building to its high and holy purpose. May the youth of this community for generations to come gather in this place to receive instruction in knowledge and training in virtue. May they find here every condition necessary to a true and enlightened education. Especially, may their teachers be examples of excellence in scholarship and character, seekers after goodness and truth, lovers of children, enthusiasts and adepts in the finest of all arts, the development and inspiration of human souls. May these rooms always be pervaded with an invigorating atmosphere of mental and moral life, and may no child pass from these schools to higher grades or to the outer world without having been made more intelligent, more thoughtful, more courageous, more virtuous, and in every way more capable of wise and just, of useful and noble living. To this end, may the blessing of God be upon child and parent, upon pupil and teacher, upon principal and superintendent and upon every one whose influence will in any degree affect the work of education as it shall be conducted within these walls.

—*Scott.*

EXPERIENCE TEACHES—It is not enough to have books, or to know where to read up for information when we want it. Practical wisdom for the purposes of life must be carried about with us, and be ready for use at call. It is not enough that we have a fund laid up at home, but not a farthing in our pocket: we must carry about with us a store of the current coin of knowledge ready for exchange on all occasions, else we are helpless when the opportunity for action occurs. The experience gathered from books is of the nature of learning; the experience gained from actual life is of the nature of wisdom; and a small store of the latter is worth vastly more than any stock of the former.

—*Smiles.*

The Teacher

Lord, who am I to teach the way
   To little children day by day,
So prone myself to go astray?

I teach them knowledge, but I know
   How faint they flicker and how low
The candles of my knowledge glow.

I teach them power to will and do,
   But only now to learn anew
My own great weakness thru and thru.

I teach them love for all mankind
   And all God's creatures, but I find
My love comes lagging far behind.

Lord, if their guide I still must be,
   Oh, let the little children see
The teacher leaning hard on Thee.

     —*Leslie Pinckney Hill.*

TRUE REPOSE—I have sought repose everywhere, and I have found it only in a little corner with a little book.

     —*St. Francois de Sales.*

RIGHTEOUSNESS—President McCosh, in his Baccalaureate sermon, said to the graduating boys: "I say to you intending lawyers, see that ye yield to no crookedness; and to you intending merchants, that ye be honorable in all your transactions; to you intending journalists, that ye write only what ye know to be true; and you, ministers of the everlasting Gospel, that your aim be to win souls to Christ; and to all that ye live soberly, righteously, and godly."

~

THE ART OF LIVING WELL — "Public instruction," said Napoleon, "should be the first object of government." "All who have meditated on the art of governing mankind," said Aristotle, "have been convinced that the fate of empires depends upon the education of youth." "Knowledge," said Daniel Webster, "does not comprise all which is contained in the large term 'education'. The feelings are to be disciplined, the passions are to be restrained, true and worthy motives are to be instilled, and pure morality inculcated under all circumstances. All this is comprised in education." "Teach," said Seneca, "the art of living well." "Reason and experience both forbid us to expect," said Washington, "that national morality can prevail in exclusion of religious principles." "Educate men without religion," said the Duke of Wellington, "and you make of them but clever devils." "Religion and liberty are inseparable," said Philip Schaff. "True religion," said Burke, "is the foundation of society. When that is once shaken by contempt the whole fabric cannot be stable or lasting."—Public Speakers Library.

~

FUNDAMENTALS—Manhood, not scholarship, is the first aim of education.
—Ernest Thompson Seton.

A NATION'S DESTINY—A nation's destiny is not in its learning or the amount of information it acquires—it's in its character. The heart of culture is the culture of the heart. The only way to form character is through religion. Find me another way and I'll accept it. The only system of education worthy of the name of system, much less education, is that one which literally and actually inculcates the eternal truth of morality, not only by teaching, but by hour-to-hour example. I do not speak as a politician. I am speaking as an expert. I am not a theorist. The reason I dare speak is that every day, every hour, I am face to face with the real thing here, with the facts.
—Talley.

~

SHAMS—As one grows older one is more impatient with subterfuges and shams generally, and increasingly desirous that the "last run" at least should be free from them. The world is apparently so confused that the least one can do for it is to keep one's mental integrity and to hold honestly to such poor wisdom as one has been able to garner on the way.
—Jane Addams.

~

EXAMPLE—Education does not mean teaching people what they do not know. It means teaching them to behave as they do not behave. It is not teaching the youth the shapes of letters and the tricks of numbers, and then leaving them to turn their arithmetic to roguery, and their literature to lust. It means, on the contrary, training them into the perfect exercise and kingly continence of their bodies and souls. It is a painful, continual and difficult work to be done by kindness, by watching, by warning, by precept, and by praise, but above all—by example.
—John Ruskin.

HUMAN SCULPTURE—A statue lies hid in a block of marble, and the art of statuary only clears away the superfluous matter and removes the rubbish. The figure is in the stone; the sculpture only finds it. What sculpture is to a block of marble, education is to a human soul. The philosopher, the saint, or the hero, the wise, the good or the great man, very often lies hid and concealed in a plebian, which a proper education might have disinterred, and have brought to light.

—*Addison.*

WISDOM—A man should never be ashamed to own he has been in the wrong, which is but saying in other words that he is wiser today than he was yesterday.

—*Pope.*

STUDYING—I would say to every person read with your pencil. Never pass a word, or an allusion, or a name you do not understand without marking it down for inquiry. Then go to your dictionary for the definition or explanation; go to the encyclopedia for information as to biographical or historical allusions. Never read about any country without having a map before you. This kind of study will fix things in your minds as no formal method of the schools ever will.

—*Beecher.*

READ the best books first, or you may not have a chance to read them at all.

—*Thoreau.*

SAFETY FIRST—The safety of our sons and daughters as they go out on the streets this very night is due to the influence of the preachers rather than to policemen and lawmakers. The safety of our nation, including all groups, depends on Christian education.—*Roger Babson.*

INTELLECT—The intellect makes religion a science; the heart feels it as a life. To the one it is philosophy; to the other, practice. The one cannot, by its very nature, find what it seeks; the other cannot miss it. Mere intellect can only see the trailing garments of God as He passes by; love lies in His bosom. Tasking himself beyond his powers, man is lost when he seeks to think out the Infinite. As a phantom is said to rise in the desert and beckon the traveler into its depths to perish, speculation tempts the mind into the trackless wastes of the unknown, to lose itself in immensity. True wisdom comes in the end to feel, with Socrates, that the highest knowledge is to know that we know nothing.—*Selected.*

Church

What is the church? The church is man
    when his awed soul goes out,
In reverence to a mystery that swathes
    him all about.
When any living man in awe gropes
    Godward in his search;
Then in that hour, that living man becomes the living church,
Then, though in wilderness or in waste,
    his soul is swept along
Down naves of prayer, through aisles of
    praise, up altar-stairs of song.
And where man fronts the Mystery with
    spirit bowed in prayer,
There is the universal church—the church
    of God is there.

From SONGS OF THE AVERAGE MAN. By Sam Walter Foss. Copyright 1907, Lothrop, Lee & Shepard Co., Inc., New York.

LEADERS — We are building many splendid churches in this country, but we are not providing leaders to run them. I would rather have a wooden church with a splendid parson than a splendid church with a wooden parson.—*Drury.*

ONE-SIDED.—I distrust the man of one book, or of one class of books. A lawyer may get no direct aid from Tennyson, but you may more safely trust your case with him, because the fact of reading such an author indicates that he covers more space in human thought. A physician cannot study human nature in Shakespeare without getting a conception of man helpful in his practice. Nor will a preacher be any the worse, but all the better, for not confining himself to works of theology. The men who think and read in various directions are the better entitled to their opinions. Read variously, and you will find after a time that one of the chief delights of reading is substantiating what you find in one department by what you find in another. One thus follows the hidden threads which bind the creation into a unity.—*T. T. Munger.*

WHO IS EDUCATED?—A professor in Chicago is reported to have given the following test to his pupils. He told them they were not really educated unless they could say Yes to all these questions:

Has your education given you sympathy with all good causes and made you espouse them?

Has it made you public-spirited?

Has it made you a brother to the weak?

Have you learned how to make friends and to keep them?

Do you know what it is to be a friend yourself?

Can you look an honest man or a pure woman straight in the eye?

Do you see anything to love in a little child?

Will a lonely dog follow you down the street?

Can you be high-minded and happy in the meaner drudgeries of life?

Do you think washing dishes and hoeing corn just as compatible with high thinking as piano playing or golf?

Are you good for anything to yourself? Can you be happy alone?

Can you look out on the world and see anything but dollars and cents?

Can you look into a mud puddle by the wayside and see anything in the puddle but mud?

Can you look into the sky at night and see beyond the stars?

Can your soul claim relationship with the Creator?

A GREAT MAN is what he is, because he was what he was.

To a Music Teacher

You cannot practice for her every day
The knowledge that you give her will not stream
On her young mind in one bright, blinding ray
But you can plant a dream.

Ah, you can plant a dream in her young heart
A dream of excellence whose light will gleam
Upon her pathway as the years depart
Your words can plant a dream.

To sow a dream and see it spread and grow
To light a lamp and watch its brightness gleam
Here is a gift that is divine I know
To give a child a dream.
—*Anne Campbell.*

INSURANCE — "Cultivate literature and useful knowledge, for the purpose of qualifying the rising generation for patrons of good government, virtue and happiness."—*George Washington.*

XII. FAITH

BELIEF—An Every-Day Creed—I *believe* in my job. It may not be a very important job, but it is *mine.* Furthermore, it is God's job, for *me.* He has a purpose in my life with reference to His plan for the world's progress. No other fellow can take my place. It isn't a big place, to be sure, but for years I have been molded in a peculiar way to fill a peculiar niche in the world's work. I could take no other man's place. He has the same claim as a specialist that I make for myself. In the end the man whose name was never heard beyond the house in which he lived, or the shop in which he worked, may have a larger place than the chap whose name has been a household word in two continents. Yes, I believe in my job. May it be kept true to the task which lies before me—true to myself and to God, who intrusted me with it.

I *believe* in my fellow-man. He may not always agree with me. I'd feel sorry for him if he did, because I myself do not believe some of the things that were absolutely sure in my own mind a dozen years ago. May he never lose faith in himself, because, if he does, he may lose faith in me, and that would hurt him more than the former, and it would really hurt him more than it would hurt me.

I *believe* in my country. I believe in it because it is made up of my fellow-men—and myself. I can't go back on either of us and be true to my creed. If it isn't the best country in the world it is partly because I am not the kind of a man that I should be.

I *believe* in my home. It isn't a rich home. It wouldn't satisfy some folks, but it contains jewels which cannot be purchased in the markets of the world. When I enter its secret chambers, and shut out the world with its care, I am a lord. Its motto is Service, its reward is Love. There is no other spot in all the world which fills its place, and heaven can be only a larger home, with a Father who is all-wise and patient and tender.

I *believe* in today. It is all that I possess. The past is of value only as it can make the life of today fuller and freer. There is no assurance of tomorrow. I must make good today!—*Charles Stelzle.*

O world, thou choosest not the better
     part!
It is not wisdom to be only wise,
And on the inward vision close the
     eyes,
But it is wisdom to believe the heart.
Columbus found a world and had no
     chart,
Save one that faith deciphered in the
     skies;
To trust the soul's invincible surmise
Was all his science and his only art.
Our knowledge is a torch of smoky pine
That lights the pathway but one step
     ahead
Across a void of mystery and dread.
Bid, then, the tender light of faith to
     shine
By which alone the mortal heart is led
Unto the thinking of the thought di-
     vine.

—GEORGE SANTAYANA.

GREAT ERAS—All great ages have been ages of belief. I mean, when there was any extraordinary power of performance, when great national movements began, when arts appeared, when heroes existed, when poems were made, the human soul was in earnest.

—*Ralph Waldo Emerson.*

AS A MAN THINKETH—A competent scientist reports the result of a test with three men in the British Army: "I asked the three men to submit themselves to a test designed to measure the effect of their mental attitude on their physical strength, this strength to be registered by a single gripping device operated by the right hand. In their normal state, these three men had an average grip of 101 pounds. When, under hypnosis, I told them they were very weak, their utmost effort registered only 29 pounds. But when, still keeping the men under hypnosis, I told them they were very strong, their average strength jumped back to the normal 101 pounds and then rose to 142 pounds. They were actually 40% stronger when they believed they were strong, and actually 70% weaker when they believed they were weak."

IN SPITE OF DUNGEON, FIRE, OR SWORD
I have loved justice; therefore have I borne
Conflict and labor, plot and biting scorn.
Guardian of Faith, for Christ's dear sake would I
Suffer with gladness and in prison die.
—*Pope Leo XIII.*

IMPOSSIBILITIES—Faith laughs at impossibilities, and says "it shall be done." Abraham's faith was adventurous when he went out, not knowing whither he went. Every promise claimed is a promice possessed. Believe, and thou shalt see. Those who are afraid of the deep will not catch many fishes. Have the courage to "launch out." We need pioneers in the realms of faith as well as in the dark places of the earth, and no other field of exploration can ever yield such rewards, for "every place where the sole of your feet shall tread upon shall be yours."
—*S. S. Times.*

BEYOND THE FACTS—There need not be in religion, or music, or art, or love, or goodness, anything that is against reason; but never while the sun shines will we get great religion, or music, or art, or love, or goodness, without going beyond reason.
—*Harry Emerson Fosdick.*

QUIETNESS
"Be still and know that I am God,"
That I who made and gave thee life
Will lead thy faltering steps aright;
That I who see each sparrow's fall
Will hear and heed thy earnest call.
 I am God.

"Be still and know that I am God,"
When aching burdens crush thy heart,
Then know I form thee for thy part
And purpose in the plan I hold.
 Trust in God.

"Be still and know that I am God,"
Who made the atom's tiny span
And set it moving to My plan,
That I who guide the stars above
Will guide and keep thee in My love.
 Be thou still.
—*Doran.*

IMPROVING—Such as do not grow in grace, decay in grace. There is no standing at a stay in religion, either we go forward or backward; if faith does not grow, unbelief will; if heavenly mindedness doth not grow, covetousness will. A man that doth not increase his stock diminisheth it; if you do not improve your stock of grace, your stock will decay. The angels on Jacob's ladder were either ascending or descending; if you do not ascend in religion, you descend.
—*T. Watson.*

HOPE!—Who is insensible to the music of that word? What bosom has not kindled under its utterance? Poetry has sung of it; music has warbled it; oratory has lavished on it its bewitching strains. Fled from the world, Hope, with her elastic dreams, said that when all other divinities fled from the world, Hope, with her elastic step and radiant countenance and lustrous attire, lingered behind. Hope! well may we personify thee, lighting up thy altar-fires in this dark world, and dropping a live coal into many desolate hearts; gladdening the sick chamber with visions of returning health; illuminating with rays, brighter than the sunbeam, the captive's cell; crowding the broken slumbers of the soldier by his bivouac-fire with pictures of his sunny home and his own joyous return. Hope! drying the tear on the cheek of woe! As the black clouds of sorrow break and fall to the earth, arching the descending drops with thine own beauteous rainbow! Ay, more, standing with thy lamp in thy hand by the gloomy realms of Hades, kindling thy torch at Nature's funeral pile, and opening vistas through the gates of glory! If Hope, even with reference to present and infinite things, be an emotion so joyous— if uninspired poetry can sing so sweetly of its delights, what must be the believer's hope, the hope which has God for its object and Heaven its consummation?

—*John MacDuff.*

God's Witnesses

I need not shout my faith. Thrice eloquent
   Are quiet trees and the green listening
     sod;
Hushed are the stars, whose power is
     never spent;
   The hills are mute: yet how they speak
     of God!

—*Charles Hanson Towne.*

FAITH and obedience are bound up in the same bundle. He that obeys God trusts God; and he that trusts God obeys God. He that is without faith is without works; and he that is without works is without faith.—*Spurgeon.*

His Strength

And, as the path of duty is made plain,
May grace be given that I may walk there-
   in,
Not like the hireling, for his selfish gain,
With backward glances and reluctant
   tread,
Making a merit of his coward dread,—
   But, cheerful, in the light around me
     thrown,
   Walking as one to pleasant service led;
   Doing God's will as if it were my own,
Yet trusting not in mine, but in His
   strength alone!

—*John Greenleaf Whittier.*

LIFT THE LATCH—Israel could not enter Canaan because of their unbelief. There is many a promised land from which we are excluded for the same reason. For instance, how many of us enjoy the "perfect peace" which is the privilege of the true believer? How many of us have got beyond "hoping" we are saved and "trusting" we are forgiven? They which have believed "do enter into rest." But this Canaan is denied to the only half-believer. He is like a foolish child lingering on a cold, wintry, tempestuous night out in the snow and the wind, while all is warm and tranquil at the fireside within— the supper spread for him, and a vacant seat placed at the table ready for him— because he cannot bring himself fully to believe that if he lifted the latch he would receive instant and joyful welcome.

—*J. Halsey.*

EQUATIONS — Two and two make four—that is mathematics; hydrogen and oxygen form water—that is chemistry; Christ crucified is the power of God unto salvation—that is revelation. But how do you know? Put two and two together and you have four: count and see. Put hydrogen and oxygen together and you have water: test and you will prove it. Believe in the Lord Jesus Christ and thou shalt be saved: believe and you will know. Each demonstration is unanswerable in its own sphere.

—*F. G. Penticost.*

WAITING

Serene, I fold my hands and wait,
    Nor care for wind, nor tide, nor sea;
I rave no more 'gainst time or fate,
    For, lo! mine own shall come to me.

I stay my haste, I make delays,
    For what avails this eager pace?
I stand amid the eternal ways,
    And what is mine shall know my face.

Asleep, awake, by night or day,
    The friends I seek are seeking me;
No wind can drive my bark astray,
    Nor change the tide of destiny.

What matter if I stand alone?
    I wait with joy the coming years;
My heart shall reap where it has sown,
    And garner up its fruit of tears.

The waters know their own, and draw
    The brook that springs in yonder heights;
So flows the good with equal law
    Unto the soul of pure delights.

The stars come nightly to the sky;
    The tidal wave comes to the sea;
Nor time, nor space, nor deep, nor high,
    Can keep my own away from me.

—*John Burroughs.*

REVERENCE — In England, as in America, audiences uniformly rise when choirs begin to sing the Hallelujah Chorus in the Oratorio of the Messiah. In Albert Hall, London, a great audience was assembled. Victoria, the Great and the Good, was present in the royal box. The audience rose, but the noble queen remained seated. Soon every eye was directed to the royal box in which sat the queen. On rolled the magnificent chorus; but the queen remained seated. Higher still rose the lofty song; onward swept the glorious music. With curious glances, the audience turned to the royal box in which the queen remained seated. Loftier still rose the celestial notes. Now the song reached the part where Christ is praised as "King of kings and Lord of lords." The swelling song puts the crown of universal dominion on His divine brow. Then the noble queen arose and stood with bowed head, as if she would cast the crown of her mighty empire at the pierced feet of her divine Lord. Creation and revelation, art and science, song and story, learning and genius, and all earthly rulers reach their noblest heights when they bend in lowliest reverence at the feet of Jesus Christ.—*McArthur.*

THE EVIDENCE

In every seed to breathe the flower,
    In every drop of dew
To reverence a cloistered star
    Within the distant blue;
To wait the promise of the bow
    Despite the cloud between,
Is Faith—the fervid evidence
    Of loveliness unseen.

—*John B. Tabb.*

OPINIONS—A string of opinions no more constitutes faith, than a string of beads constitutes holiness.—*J. Wesley.*

EVIDENCE—Thousands and tens of thousands have gone through the evidence which attests the resurrection of Christ, piece by piece, as carefully as ever a judge summed up on the most important case. I have myself done it many times over, not to persuade others, but to satisfy myself. I have been used for many years to study the history of other times, and to examine and weigh the evidence of those who have written about them, and I know of no fact in the history of mankind which is proved by better and fitter evidence and every kind.—*Arnold.*

ATTAINMENT

Use all your hidden forces. Do not miss
The purpose of this life, and do not wait
For circumstance to mold or change your
    fate.
In your own self lies destiny. Let this
Vast truth cast out all fear, all prejudice,
All hesitation. Know that you are great,
Great with divinity. So dominate
Environment, and enter into bliss.—
Love largely and hate nothing. Hold no
    aim
That does not chord with universal good.
Hear what the voices of the silence say,
All joys are yours if you put forth your
    claim,
Once let the spiritual laws be understood,
Material things must answer and obey.
        —*Ella Wheeler Wilcox.*

THE OLD-TIME RELIGION —
Someone has said, "If we could get religion like a Baptist, experience it like a Methodist, be positive about it like a Disciple, be proud of it like an Episcopalian, pay for it like a Presbyterian, propagate it like an Adventist, and enjoy it like a Negro—that would be some religion!"
        —*Harry Emerson Fosdick.*

GREATEST — My greatest loss — To lose my soul.
    My greatest gain—Christ my Savior.
    My greatest object—To glorify God.
    My greatest pride—A crown of glory.
    My greatest work—To win souls for Christ.
    My greatest joy—The joy of God's salvation.
    My greatest inheritance—Heaven and its glories.
    My greatest victory — Over death through Christ.
    My greatest neglect—To neglect so great salvation.
    My greatest crime—To reject Christ the only Savior.
    My greatest privilege — Power to become a son of God.
    My greatest bargain—The loss of all things to win Christ.
    My greatest profit—Godliness in this life and that to come.
    My greatest peace — That peace that passeth understanding.
    My greatest knowledge—To know God and Jesus Christ whom He hath sent.
        —*Dinger.*

MY CREED

I would be true, for there are those that
    trust me;
  I would be pure, for there are those who
    care;
I would be strong, for there is much to
    suffer;
I would be brave, for there is much to
    dare.
I would be friend of all — the foe — the
    friendless;
  I would be giving, and forget the gift;
I would be humble, for I know my weakness;
  I would look up—and laugh—and love
    —and lift.
        —*Howard Arnold Walter.*

MOTIVE POWER—Roger W. Babson says: "A man's religion may be strengthened by connection with a live church. But your religion must be part of you, something you feel in your heart and practise in your life." Then he adds: "Religion changes a human being from a small ineffective detached unit, into a part of a mighty whole. It makes him serve others, and this service is returned to him in kind."

There Is No Unbelief

There is no unbelief;
Whoever plants a seed beneath the sod
And waits to see it push away the clod—
He trusts in God.

There is no unbelief;
Whoever says when clouds are in the sky,
"Be patient, heart; light breaketh by and by,"
Trusts the Most High.

There is no unbelief;
Whoever sees 'neath winter's field of snow,
The silent harvest of the future grow—
God's power must know.

There is no unbelief;
Whoever says "tomorrow," "the unknown,"
"The future," trusts the power alone
He dares disown.

There is no unbelief;
The heart that looks on when the eyelids close,
And dares to live when life has only woes,
God's comfort knows.

There is no unbelief;
For thus by day and night unconsciously
The heart lives by that faith the lips deny.
God knoweth why!
—*Elizabeth York Case.*

THE STAR — Christ is our star of Hope. I want my death-bed to be under that star. All other light will fail. The light that falls from the scroll of fame, the light that flashes from the gem in the beautiful apparel, the light that flashes from the lamps of a banquet—but this light burns on and on. Paul kept his eye on that star until he could say, "I have finished my course." Edward Payson kept his eye on that star until he could say, "The breezes of Heaven fan my brow." John Tennant kept his eye on that star until he could say, "Welcome Lord Jesus, welcome eternity." No other star ever pointed a man into so safe a harbor.
—*Talmage.*

Trust

Build a little fence of trust
Around today;
Fill each space with loving work
And therein stay;
Look not through the sheltering bars
Upon tomorrow,
God will help thee bear what comes,
Of joy or sorrow.
—*Mary Frances Butts.*

EXPERT ADVICE—It is the testimony of people who have tried Christianity. Whenever we wish to know anything we go to one who knows. We seek an expert. If we wish to know something about bridges, we go to a bridge builder. If it be medicine, we go to a physician; law, to a lawyer; agriculture, to a specialist in that department. Why not follow the same rule in religious investigations? Instead of asking an agnostic, whose boast is that he knows nothing about Christianity, let us have the testimony of one who has tried it and who out of his personal experience can say: "I know Whom I have believed."—*Vance.*

NO EASY WAY — There are very few things in this world worth having which can be had cheaply. What we have come to call the strenuous life is essential to all acquisition. One can not get his living for the asking; he must work for his living. Why should it require less persistency and alertness to find a God than is necessary to find a dollar? I once heard a young man remark that the name of God had lost to him all significance. When, however, he was asked whether his interests, reading, and companionships had been such as to keep the spiritual life real and near, he was frank enough to answer that he had never given a thought to such matters for years. He had been living in quite another world, but he fancied that if religion were real, it would somehow break into his world by force.—*Francis G. Peabody.*

Dependence on God

Lord, I am like to mistletoe,
Which has no root and cannot grow
Or prosper, but by that same tree
It clings about; so I by Thee.
What need I then to fear at all
So long as I about Thee crawl?
But if that tree should fall and die,
Tumble shall Heaven, and so down will I.
—*Robert Herrick.*

REVERENCE — The most striking fact in modern life is the growing reverence for the teachings and character of Jesus Christ. As once his brothers' sheaves bowed down before Joseph's sheaf, so today art, literature, law, trade, reform, manifest more and more reverence for that Divine Teacher whose sublime figure already fills the whole horizon, and whose teachings are founded as surely as the mountains and stars.
—*Newell Dwight Hillis.*

THE SILVER CORD — Faith is the silver thread upon which the pearls of the graces are to be strung. Break that, and you have broken the string—the pearls lie scattered on the ground; nor can you wear them for your own adornment. Faith is the mother of virtues. Faith is the fire which consumes sacrifice. Faith is the water which nurtures the root of piety. If you have not faith, all your graces must die. And in proportion as your faith increases, so will all your virtues be strengthened, not all in the same proportion, but all in some degree.—*C. H. Spurgeon.*

SUPPORT — Dr. Griffith Thomas told of the long-time search of the great missionary John G. Paton for a word to use for faith, or belief, when he was making a translation of the Scriptures into the language of those to whom he was seeking to bring Christ. Apparently there was no native word for "believe." For a long time Dr. Paton was well nigh baffled. One day, while working on the translation, a native came into his study, and, tired out, flung himself down on a chair, rested his feet on another chair, and lay back full length, saying as he did so something about how good it was to lean his whole weight on those chairs. Instantly Dr. Paton noted the word the man had used for "lean his whole weight on." The missionary had his word for "believe!" He used it once, and thereafter, in translating the Scriptures. Try it for yourself and see, in any verse that uses the word "believe." "For God so loved the world, that he gave his only begotten Son, that whosoever leans his whole weight on him should not perish, but have eternal life." (John 3:16.) "What must I do to be saved? . . . Lean thy whole weight on the Lord Jesus, and thou shalt be saved." (Acts 16:30, 31.)—*S. S. Times.*

HERITAGE—Paul is yours to lay, as a wise master-builder, the foundation of your faith. Apollos is yours to build on that foundation, to enrich you with his learning, and inspire you with his eloquence. Cephas is yours, with his impetuous devotion, and his stirring reminiscences, and his zeal and experience; all that these have, and all that they are, all that in them can minister to your growth in grace are made over to you. Every variety of Christian sentiment and character is yours if you are Christians at all. You, as joint-heirs with Christ, have a vested right in them which can never be taken away. You, though to the eye of man you may have nothing, in truth possess all things.—*Duckworth.*

The Monitor

A curious child, who dwelt upon a tract
Of inland ground, applying to his ear
The convolutions of a smooth-lipped shell;
To which, in silence hushed, his very soul
Listened intensely; and his countenance
    soon
Brightened with joy; for murmurings from
    within
Were heard, sonorous cadences! whereby
To his belief, the monitor expressed
Mysterious union with his native sea.
Even in such a shell the Universe itself
Is to the ear of Faith: and there are times,
I doubt not, when to you it doth impart
Authentic tidings of invisible things;
Of ebb and flow and ever-during power;
And central peace, subsisting at the heart
Of endless agitation.
    —*William Wordsworth.*

DOUBTS—I will listen to any one's convictions, but pray keep your doubts to yourself.—*Goethe.*

DOUBT—It is impossible for that man to despair who remembers that his Helper is omnipotent.—*Jeremy Taylor.*

TIGHTENED CORDS—Failure will hurt but not hinder us. Disillusion will pain but not dishearten us. Sorrows will shake us but not break us. Hope will set the music ringing and quicken our lagging pace. We need hope for living far more than for dying. Dying is easy work compared with living. Dying is a moment's transition; living, a transaction of years. It is the length of the rope that puts the sag in it. Hope tightens the cords and tunes up the heart-strings. Work well, then; suffer patiently, rejoicing in hope. God knows all, and yet is the God of Hope. And when we have hoped to the end here, He will give us something to look forward to, for all eternity. For "hope abideth."—*Babcock.*

Foolish Pride

When I complained that I had lost my
    hope
Of life eternal with eternal God;
When I refused to read my horoscope
In the unchanging stars, or claim abode
With powers and dominations—but, poor
    clod,
Clung to the earth and grovelled in my
    tears,
Because I soon must lie beneath the sod
And close the little number of my years,—
Then I was told that pride had barred the
    way
And raised this foul rebellion in my head.
Yet, strange rebellion! I, but yesterday,
Was God's own son in His own likeness
    bred.
And thrice strange pride! who thus am
    cast away
And go forth lost and disinherited.
    —*Wilfred Scawen Blunt.*

LOYALTY — There is related in the book, "The Czar," a story of a Russian officer taken prisoner by the French. They got an iron and branded him on the hand with an "N." When he asked what it meant, they said, "It means that you belong, body and soul, to the Emperor Napoleon." The soldier, seizing an axe, severed his hand from the wrist and said, "Take what belongs to you; I am for the Czar, and belong to him." Whether fact or fiction, it shows what entire consecration means, and the kind of loyalty, whole-souled loyalty, Jesus claims for Himself.
—*Chapman.*

HOLDING

In the bitter waves of woe,
Beaten and tossed about
By the sullen winds that blow
From the desolate shores of doubt,
Where the anchors that faith has cast
Are dragging in the gale,
I am quietly holding fast
To the things that cannot fail.
—*Washington Gladden.*

LIMITATIONS — A child might say to a geographer, "You talk about the earth being round! Look on this great crag; look on that deep dell; look on yonder great mountain, and the valley at its feet, and yet you talk about the earth being round." The geographer would have an instant answer for the child. His view is comprehensive; he does not look at the surface of the world in mere detail; he does not deal with inches, and feet, and yards; he sees a larger world than the child has had time to grasp. He explains what he means by the expression, "The earth is a globe," and justifies his strange statement. And so it is with God's wonderful dealings towards us; there are great

rocks and barren deserts, deep, dank, dark pits, and defiles, and glens, and dells, rugged places that we cannot smooth over at all, and yet when He comes to say to us at the end of the journey, "Now look back; there is the way that I have brought you," we shall be enabled to say, "Thou has gone before us and made our way straight."—*Joseph Parker.*

CONVICTION—A man without convictions is a tramp on the road that leads to the land of nowhere.—*Evangelist.*

TRANSCENDENT — We do not have to go to the universe to prove the existence of God from design. We do not have to dig down into the bowels of the earth, nor go up to the stars for proofs of the divine existence. He is not far from every one of us. As Paul says, "In Him we move and have our being;" and as Tennyson says, "Closer is He than breathing; and nearer than hands and feet." God is here. There is no escaping Him. Man is under moral law as well as physical, and if he violates the one code or the other, the penalty will in each case be inflicted. I put my hand in the fire and feel physical pain; that is proof that I have a physical system. I perform a bad action and feel the sting of conscience and the pangs of remorse; that is equally a proof that I have a moral nature. Who made the act?—I did. Who made the pain?—Some one not myself, whom I call God.—*Parkhurst.*

It fortifies my soul to know
That though I perish, truth is so;
That, howso'er I stray and range,
Whate'er I do, Thou dost not change.
I steadier step when I recall
That, if I slip, Thou dost not fall.
—*Arthur Hugh Clough.*

Charity

The place of Charity,
like that of God, is
everywhere. — *Quarles.*

XIII. FAULT FINDING

FUTILE — A wicked man who reproaches a virtuous one is like one who looks up and spits at Heaven; the spittle soils not the Heaven, but comes back and defiles his own face.

—*Sakya-Muni.*

A MIRROR—Search thy own heart; what paineth thee in others in thyself may be.—*Whittier.*

Do you want to know the man against whom you have most reason to guard yourself? Your looking-glass will give a very fair likeness of his face.—*Whateley.*

THE EASIEST WAY — Napoleon said that the man who never makes a mistake never makes war. Those who content themselves with pointing out the mistakes and blunders of those who are in the struggle, are making, themselves, the greatest of all blunders. Nothing is easier than fault-finding. No talent, no self-denial, no brains, no character are required to set up in the grumbling business.—*Robert West.*

CONSIDERATE — There is a good thought in the following incident from a late book: "A dear old friend of mine used to say with the truest Christian charity, when he heard any one being loudly condemned for some fault: 'Ah! well, yes, it seems very bad to me, because that's not my way of sinning'."

—*Williams.*

EVEN IN PARADISE—Some would find fault with the morning-red, if they ever got up early enough. . . The fault-finder will find faults even in Paradise.

—*Thoreau.*

PATIENCE—Endeavor to be always patient of the faults and imperfections of others, for thou hast many faults and imperfections of thy own that require a reciprocation of forbearance. If thou art not able to make thyself that which thou wishest to be, how canst thou expect to mould another in conformity to thy will?

—*Thomas a' Kempis.*

CONFESSION — We confess our little faults only to persuade others that we have no great ones.

—*La Rochefoucauld.*

The Anvil Outlasts the Hammer.—

TRUE RELIGION

I remember that in the time of childhood I was very religious; I rose in the night, was punctual in the performance of my devotions, and abstinent. One night I had been sitting in the presence of my father, not having closed my eyes during the whole time, and with the holy Koran in my embrace, whilst numbers around us were asleep. I said to my father: "Not one of these lifteth up his head to perform his genuflexions, but they are all so fast asleep you would say they are dead." He replied: "Life of your father, it were better if thou also wert asleep than to be searching out the faults of mankind. The boaster sees nothing but himself, having a veil of conceit before his eyes. If he were endowed with an eye capable of discerning God, he would not discern any person weaker than himself."

SAADI—*The Gulistan.*

RID THE WORLD OF A RASCAL
—Make yourself an honest man, and then you may be sure that there is one rascal less in the world.—*Carlyle.*

DEAD LEAVES—You will find it less easy to uproot faults, than to choke them by gaining virtues. Do not think of your faults; still less of others' faults; in every person who comes near you look for what is good and strong: honor that; rejoice in it; and, as you can, try to imitate it; and your faults will drop off, like dead leaves, when their time comes.—*Ruskin.*

NEVER MIND
Some people think so many things;
So many things that are not so;
Never mind their taunts and stings;
You and I, dear—know.
—Ruth Mason Rice.

BLAMELESS — Let him who would move and convince others, be first moved and convinced himself.—*T. L. Cuyler.*

If you would lift me, you must be on higher ground.—*Emerson.*

I can easier teach twenty what were good to be done, than to be one of the twenty to follow mine own teachings.
—Shakespeare.

It is easier to be wise for others than for ourselves.—*La Rochefoucauld.*

CRITICISM — Of course, there are some folks who do not seem to be able to cooperate. Their long suit is criticism—destructive and not constructive criticism, at that. To such I would quote the words of Edmund Burke: "Applaud us when we run, console us when we fall, cheer us when we recover, but for God's sake, let us pass on!"

REVENGE—A little girl was making faces at a bulldog. Her mother reprimanded her. "Well, he started it," said the girl. No doubt the girl was right, for it is no trouble for a bulldog to look ugly. The weakness was in the girl's conclusion drawn from the dog's face. The dog was probably innocent, but if not, the girl gained nothing by competing with him in making faces. The person who proceeds on the theory that he must return every ugly face he sees, or every ugly act which is directed toward him, will have a never-ending and profitless job. Hate has injurious effects on the person who resents, so that he is the chief sufferer.—*Telescope.*

CRITICS — How humiliating it is to find that I am pained when I learn that N or M does not like my preaching, yet am so calmed when all the alphabet, for years, rejected my Master's message.
—J. W. Alexander.

STRIKE AN AVERAGE — I have long been disposed to judge men by their average. If it is reasonably high, I am charitable with faults that look pretty black.—*Ed Howe.*

GOSSIP
There is so much good in the worst of us,
And so much bad in the best of us,
That it ill becomes any of us
To find fault with the rest of us.

SLANDER—Life would be a perpetual flea hunt if a man were obliged to run down all the innuendoes, inveracities, insinuations and misrepresentations which are uttered against him.
—Henry Ward Beecher.

TEMPTATION is like a winter torrent, difficult to cross. Some, then, being most skilful swimmers, pass over, not being whelmed beneath temptations, nor swept down by them at all, while others who are not such, entering into them, sink in them. As, for example, Judas, entering into the temptation of covetness, swam not through it, but, sinking beneath it, was choked both in body and spirit. Peter entered into the temptation of the denial, but having entered it, he was not overwhelmed by it, but manfully swimming through it he was delivered.—*Cyril.*

Three Gates

If I am tempted to reveal
  A tale someone to me has told
About another, let it pass,
  Before I speak, three gates of gold.

Three narrow gates: First, is it *true?*
  Then, is it *needful?* In my mind
Give truthful answer, and the next
  Is last and narrowest, Is it *kind?*

And if, to reach my lips at last,
  It passes through these gateways, three,
Then I may tell the tale, nor fear
  What the result of speech may be.
                    —*Beth Day.*

A FUNDAMENTAL LAW — We are too hasty to believe every evil report. Many an innocent person has been injured by a tale that was without foundation. It is a serious matter to do an injustice to a fellow man by a report that we spread. The first thing, the least thing that one can do before he passes on a story that has come to him, is to stop long enough to ask if it is true. One of the ten fundamental laws of character is, "Thou shalt not bear false witness against thy neighbor."

THE RESPONSIBILITY of tolerance lies with those who have the wider vision.
                    —*George Eliot.*

BUSYBODIES — Most of us are fearless critics of other men's conduct and meticulous denouncers of other men's sins. To mind other people's business is a common pastime of our day. There are very few of us who are not deeply concerned over the reform of—somebody else.

Now there is no more lovely experience than to feel the personal interest of a friend in you and your affairs. But there is no more irritating experience than to be aware of unfriendly meddling and prying into your private affairs.

The man who cannot respect personality is hardly qualified to be listened to on any subject.

I FIND the doing of the will of God leaves me no time for disputing about His plans.—*Macdonald.*

DESERVING—To be suspicious is to invite treachery.—*Voltaire.*

TOLERANT SYMPATHY — There are two kinds of tolerance.

The one comes from indifference. It is a supercilious thing. "No matter what you believe," it seems to say, "you will have to take the consequences. That does not affect me, because I have the right creed."

The other kind of tolerance comes through sympathy. "You and I do not profess the same doctrines," it says, "but we seek the same end,—the glory of God and the good of our fellow men. Our points of view, our circumstances, our educations have been different. The road is not easy. Let us help one another."

RECOGNIZING GREATNESS — There is an old maxim to the effect that only good should be spoken of the dead. It is a noble half-truth and ought to be considered by those who are inclined to injure the good names of people whose voices are stilled in death.

But why should generous praise wait for death? Why can we not introduce the element of eternity into our judgment of living men so that greatness may be recognized and encouraged before it takes its difficult journey into the valley of the shadow?

ABSURDITY — What an absurd thing it is to pass over all the valuable parts of a man, and fix our attention on his infirmities.—*Addison*.

SELF-DISCOVERY

"Within my earthly temple there's a
  crowd;
There's one of us that's humble, one that's
  proud;
There's one that's brokenhearted for his
  sins
And one who, unrepentant, sits and grins;
There's one who loves his neighbor as
  himself
And one who cares for naught but fame
  and pelf.
From such corroding care I would be free
If once I could determine which is me."

VAGARY—Worldly fame is but a breath of wind that blows now this way, and now that, and changes name as it changes direction.—*Dante*.

HOW IMMENSE appear to us the sins that we have not committed.
                    —*Madame Necker*.

FERTILIZING—It is not so much the being exempt from faults, as having overcome them, that is an advantage to us; it being with the follies of the mind as with the weeds of the field, which if destroyed and consumed upon the place of their birth, enrich and improve it more than if none had sprung there before.
                    —*Pope*.

FRIEND—I joked about every prominent man in my lifetime, but I never met one I didn't like.—*Will Rogers*.

DIARY OF A LEGISLATIVE BODY:

"Monday—Soak the rich.

"Tuesday—Begin hearing from the rich.

"Tuesday Afternoon — Decide to give the rich a chance to get richer.

"Wednesday—Tax Wall Street stock sales.

"Thursday — Get word from Wall Street: 'Lay off us or you will get no campaign contributions.'

"Thursday Afternoon — Decide: 'We are wrong about Wall Street.'

"Friday—Soak the little fellow.

"Saturday Morning—Find out there is no little fellow. He has been soaked until he is drowned.

"Sunday—Meditate.

"Next Week—Same procedure, only more talk and less results."—*Will Rogers*.

EVERYONE is eagle-eyed to see another's faults and deformity.—*Dryden*.

HE CENSURES GOD who quarrels with the imperfections of men.—*Burke*.

XIV. FRIENDSHIP

TALISMAN—Friendship, in its truest sense, is next to love the most abused of words. One may call many "friend" and be still ignorant of that sentiment, cooler than passion, warmer than respect, more just and generous than either, which recognizes a kindred spirit in another, and, claiming its right, keeps it sacred by the wise reserve that is to friendship what the purple bloom is to the grape, a charm which once destroyed can never be restored.

—*J. Alcott.*

A TRUE FRIEND is somebody who can make us do what we can.—*Emerson.*

A friend hath the skill and observation of the best physician; the diligence and vigilance of the best nurse; and the tenderness and patience of the best mother.

—*Clarendon.*

GOOD MAN—You may depend upon it that he is a good man whose intimate friends are all good, and whose enemies are decidedly bad.—*Lavater.*

SHINING ARMOR—A blessed thing it is for any man or woman to have a friend; one human soul whom we can trust utterly; who knows the best and the worst of us, and who loves us in spite of all our faults; who will speak the honest truth to us, while the world flatters us to our face, and laughs at us behind our back; who will give us counsel and reproof in the day of prosperity and self-conceit; but who, again, will comfort and encourage us in the day of difficulty and sorrow, when the world leaves us alone to fight our own battle as we can.

—*Kingsley.*

THE GREATEST BOON—For true friendship, it is not enough to have emptied a brotherly glass to each other. to have sat on the same form at school, to have met frequently at the same cafe, to have conversed courteously in the street, to have sung the same songs at the same club, to have worn the same colors as politicians, to have extolled one another in the press. Friendship, indeed, is one of the greatest boons God can bestow on man. It is a union of our finest feelings; a disinterested binding of hearts, and a sympathy between two souls. It is an indefinable trust we repose in one another, a constant communication between two minds, and an unremitting anxiety for each other's souls.—*J. Hill.*

Because you love me, I have found
New joys that were not mine before;
New stars have lightened up my sky
With glories growing more and more.
Because you love me I can rise
To the heights of fame and realms
of power;
Because you love me I may learn
The highest use of every hour.

Because you love me I can choose
To look through your dear eyes and
see
Beyond the beauty of the Now
Far onward to Eternity.

Because you love me I can wait
With perfect patience well possessed;
Because you love me all my life
Is circled with unquestioned rest;
Yes, even Life and even Death
Is all unquestioned and all blest.
—*Pall Mall Magazine.*

A FRIEND IS A PERSON—

Who will help you in the hour of sickness;

Who will lend you a dollar without deducting the interest;

Who will help you up hill when you are sliding down;

Who will defend you in the hour when others speak evil of you;

Who will believe in your innocence until you admit your guilt;

Who will say behind your back what he says to your face;

Who will shake hands with you wherever he meets you, even though you wear patches; and

Who will do all these things without expecting any return.

—*Dorothy C. Retsloff.*

OLD FRIENDSHIP

Beautiful and rich is an old friendship,
Grateful to the touch as ancient ivory,
Smooth as aged wine, or sheen of tapestry
Where light has lingered, intimate and
    long.
Full of tears and warm is an old friend-
    ship
That asks no longer deeds of gallantry,
Or any deed at all—save that the friend
    shall be
Alive and breathing somewhere, like a
    song.
                    —*Eunice Tietjens.*

Reprinted from LEAVES IN WINDY WEATHER by Eunice Tietjens, by permission of Alfred A. Knopf, Inc. Copyright 1926, by Alfred A. Knopf, Inc.

THE LANGUAGE OF FRIEND-SHIP is not words, but meanings. It is an intelligence above language.

WE DO NOT WISH for friends to feed and clothe our bodies—neighbors are kind enough for that—but to do the like office for our spirits.—*Thoreau.*

THESE THREE—Three men are my friends—he that loves me, he that hates me, he that is indifferent to me. Who loves me, teaches me tenderness; who hates me, teaches me caution; who is indifferent to me, teaches me self-reliance.
                    —*Dinger.*

SPENDTHRIFTS—Never cast aside your friends if by any possibility you can retain them. We are the weakest of spendthrifts if we let one friend drop off through inattention, or let one push away another, or if we hold aloof from one for petty jealousy or heedless slight or roughness. Would you throw away a diamond because it pricked you? One good friend is not to be weighed against the jewels of all the earth. If there is coolness or unkindness between us, let us come face to face and have it out. Quick, before the love grows cold. Life is too short to quarrel in, or carry black thoughts of friends. It is easy to lose a friend, but a new one will not come for calling, nor make up for the old one when he comes.
                    —*Anonymous.*

FLATTERY — The friend who holds up before me the mirror, conceals not my smallest faults, warns me kindly, reproves me affectionately, when I have not performed my duty, he is my friend, however little he may appear so. Again, if a man flattering praises and lauds me, never reproves me, overlooks my faults, and forgives them before I have repented, he is my enemy, however much he may appear my friend.—*Herder.*

INDISPENSABLE — So long as we love, we serve. So long as we are loved by others I would almost say we are indispensable; and no man is useless while he has a friend.—*R. L. Stevenson.*

COMPANIONSHIP — Christ asked His disciples to watch with Him in Gethsemane. Tender touch of nature, to make Him with the whole world kin. Two infants will walk hand in hand "in the dark" where neither would go alone. Invalids, who have counted the strokes of midnight's wakeful hours, conjured by the wall flashes and flickers of dim lamps, and need no other service, cry out, Father! Mother! Some one! We sit by them, long and patiently, perhaps dozing, disciple-like, as we hold their hands, saying and doing nothing, but being near them. Through the streets of Paris, between prison and block, the most desperate were often observed sitting upon the cart's edge, hand in hand. Triumph wants friends also. Jesus wants our sympathy still in His warfare with sin on the earth. He who so wanted the society of men will have His own with Him where He is, at last and forever.—*Evans.*

EACH MAN can interpret another's experience only by his own.—*Thoreau.*

THREE KINDS — There are three kinds of friendships which are advantageous, and three which are injurious. Friendship with the upright, friendship with the sincere, and friendship with the man of much information—these are advantageous. Friendship with a man of specious airs, friendship with the insinuatingly soft, friendship with the glib-tongued—these are injurious.—*Confucius.*

BEAUTY HINT NO. 2—Said Mrs. Browning, the poet, to Charles Kingsley, the novelist, "What is the secret of your life? Tell me, that I may make mine beautiful also." Thinking a moment, the beloved old author replied, "I had a friend."

GOD'S BEST GIFT — Blessed are they who have the gift of making friends, for it is one of God's best gifts. It involves many things, but above all, the power of going out of one's self, and appreciating whatever is noble and loving in another.
—*Thomas Hughes.*

In Tune

I don't remember when I first began
To call you "friend." One day, I only
    know,
The vague companionship that I'd seen
    grow
So imperceptibly, turned gold, and ran
In tune with all I'd thought, or dared to
    plan.
Since then, you've been to me like music,
    low,
Yet clear; a fire that throws its warm,
    bright glow
On me as on each woman, child, and
    man,
And common thing that lies within its
    rays;
You've been like wholesome food that
    stays the cry
Of hungry, groping minds; and like a
    star—
A self-sufficient star—you make me raise
My utmost being to a higher sky,
In tune, like you, with earth, yet wide,
    and far.
—*Florence Steigerwalt.*

PERFECTION — Friendship is the highest degree of perfection in society.
—*Montaigne.*

A FRIEND is one who incessantly pays us the compliment of expecting from us all the virtues, and who can appreciate them in us.—*Thoreau.*

FRIEND—A friend is one who needs us and one whom we need. Around us may be many whose companionship we enjoy, but were they suddenly to drop out of their places there would be no soreness, no sense of deprivation, no lack of comfort. We do not need them, neither do they need us. A friend is one to whom we cling, though many leagues of space separate us. Though days pass with no sight of his face or word from his pen, we know our friend loves us and that when we meet again we will be on the same old terms: we shall begin where we left off. A friend is one in whom we can confide. The secret chambers of our soul open to his touch on the latch. Thousands imagine their friends are numbered by scores, but if subjected to these tests every one of them would fall into the great sea of common humanity.—*Dinger.*

IGNORANCE with love is better than wisdom without it.

COMPARISONS

Friendship — Like music heard on the
    waters,
Like pines when the wind passeth by,
Like pearls in the depths of the ocean,
Like stars that enamel the sky,
Like June and the odor of roses,
Like dew and the freshness of morn,
Like sunshine that kisseth the clover,
Like tassels of silk on the corn,
Like mountains that arch the blue
    heavens,
Like clouds when the sun dippeth low,
Like songs of birds in the forest,
Like brooks where the sweet waters flow,
Like dreams of Arcadian pleasures,
Like colors that gratefully blend,
Like everything breathing of kindness—
Like these is the love of a friend.
          —*A. P. Stanley.*

TRIBUTE — I love you not only for what you are, but for what I am when I am with you. I love you not only for what you have made of yourself, but for what you are making of me. I love you for the part of me that you bring out.

I love you for putting your hand into my heaped-up heart, and passing over all the foolish and frivolous and weak things which you cannot help dimly seeing there, and for drawing out into the light all the beautiful, radiant belongings, that no one else had looked quite far enough to find.

I love you for ignoring the possibilities of the fool and weakling in me, and for laying firm hold on the possibilities of good in me. I love you for closing your eyes to the discords in me, and for adding to the music in me by worshipful listening.

I love you because you are helping me to make of the lumber of my life not a tavern but a Temple, and of the words of my every day not a reproach but a song.

I love you because you have done more than any creed could have done to make me good, and more than any fate could have done to make me happy. You have done it just by being yourself. Perhaps that is what being a friend means after all.

HE THAT DOES a base thing for a friend burns the golden thread which ties their hearts together.—*Jeremy Taylor.*

"Hello" only lasts for a minute,
    It's a short, brisk, queer little word.
But, say! there's a lot of cheer in it;
    It's like the first chirp of a bird
In spring, when the hilltops are greening,
    Right after the cold and the snow.
I think when it comes to real meaning,
    There isn't a word like "Hello!"
          —*Ralph Bricker.*

XV. HAPPINESS

ALTERNATIVES—There are two ways of being happy; we may either diminish our wants or augment our means. Either will do, the result is the same. And it is for each man to decide for himself, and do that which happens to be the easiest. If you are idle or sick or poor, however hard it may be for you to diminish your wants, it will be harder to augment your means. If you are active and prosperous or young or in good health, it may be easier for you to augment your means than to diminish your wants. But if you are wise, you will do both at the same time, young or old, rich or poor, sick or well. And if you are very wise, you will do both in such a way as to augment the general happiness of society.—*Benjamin Franklin.*

TASTE—Happiness lies in the taste, and not in things; and it is from having what we desire that we are happy—not from having what others think desirable.
—*La Rochefoucauld.*

HABITS — Gentleness and cheerfulness, these come before all morality; they are the perfect duties . . . If your morals make you dreary, depend upon it they are wrong. I do not say "Give them up," for they may be all you have; but conceal them like vice, lest they should spoil the lives of better and simpler people.
—*Robert Louis Stevenson.*

CHEERFULNESS — The difference between polished iron and iron that is unpolished is the difference between cheerfulness and no cheerfulness. Cheerfulness in a man is that which when people meet him makes them happy.—*Beecher.*

THE SEARCH—If you ever find happiness by hunting for it, you will find it as the old woman did her lost spectacles, safe on her own nose all the time.
—*Josh Billings.*

LOAF AND INVITE YOUR SOUL —There is such a thing as taking ourselves and the world too seriously, or at any rate too anxiously. Half of the secular unrest and dismal, profane sadness of modern society comes from the vain idea that every man is bound to be a critic of life, and to let no day pass without finding some fault with the general order of things, or projecting some plan for its general improvement. And the other half comes from the greedy notion that a man's life does consist, after all, in the abundance of things that he possesseth, and that it is somehow or other more respectable and pious to be always at work trying to make a larger living, than it is to lie on your back in the green pastures and beside the still waters, and thank God that you are alive.—*Henry Van Dyke.*

Who drives the horses of the sun
  Shall lord it but a day;
Better the lowly deed were done,
  And kept the humble way.

The rust will find the sword of fame,
  The dust will hide the crown;
Ay, none shall nail so high his name
  Time will not tear it down.

The happiest heart that ever beat
  Was in some quiet breast
That found the common daylight sweet
  And left to Heaven the rest.
—JOHN VANCE CHENEY.

LAUGH, PREACHER, LAUGH—
Ministers are not martyrs. Most ministers have a saving sense of humor and look on the sunny side of life. When Monday morning rolls along, and it is so-called "Ministers' Blue Monday" they get together like birds of a feather. In those ministers' conferences from time to time the preachers are boys again and swap yarns and experiences. In some of these meetings the cream of humor comes to the top.

One summer while vacationing in New York City my eye fell on the announcement in a prominent paper, offering a prize for the funniest experience on the part of the readers. In due time I sent in mine. A few days later a beautiful check was received for my prize-winning experience. Here it is: I had preached in a certain church on Sunday. On Friday I received the following letter: "Dear Brother: Since I heard you preach I have gotten so that I can not walk. Please get me a wheelchair." If any preacher wishes to go in the wheelchair business I will send him some of my old sermons.

A friend of mine married a couple. The girl weighed probably close to 300 pounds. The man would not weigh more than a hundred, judging from his diminutive size. When the time came for the presentation of the wedding ring the little groom was about to place the band of gold on the ring finger of the colossal bride. It did not fit, whereupon the little fellow exclaimed: "Oh baby, it does not fit." The preacher was asked to furnish a file, and the little groom, who was a mechanic as well as an ardent lover, filed the ring off until it fitted, whereupon the ceremony was completed.

A very pompous preacher, whose bay window was the only sign of his greatness and who had a fairly good opinion of himself, was trying to make a gathering of people laugh at the expense of a preacher who was not quite so corpulent as he. The preacher of small stature had a reputation of being a hearty eater. He had also the reputation of being witty. Listen to the historic dialogue: "A great deal of good food has been wasted on Brother Little; it does not seem to have done him much good." Laughter. Whereupon Brother Little quietly arose saying: "Mr. Chairman, food affects different people in different ways. For instance, in some people it makes tissue, in other blood, in others bone, in others muscle. In my case it makes brain. In the case of Brother Big it all goes to his stomach!" Convulsing laughter.

Although this is only the beginning of a much longer story I will close with an incident that occurred in a community in which I was pastor. One of our members was quite sick. In the yard of her home an immense hog attracted curious people from far and near. Annoyed by the constant stream of visitors, a member of the family put the following notice in the newspaper: "Mrs. Z. is very ill. Please do not come to see the big hog until she is better."—*Marinus James.*

❦

VALUES—A laugh is worth one hundred groans in any market.
—*Charles Lamb.*

❦

A WILD GOOSE CHASE — Happiness in this world, when it comes, comes incidentally. Make it the object of pursuit, and it leads us a wild goose chase, and is never attained. Follow some other object, and very possibly we may find that we have caught happiness without dreaming of it; but likely enough it is gone the moment we say to ourselves, "Here it is!" Like the chest of gold that treasure-seekers find.
—*Nathaniel Hawthorne.*

LAUGHTER—while it lasts, slackens and unbraces the mind, weakens the faculties, and causes a kind of remissness and dissolution in all the powers of the soul; and thus far it may be looked upon as a weakness in the composition of human nature. But if we consider the frequent reliefs we receive from it, and how often it breaks the gloom which is apt to depress the mind and dampen our spirit, with transient, unexpected gleams of joy, one would take care not to grow too wise for so great a pleasure of life.—*Addison.*

PLEASANT—You have not fulfilled every duty, unless you have fulfilled that of being pleasant.—*Charles Buxton.*

MISERABLE—If you want to be miserable think about yourself, about what you want, what you like, what respect people ought to pay you and what people think of you.—*Charles Kingsley.*

HAPPINESS

I asked professors who teach the meaning
　　of life to tell me what is happiness.
And I went to famous executives who boss
　　the work of thousands of men.
They all shook their heads and gave me
　　a smile as though I was trying to fool
　　with them.
And then one Sunday afternoon I wandered out along the Desplaines river
And I saw a crowd of Hungarians under
　　the trees with their women and children and a keg of beer and an accordion.　　　　—*Carl Sandburg.*

From *CHICAGO POEMS* by Carl Sandburg, by permission of the publishers, Henry Holt and Company, Inc. Copyright, 1916 by Henry Holt and Company. Copyright, 1943 by Carl Sandburg.

SUNSHINE — Those who bring sunshine to the lives of others cannot keep if from themselves.—*James M. Barrie.*

MOVING MOUNTAINS — If you only laugh, things don't come so hard. If you laugh at it, the trouble will not seem so real. I know, for I laugh away a mountain.

Jesus told of the faith that removes mountains. May not cheerfulness in the face of difficulty and privation be an evidence of that wonder working faith?
　　　　—*John T. Faris.*

RADIANT WITNESSES—We do not please God more by eating bitter aloes than by eating honey. A cloudy, foggy rainy day is not more heavenly than a day of sunshine. A funeral march is not so much like the music of angels as the songs of birds on a May morning. There is no more religion in the gaunt, naked forest in winter than in the laughing blossoms of the spring, and the rich ripe fruits of autumn. It was not the pleasant things in the world that came from the devil, and the dreary things from God! It was "sin brought death into the world and all our woe;" as the sin vanishes the woe will vanish too. God Himself is the ever-blessed God. He dwells in the light of joy as well as of purity, and instead of becoming more like Him as we become more miserable, and as all the brightness and glory of life are extinguished, we become more like God as our blessedness becomes more complete. The great Christian graces are radiant with happiness. Faith, hope, charity, there is no sadness in them; and if penitence makes the heart sad, penitence belongs to the sinner; not to the saint; as we become more saintly, we have less sin to sorrow over.
　　　　—*R. W. Dale.*

PERFUME—Happiness is a perfume you cannot pour on others without getting a few drops on yourself.

TRUE CONTENT—Be content with your surroundings but not with yourself till you have made the most of them.

GLADNESS—The men whom I have seen succeed best in life have always been cheerful and hopeful men, who went about their business with a smile on their faces, and took the changes and chances of this mortal life like men, facing rough and smooth alike as it came.
—*Charles Kingsley.*

THE POWER BEHIND evolution is the mightiest and surest thing in existence. It is the most dependable thing in the Cosmos. It attends every instant upon man's willingness to cooperate with it, ready to respond richly to his most timid demands. It puts its shoulder to the wheel alongside the weakest and most debased of mortals. . . . The cry of hunger is a manifesto more powerful than the parchment of princes, because it is a voice from Nature. The Law is consistently beneficient. There is such a thing as perfect justice to every man. The greatest good to the greatest number is a sophistical make-shift. Its euphonious persuasiveness has captivated the superficial logic of a science which accepted expedients for principle. But in the light of new truth it is a clear and a most thrilling fact, that good and happiness and justice belong to every single man, and to one as much as another. The new philosophy makes for the universal good without a single creature forgotten; according to himself shall each man share in the universal and appropriable allgood.—*Annie F. Cantwell.*

NOT ENOUGH — Be not simply good, but good for something.—*Thoreau.*

GRIEF—Happiness is to feel that one's soul is good; there is no other, in truth, and this kind of happiness may exist even in sorrow, so that there are griefs preferable to every joy, and such as would be preferred by all those who have felt them.
—*Joseph Joubert.*

CHEER—Among Christians so much prominence has been given to the disciplinary effects of sorrow, affliction, bereavement, that they have been in danger of overlooking the other and more obvious side that by every joy, by every favor, by every sign of prosperity—yea, and by these chiefly—God designs to educate and discipline His children. This one-sided view of the truth has made many morbid, gloomy Christians, who look for God's hand only in the lightning and never think of seeing it in the sunlight. They only enjoy themselves when they are miserable.
—*F. E. Clark.*

CLASSIFICATION — Man is the merriest specie of the creation; all above or below him are serious.—*Addison.*

COMPLETE — The out-and-out Christian is a joyful Christian. The half-and-half Christian is the kind of Christian that a great many of you are—little acquainted with the Lord. Why should we live halfway up the hill and swathed in the mists, when we might have an unclouded sky and a radiant sun over our heads if we would climb higher and walk in the light of His face?
—*Alexander Maclaren.*

THE SECRET—The secret of happiness is not in doing what one likes, but in liking what one has to do.—*Barrie.*

XVI. HOME

NEGLECT—A story is told of a young man who stood at the bar of justice to be sentenced for forgery. The judge had known the young man from childhood, for his father had been a famous legal light and his work on the Law of Trusts was the most exhaustive work on the subject. "Do you remember your father," asked the judge, sternly, "that father whom you have disgraced?" The prisoner answered, "I remember him perfectly. When I went to him for advice or companionship, he would look up from his book on the Law of Trusts and say, 'Run away, boy, I am busy.' My father finished his book, and here I am." The great lawyer had neglected his own trust with awful results.

—*Public Speakers Library.*

JOYS OF HOME

Curling smoke from a chimney low,
And only a few more steps to go.
Faces pressed at a window pane
Watching for someone to come again.
And I am the someone they want to see—
These are the joys life gives to me.

So let me come home at night and rest
With those who know I have done my
    best;
Let the wife rejoice and my children
    smile,
And I'll know by their love that I'm worth
    while.
For this is conquest and world success—
A home where abideth happiness.

—*Edgar A. Guest.*

"Joys of Home" is from the book "When Day is Done" by Edgar A. Guest, copyright 1921 by The Reilly & Lee Co., Chicago.

PEACE AT HOME—He is happiest, be he king or peasant, who finds peace in his home.—*Goethe.*

ADOPTION—When Christ receives a soul into His love, He puts upon him the ring of adoption. Adopted! Why, then, we are brothers and sisters to all the good of earth and Heaven, we have the family name and the family dress; and the Father looks down upon us, robes us, defends and blesses, and the insignia of eternal glory is our coat of arms.

—*Gallaway.*

SELF-RELIANCE — If you would have your son be something in the world, teach him to depend on himself. Let him learn that it is by close and strenuous personal application he must rise—that he must, in short, make himself, and be architect of his own fortune.—*Edwards.*

THE WATCHER

She always leaned to watch for us,
    Anxious if we were late,
In winter by the window,
    In summer by the gate;

And though we mocked her tenderly,
    Who had such foolish care,
The long way home would seem more
    safe
    Because she waited there.

Her thoughts were all so full of us,
    She never could forget!
And so I think that where she is
    She must be watching yet,

Waiting till we come home to her,
    Anxious if we are late—
Watching from Heaven's window,
    Leaning from Heaven's gate.

—MARGARET WIDDEMER.

From CROSS CURRENTS by Margaret Widdemer, copyright, 1921, by Harcourt, Brace and Company, Inc. Reprinted by permission.

LOVE has many ways of expressing itself, but in general the ways are two —the practical and the sentimental. Which is the higher and better way? It is merely a question of appropriateness under the circumstances. Love must express itself very often in coal, and cornmeal, and salt pork, and clothes. But let it not be concluded that love may not express itself in acts of pure sentiment. The soul has needs. Sympathy and tenderness and friendship are just as real and more enduring, than coal and wood. Sometimes a flower is more important than flour; sometimes a word of cheer is better than gold.—*Ferral.*

Measuring Rods

I know what mother's face is like,
  Though it I cannot see:
It's like the music of a bell,
It's like the way the roses smell,
It's like the stories fairies tell—
  It's all of these to me.

I know what father's face is like,
  I am sure I know it all:
It's like his whistle in the air,
It's like his step upon the stair,
It's like his arms that take much care,
  And never let me fall.

And so I know what God is like,
  The God whom no one sees:
He's everything my mother means,
He's like my very sweetest dreams,—
He's everything my father seems,
  But greater than all these.

A BOTANY LESSON — If we had paid no more attention to our plants than we have to our children, we would now be living in a jungle of weeds.
  —*Luther Burbank.*

HOME-GROWN—Happiness grows at our own firesides, and is not to be picked in strangers' gardens.
  —*Douglas Jerrold.*

Apotheosis

("A mother's kiss made me a painter."—Benjamin West.)

Bent breathless o'er a sleeping baby's bed,
A boy whose fingers twitched with restless zeal,
Thrilled as he watched the fitful light reveal
The smile that cross those tender lips had spread.
It seemed to him to be God's very seal.
Those trembling fingers seized a coal still red
And strove to tell in lines what his heart said;—
A boy's crude sketch of innocence ideal.

A mother paused from tasks dark found undone,
And with her worn hand roughly touched his cheek;
Then made her boy an artist with a kiss.
The source of genius is not hard to seek:
Its falt'ring sparks are fanned to flame each one
By trust like this shown in a mother's kiss.

  —*Clyde Francis Lytle.*

A LITTLE CHILD SHALL LEAD THEM — In the old days there were angels who came and took men by the hand, and led them away from the city of destruction. We see no white-winged angels now. But yet men are led away from threatening destruction: a hand is put into theirs, which leads them forth gently toward a calm, bright land, so that they look no more backward; and the hand may be a little child's.
  —*George Eliot.*

IS THERE A SANTA CLAUS?—

Dear Editor,—I am eight years old. Some of my little friends say there is no Santa Claus. Papa says "If you see it in *The Sun*, it's so." Please tell me the truth; is there a Santa Claus?

—*Virginia O'Hanlon.*

115 West Ninety-fifth St.

Virginia, your little friends are wrong. They have been affected by the scepticism of a sceptical age. They do not believe except they see. They think that nothing can be which is not comprehensible by their little minds.

All minds, Virginia, whether they be men's or children's, are little. In this great universe of ours man is a mere insect, an ant, in his intellect, as compared with the boundless world about him, as measured by the intelligence capable of grasping the whole of truth and knowledge.

Yes, Virginia, there is a Santa Claus. He exists as certainly as love and generosity and devotion exist, and you know that they abound and give to our life its highest beauty and joy. Alas! how dreary would be the world if there were no Santa Claus. It would be as dreary as if there were no Virginias. There would be no childlike faith then, no poetry, no romance, to make tolerable this existence. We should have no enjoyment, except in sense and sight. The eternal light with which childhood fills the world would be extinguished.

Not believe in Santa Claus! You might as well not believe in fairies! You might get your papa to hire men to watch in all the chimneys on Christmas Eve to catch Santa Claus, but even if they did not see Santa Claus coming down, what would that prove? Nobody sees Santa Claus, but that is no sign there is no Santa Claus.

The most real things in the world are those that neither children nor men can see. Did you ever see fairies dancing on the lawn? Of course not, but that's no proof that they are not there. Nobody can conceive or imagine all the wonders there are unseen and unseeable in the world.

You may tear apart the baby's rattle and see what makes the noise inside, but there is a veil covering the unseen world which not the strongest man, nor even the united strength of all the strongest men that ever lived, could tear apart. Only faith, fancy, poetry, love, romance, can push aside that curtain and view and picture the supernal beauty and glory beyond. Is it all real? Ah, Virginia, in all this world there is nothing else real and abiding.

No Santa Claus! Thank God! he lives, and he lives forever. A thousand years from now, Virginia, nay, ten times ten thousand years from now, he will continue to make glad the heart of childhood.—*Casual Essays of the Sun.*

PATIENCE

If we knew the baby fingers,
　Pressed against the window pane,
Would be cold and stiff tomorrow—
　Never trouble us again—
Would the bright eyes of our darling
　Catch the frown upon our brow?
Would the prints of rosy fingers
　Vex us then as they do now?

Ah, those little ice-cold fingers,
　How they point our memories back
To the hasty words and actions
　Strewn along our backward track!
How those little hands remind us,
　As in snowy grace they lie,
Not to scatter thorns—but roses
　For our reaping by-and-by.

—*Selected.*

HEART'S EASE — Every house where love abides and friendship is a guest, is surely home, and home, sweet home, for there the heart can rest.

—*Henry Van Dyke.*

To My Father

It matters not that Time has shed
His thawless snow upon your head,
For he maintains, with wondrous art,
Perpetual summer in your heart.

—*William Hamilton Hayne.*

ALL THE WORLD.—There is an enduring tenderness in the love of a mother to a son that transcends all other affections of the heart! It is neither to be chilled by selfishness, nor daunted by danger, nor weakened by worthlessness, nor stifled by ingratitude. She will sacrifice every comfort to his convenience; she will surrender every pleasure to his enjoyment; she will glory in his fame, and exult in his prosperity—and if misfortune overtake him he will be the dearer to her from misfortune; and if disgrace settle upon his name she will still love and cherish him in spite of his disgrace; and if all the world beside cast him off she will be all the world to him.—*Washington Irving.*

Road Maps

Would ye learn the road to Laughter-
town,
O ye who have lost the way?
Would ye have young heart though your
hair be gray?
Go learn from a little child each day.
Go serve his wants and play his play,
And catch the lilt of his laughter gay,
And follow his dancing feet as they stray;
For he knows the road to Laughtertown,
O ye who have lost the way!

—*Katherine D. Blake.*

A Boy to Train

The man who has a boy to train,
  Has work to keep him night and day.
There's much to him he must explain,
  And many a doubt to clear away;
His task is one which calls for tact
  And friendship of the finest kind,
Because, with every word and act,
  He molds the little fellow's mind.
He must be careful of his speech,
  For careless words are quickly learned;
He must be wise enough to teach
  What corners may be safely turned.

"A Boy to Train" is copyrighted by Edgar A. Guest. Used by permission of the publishers, The Reilly & Lee Co., Chicago.

What Would You Take?

What would you take for that soft little
    head
  Pressed close to your face at time for
    bed;
For that white, dimpled hand in your own
  held tight,
  And the dear little eyelids kissed down
    for the night?
      What would you take?

What would you take for that smile in
  the morn,
  Those bright, dancing eyes and the face
    they adorn;
For the sweet little voice that you hear all
  day
  Laughing and cooing—yet nothing to
    say?
      What would you take?

What would you take for those pink little
  feet,
  Those chubby round cheeks, and that
    mouth so sweet;
For the wee tiny fingers and little soft toes,
  The wrinkly little neck and that funny
    little nose?
      Now, what would you take?

—*Good Housekeeping.*

NEIGHBOR—What is meant by our neighbor we cannot doubt; it is every one with whom we are brought into contact. First of all, he is literally our neighbor who is next to us in our own family and household; husband to wife, wife to husband, parent to child, brother to sister, master to servant, servant to master. Then it is he who is close to us in our own neighborhood, in our own town, in our own parish, in our own street. With these all true charity begins. To love and be kind to these is the very beginning of all true religion. But, beside these, as our Lord teaches, it is every one who is thrown across our path by the changes and chances of life; he or she, whosoever it be, whom we have any means of helping —the unfortunate stranger whom we may meet in traveling, the deserted friend whom no one else cares to look after.

—*A. P. Stanley.*

Motto for Every Home

Whoe'er thou art that entereth here,
Forget the struggling world
And every trembling fear.

Take from thy heart each evil thought,
And all that selfishness
Within thy life has wrought.

For once inside this place thou'lt find
No barter, servant's fear,
Nor master's voice unkind.

Here all are kin of God above—
Thou, too, dear heart: and here
The rule of life is love.

IMMEDIACY — He who helps a child helps humanity with an immediateness which no other help given to human creature in any other stage of human life can possibly give again.—*Phillips Brooks.*

Restoration

Could every time-worn heart but see Thee
once again,
A happy, human child, among the homes
of men,
The age of doubt would pass—the vision
of Thy face
Would silently restore the childhood of
the race.

—*Henry Van Dyke.*

The Bravest Battle

The bravest battle that ever was fought!
Shall I tell you where and when?
On the maps of the world you will find
it not;
'Twas fought by the mothers of men.

Nay, not with cannon or battle-shot,
With a sword or noble pen;
Nay, not with eloquent words or thought
From mouths of wonderful men!

But deep in a walled-up woman's heart—
Of a woman that would not yield,
But bravely, silently bore her part—
Lo, there is that battlefield!

No marshaling troops, no bivouac song,
No banner to gleam and wave;
But oh! these battles, they last so long—
From babyhood to the grave.

Yet, faithful still as a bridge of stars,
She fights in her walled-up town—
Fights on and on in the endless wars,
Then, silent, unseen, goes down.

Oh, ye with banners and battle-shot,
And soldiers to shout and praise!
I tell you the kingliest victories fought
Were fought in those silent ways.

O spotless woman in a world of shame,
With splendid and silent scorn,
Go back to God as white as you came—
The kingliest warrior born!

—*Joaquin Miller.*

BUT ONLY ONE MOTHER—Most of all the other beautiful things in life come by twos and threes, by dozens and hundreds. Plenty of roses, stars, sunsets, rainbows, brothers and sisters, aunts and cousins, but only one *mother* in the whole world.—*Kate Douglas Wiggin.*

Boy

For the time when a boy is in danger
Of going a little bit wild
Is when he's too young to be married
Too old to be known as child.
A bird of the wild grass thicket
Just out of the parent tree flown.

Too large to keep in the old nest,
Too small to have one of its own.
When desolate, 'mid his companions,
His soul is a stake to be won,
'Tis then that the devil stands ready
To get a good place to catch on.

—*Selected.*

THE WATCHMAN — Nothing is sweeter than love, nothing more courageous, nothing higher, nothing wider, nothing more pleasant, nothing fuller nor better in Heaven and earth, because love is born of God, and cannot rest but in God, above all created things. Love feels no burden, thinks nothing of trouble, attempts what is above its strength, pleads no excuse of impossibility . . . It is therefore able to undertake all things, and it completes many things, and warrants them to take effect, where he who does not love would faint and lie down. Love is watchful and sleeping, slumbereth not. Though weary, it is not tired; though pressed, it is not straitened; though alarmed, it is not confounded; but, as a lively flame and burning torch, it forces its way upwards and securely passes all.

—*Thomas a' Kempis.*

Son

When I look out upon the florid years
    Ensnared in dreams, and castles vainly built
Encumbered with uncertainty and fears
    Of doing — comes propinquity with guilt:
That my own duty, Son, be not well done;
    That should you fail your boyish hands, full grown,
Will mark me cause; that fortunes never won,
    And favors lost, or wisdom scantly known
Shall stand between us: this your credo make:
    To live the truth in speech and deed; to spend
Long efforts toward good courtesy, and take
    Great pains with kindness; all your days commend
To glad God-fearing work, and rightly none
    Shall put a contemny upon you, Son.
        —*Lillian Arline Walbert.*

THE MODEL—Did you ever watch a little child take a lesson in model drawing? Never two strokes of the pencil without a glance at the model. And the first law and the last law of the imitation of Christ is just this—"looking unto Jesus."
        —*George Jackson.*

My Boy

"So let him live,
Love work, love play,
Love all that life can give;
And when he grows too weary to feel joy,
Leave life, with laughter, to some other boy."
        —*Charles C. Wakefield.*

MUTUAL HELP—The family is a school of mutual help. Each member depends on every other. Today the robust father holds the "wee laddie" on his knee, or leads him up the stairway of that schoolroom in which he is to be taught his alphabet. But there is a tomorrow coming by and by when the lisper of the A B C will be the master of a home of his own—with an infirm, gray-haired parent dozing away his sunset years in an armchair. Each helps the other when and where the help is most needed. And every word and deed of unselfish love, comes back in blessings on its author. God puts helpless babes, and infirm parents into our families for this purpose (among others) that the strong may bear the burden of the weak, and in bearing them may grow stronger themselves in Bible graces.—*Cuyler.*

My Mother

She was as good as goodness is,
    Her acts and all her words were kind,
And high above all memories
    I hold the beauty of her mind.
                    —*Frederic Hentz Adams.*

A STANDARD—There is nothing by which men display their character so much as in what they consider ridiculous.
                    —*Goethe.*

Boundless

They talk about a woman's sphere
As though it had a limit;
There's not a place in earth or Heaven,
There's not a task to mankind given,
There's not a blessing or a woe,
There's not a whispered yes or no,
There's not a life, or death, or birth,
That has a feather's weight of worth—
    Without a woman in it.

FORGIVE—We may, if we choose, make the worst of one another. Every one has his weak points; every one has his faults; we may make the worst of these; we may fix our attention constantly upon these. But we may also make the best of one another. We may forgive, even as we hope to be forgiven. We may put ourselves in the place of others, and ask what we should wish to be done to us, and thought of us, were we in their place. By loving whatever is lovable in those around us, love will flow back from them to us, and life will become a pleasure instead of a pain; and earth will become like Heaven; and we shall become not unworthy followers of Him whose name is Love.

Memories

Like a richly colored flame whose bright
    tip
Draws upward, but is brushed by erring
    storm,
Then relentingly seeks the earth's dark
    form
And buries its deep desires bit by bit;
Thus your life ebbed—though trembling,
    pleading lips
Cried proffering words to a Triune God.
In vain I watched for one familiar nod,
Then pressed my mouth to thin black
    hairy wisps.

Memories? Mother! How can I forget?
Your smiling eyes with sad mystery
    tinged;
Your helping hands, though labor
    wrought with tasks;
Mother! Your clear high laughter had a
    depth
That thrilled my heart, and lifted silence
    winged
With boundless joy. Thank God! Memories last!
                    —*Hilda A. Dammtrch.*

XVII. IMMORTALITY

RELEASE—Man is like a bird in a cage until he lives for eternity. He is like a prisoner in a cell until he gives the eternal within him expression. Just as the ripples of the meadow-brook reproduce the swell of the ocean tides towards which the brook flows; and just as the music of the rivulet in its eddies echoes the lap of the mighty sea on the beach where some day the rivulet will measure its waters; so the voices within us are the voices of the larger life for which we are destined and towards which we are going.—*Vance.*

Death, be not proud, though some have called thee

Mighty and dreadful, for thou art not so;

For those, whom thou think'st thou dost overthrow,

Die not, poor Death, nor yet canst thou kill me.

From rest and sleep, which but thy pictures be,

Much pleasure, then from thee much more, must flow,

And soonest our best men with thee do go,

Rest of their bones, and soul's delivery.

Thou art slave to fate, chance, kings, and desperate men,

And dost with poison, war, and sickness dwell,

And poppy, or charms, can make us sleep as well,

And better than thy stroke. Why swell'st thou then?

One short sleep past, we wake eternally,

And Death shall be no more; Death, thou shalt die.

—JOHN DONNE.

WHISPERS OF HOPE—Immortality is a word that Hope through all the ages has been whispering to Love. The miracle of thought we can not understand. The mystery of life and death we can not comprehend. This chaos called world has never been explained. The golden bridge of life from gloom emerges, and on shadow rests. Beyond this we do not know. Fate is speechless, destiny is dumb, and the secret of the future has never yet been told. We love; we wait; we hope. The more we love, the more we fear. Upon the tenderest heart the deepest shadows fall. All paths, whether filled with thorns or flowers, end here. Here success and failure are the same. The ray of wretchedness and the purple robe of power all differences and distinction lose in this democracy of death. Character survives; Goodness lives; Love is immortal.—*Robert G. Ingersoll.*

THE GOOD—Our hope for eternal life in the hereafter does not spring from a longing for a spiritual existence, but grows out of our love for life upon this earth, which we have tried and found good.—*Robert J. Shores.*

LIFE ETERNAL!—How shall I express my thought of it? It is not mere existence, however prolonged and free from annoyance. It is not the pleasures of the senses, however vivid. It is not peace. It is not happiness. It is not joy. But it is all these combined into one condition of spiritual perfection—one emotion of indescribable rapture—the peace after the storm has gone by, the soft repose after the grief is over, the joy of victory when the conflict is ended.—*Hill.*

THE MUDDY VESTURE OF DECAY—Death means just this; no more and no less. As Maclaren has vigorously said: "Strip the man of the disturbances that come from a fevered body, and he will have a calmer soul. Strip him of the hindrances which come from a body that is like an opaque tower around his spirit, with only a narrow crevice here and a narrow door there—five poor senses with which he is connected with the outer universe—and, surely, the spirit will have wider avenues out to God. It will have larger powers of reception, because it has become rid of the closer confinements of the fleshly tabernacle. They who die in Jesus live a larger, fuller, nobler life, by the very cessation of care, change, strife, and struggle. Above all, they live a fuller, grander life, because they sleep in Jesus' and are gathered into His embrace, and awake with Him, clothed with white robes, awaiting the adoption—to wit, the redemption of the body."

SYMPATHY—If a friend of mine . . . gave a feast, and did not invite me to it, I should not mind a bit . . . But if . . . a friend of mine had a sorrow and refused to allow me to share it, I should feel it most bitterly. If he shut the doors of the house of mourning against me, I would move back again and again and beg to be admitted, so that I might share in what I was entitled to share. If he thought me unworthy, unfit to weep with him, I should feel it as the most poignant humiliation, as the most terrible mode by which disgrace could be inflicted on me . . . . he who can look on the loveliness of the world and share its sorrow, and realize something of the wonder of both, is in immediate contact with divine things, and has got as near to God's secret as any one can get.—*Oscar Wilde.*

WHY WE BELIEVE—If there be an argument which stirs me to indignation at its futility, and to wonder that any mortal ever regarded it as of the slightest force: it is that which is set out in the famous soliloquy in Cato, as to the immortality of the soul. Will any sane man say, that if in this world you wish for a thing very much, and anticipate it very clearly and confidently, you are therefore sure to get it? If that were so, many a little schoolboy would end by driving his carriage and four who ends by driving no carriage at all. No: we cling to the doctrine of a future life: we could not live without it: but we believe it, not because of undefined longings within ourselves, not because of reviving plants and flowers, not because of the chrysalis and the butterfly: but because our Savior Jesus Christ hath abolished death, and brought light and immortality to light through the gospel.—*A. K. H. Boyd.*

Hope Sees a Star

Life is a narrow vale between the cold and barren peaks of two eternities.

We strive in vain to look beyond the heights.

We cry aloud—and the only answer is the echo of our wailing cry.

From the voiceless lips of the unreplying dead there comes no word.

But in the night of death Hope sees a star, and listening Love can hear the rustling of a wing.

He who sleeps here, when dying, mistaking the approach of death for the return of health, whispered with his latest breath, "I am better now."

Let us believe, in spite of doubts and fears, that these dear words are true of all the countless dead.

—Robert G. Ingersoll, at his brother's grave, June 2, 1879.

FROM A FULL HEART—Never let the seeming worthlessness of sympathy make you keep back that sympathy of which, when men are suffering around you, your heart is full. Go and give it without asking yourself whether it is worth while to give it. It is too sacred a thing for you to tell what it is worth. God, from whom it comes, sends it through you to His needy child.—*Phillips Brooks.*

REVISED EDITION

The Body
of
Benjamin Franklin, Printer
(Like the cover of an old book,
Its contents torn out,
And stripped of its lettering and gilding,)
Lies here food for worms.
Yet the work itself shall not be lost,
For it will (as he believes) appear once
more
In a new
And beautiful Edition
Corrected and Amended
By
The Author
(*Franklin's self-written epitaph*)

CHARTED—It is not darkness you are going to, for God is Light. It is not lonely, for Christ is with you. It is not an unknown country, for Christ is there.
—*Charles Kingsley.*

EVOLUTION

Out of the dusk a shadow,
  Then a spark;
Out of the cloud a silence,
  Then, a lark;
Out of the heart a rapture,
  Then, a pain;
Out of the dead, cold ashes,
  Life again.
—*John Banister Tabb.*

HEAVEN—When I was a boy I used to think of Heaven as a glorious golden city, with jewelled walls, and gates of pearl, with nobody in it, but the angels, and they were all strangers to me. But after a while my little brother died; then I thought of Heaven as that great city, full of angels, with just one little fellow in it that I was acquainted with. He was the only one I knew there, at that time. Then another brother died, and there were two in Heaven that I knew. Then my acquaintance began to die, and the number of my friends in Heaven grew larger all the time. But, it was not till one of my own little ones was taken that I began to feel that I had a personal interest in Heaven. Then a second went, and a third, and a fourth; and so many of my friends and loved ones have gone there, that it seems as if I know more in Heaven than I know on earth. And now, when my thoughts turn to Heaven, it is not the gold and the jewels, and the pearls that I think of—but the loved ones there. It is not the place so much as the company that makes Heaven seem beautiful.—*Selected.*

ONLY THE BODY — Plato in his Phaedon represents Socrates as saying in the last hour of his life to his inconsolable followers, "You may bury me if you can catch me." He then added with a smile, and an intonation of unfathomable thought and tenderness, "Do not call this poor body Socrates. When I have drunk the poison, I shall leave you, and go to the joys of the blessed. I would not have you sorrow at my hard lot, or say at the interment, 'Thus we lay out Socrates;' or, 'Thus we follow him to the grave, and bury him.' Be of good cheer: say that you are burying my body only."
—*R. J. Cooke.*

FIGURES OF DEATH—You cannot find in the New Testament any of those hateful representations of dying which men have invented, by which death is portrayed as a ghastly skeleton with a scythe, or something equally revolting. The figures by which death is represented in the New Testament are very different. There are two of them which I think to be exquisitely beautiful. One is that of falling asleep in Jesus. When a little child has played all day long, and becomes tired out, and the twilight has sent it in weariness to its mother's knee, where it thinks it has come for more excitement, then, almost in the midst of its frolicking, and not knowing what influence is creeping over it, it falls back in the mother's arms, and nestles close to the sweetest and softest couch that ever cheek pressed, and, with lengthening breath, sleeps; and she smiles and is glad, and sits humming unheard joy over its head. So we fall asleep in Jesus. We have played long enough at the games of life, and at last we feel the approach of death. We are tired out, and we lay our head back on the bosom of Christ and quietly fall asleep.—*H. W. Beecher.*

DISSOLVED — In the laboratory of Faraday a workman one day knocked into a jar of acid a silver cup. It disappeared, was eaten by the acid, and could not be found. The question came up as to whether it could ever be found. The great chemist came in and put certain chemicals into the jar and every particle of the silver was precipitated to the bottom. The mass was then sent to a silversmith and the cup was restored. So a precious soul who has fallen into the sink of iniquity, lost, dissolved in sin can only be restored by the Great Chemist—"Jesus only."
—*S. S. Times.*

RESURRECTION — We see in the Risen Christ the end for which man was made and the assurance that the end is within reach. Christ rose from the grave changed and yet the same; and in Him we have the pledge and type of our rising.

AWAY

I cannot say, and I will not say
That he is dead. He is just away!

With a cheery smile and a wave of the hand,
He has wandered into an unknown land.

And left us dreaming how very fair
It needs must be, since he lingers there.

And you—oh you, who the wildest yearn
For the old time step and the glad return—

Think of him faring on, as dear
In the love of There as the love of Here;

And loyal still, as he gave the blows
Of his warrior strength to his country's foes—

Mild and gentle, as he was brave,
When the sweetest love of his life he gave

To simple things; where the violets grew
Pure as the eyes they were likened to,

The touches of his hands have strayed
As reverently as his lips have prayed;

When the little brown thrush that harshly chirred
Was dear to him as the mocking-bird;

And he pitied as much as a man in pain
A writhing honey-bee wet with rain.

Think of him still as the same, I say:
He is not dead—he is just—away!
—*James Whitcomb Riley.*

From AFTERWHILES, by permission of the publishers, The Bobbs Merrill Company.

THE SOUL SURVIVES—The arguments from reason by which the immortality of the soul is maintained are well known. But there is another argument, the scope of which has been so immensely enlarged in modern times that the disregard of it by the ancients does not count against its inherent validity. This is the general consent of the race. The future existence of the soul has been held as a matter of popular belief by the people of every age and country. It is found among the Chinese, the Egyptians, the Hindus, the Persians, the Greeks and Romans, the Druids, the Celts, the Germans, the Slavs, and a great variety of uncivilized tribes in North America and South, in the centre of Africa, and in the islands of the sea. There are exceptions, but these are just enough to confirm the rule. The great body of the human family in every age have held, as they hold now, that the soul survives the body; and there is no way of accounting for this unanimity but by admitting the truth of the doctrine. Either it was derived by tradition from our original ancestors, who obtained it from their Creator, or its evidences lie so deeply impressed upon the constitution of man that they compel assent. A judgment held so long, so widely, and by such different races, must be deemed to be correct.—*G. F. Wright.*

VESPERS

I know the night is near at hand:
The mists lie low on hill and bay,
The Autumn sheaves are dewless, dry;
But I have had the day.

Yes, I have had, dear Lord, the day;
When at Thy call I have the night,
Brief be the twilight as I pass
From light to dark, from dark to light.
—*Silas Weir Mitchell.*

CONQUERORS — In this world, he that is today conqueror may tomorrow himself be defeated. Pompey is eclipsed by Caesar, and then Caesar falls by the hands of conspirators; Napoleon conquered nearly all Europe, and was then himself conquered. But the Christian's conquest of death is absolute. The result is final. He has vanquished the last enemy, and has no more battles to fight.—*Foster.*

Death to a good man is but passing through a dark entry, out of one little dusky room of his Father's house into another that is fair and large, lightsome and glorious, and divinely entertaining.
—*A. Clarke.*

You have felt the exhilarating change from a convalescent chamber to a bright spring day, with its balmy air, its flowers and fragrance and songs. How fresh the burst of devout feeling in a pious mind amid such a scene! What, then, must be the transition from the gloom of a sick-chamber, and the last of life's struggles, into the tranquillity and joy of the presence of the Lord?—*J. Graham.*

HEAVEN SATISFIES — If a child were to ask me if there would be harps and pianos—yes, and hobby-horses, in Heaven, I would tell him "yes;" that is, if he was fond of those things; because that would be the truest answer I could make him. What I should mean by it would be, that there would be that there which would just as nicely fit into his Heavenly desires as the hobby-horse does into his earthly desires. Heaven means satisfaction. And if it takes a hobby-horse to satisfy him now, and I tell him there will be nothing of that kind there, then to him I make Heaven unsatisfactory and so falsify the fact. There is an untruthful way of telling the truth and a truthful way of telling an untruth.—*Parkhurst.*

MORTALITY — I was walking one day in Westminster Abbey. As I paused to survey the monuments of the illustrious departed that are gathered there, my attention was arrested by the appearance of the pavement near to where I stood. A beautiful many-colored light rested upon it, and gave it an aspect that I could not but linger to behold. The cause was apparent. A painted window above me explained the reason. And the pavement, beautiful as it appeared, had no color in itself; it was the window above that gave it the beauteous hue. How many are like that pavement! They appear beautiful, and we are apt to mistake it for "the beauty of holiness;" but it is in a borrowed light—contact with the wise and good it may be; remove that, and their true color appears.—*Selected.*

GETTING READY — There is only one way to get ready for immortality, and that is to love this life and live it as bravely and faithfully, and cheerfully as we can.—*Henry Van Dyke.*

MORTALITY—It is the custom of the Chinese to keep their coffins in their houses where they can be often seen. The ancient Egyptians, at all their feasts, served their guests with some part of a skeleton to put them in mind of their mortality. And, on the day of his coronation, one of the emperors of Constantinople, among other gifts of great value, received the present of a gravestone, to remind him of the coming day when the crown would be taken from his head. And, in the midst of life and health, it would be good for us if we would often think of that hour that will finish our discipline and fix our destiny.
—*Public Speakers Library.*

INTIMATION OF IMMORTALITY—It has always seemed to me a major tragedy that so many people go through life haunted by the fear of death—only to find when it comes that it's as natural as life itself. For very few are afraid to die when they get to the very end. In all my experience only one seemed to feel any terror—a woman who had done her sister a wrong which it was too late to right.

Something strange and beautiful happens to men and women when they come to the end of the road. All fear, all horror disappears. I have often watched a look of happy wonder dawn in their eyes when they realized this was true. It is all part of the goodness of nature and, I believe, of the illimitable goodness of God.
—*A Veteran Nurse.*

Disguise

Out of the pain of night-watching removed
Into the sleep that God gives His beloved,
Into the dawn of a glad resurrection,
Into the house of unbroken affection,
Into the joy of her Lord—thence confessing
Death in disguise is His angel in blessing.
—*Selected.*

THE CROSSING — They that love beyond the world can not be separated by it. Death can not kill what never dies.

Nor can spirits ever be divided, that love and live in the same divine principle, the root and record, of their friendship . . . Death is but crossing the world, as friends do the seas; they live in one another still . . .

This is the comfort of friends, that though they may be said to die, yet their friendship and society are, in the best sense, ever present because immortal.
—*William Penn.*

TRANSITION — We are all of us going to die sometime. . . . Some—and this, I assume, means the majority — in times of health put from them all contemplation of death as a concrete fact; even so, though, there must be hours when they speculate upon it as applying to themselves. So to all such, I, who have skirted the Valley of the Shadow, say that if my own experience is typical — and it surely must have been — then those among us whose lot it will be to face the finish while still in reasonable possession of our faculties will face it without fear and without bitterness, without reluctance and without repinings, without sufferings, whether physical or mental; we shall find it, at the last, but a peaceful transition, an eternal change mercifully accomplished.

—*Irvin S. Cobb.*

The Junk Man

I am glad God saw Death
And gave Death a job taking care of all
    who are tired of living:
When all the wheels in a clock are worn
    and slow and the connections loose
And the clock goes on ticking and telling
    the wrong time from hour to hour
And people around the house joke about
    what a bum clock it is,
How glad the clock is when the big Junk
    Man drives his wagon
Up to the house and puts his big arms
    around the clock and says:
      "You don't belong here,
      You gotta come
      Along with me,"
How glad the clock is then, when it feels
    the arms of the Junk Man close
    around it and carry it away.

—*Carl Sandburg.*

From CHICAGO POEMS by Carl Sandburg, by permission of the publishers, Henry Holt and Company, Inc. Copyright, 1916 by Henry Holt and Company. Copyright, 1943 by Carl Sandburg.

CHARACTER (*Alone Remains*)—In the U. S. Mint there was recently a curiously-engraved medal of elaborate design and the minutest detail. Even the lace on the figure was wrought out with marvelous painstaking. The expense of the medal was $6,500, yet its value there was only the bare metal, about one-twentieth. So men pass with the world at high valuation. Culture, refinement, wealth, social standing, official influence, titular distinctions, give them a temporary importance, but death soon will bring them to the crucible of a final judgment, at which all these extrinsic and adventitious characteristics pass for nothing.

Anticipations

I love preliminary things:
The tuning-up of flutes and strings;
The little scales musicians play
In varying keys to feel their way;
The hum—the hush in which it dies;
But most to see the curtain rise.

I love preliminary things:
The little box the postman brings;
To cut the twine, to break the seals,
And wonder what the lid reveals;
To lift the folds in which it lies
And watch the gift materialize.

The snowdrop and the daffodil,
The catkins hanging straight and still,
The blossom on the orchard trees—
Do you know greater joys than these?
Each represents the hope that springs
In all preliminary things.

—*J. R. J.*

Death

Fearest the shadow? Keep thy trust;
    Still the star-worlds roll.
Fearest death? Sayest, "Dust to dust"?
    No; say "Soul to soul!"

—*John Vance Cheney.*

RENOVATION — If a man has a statue decayed by rust and age, and mutilated in many of its parts, he breaks it up and casts it into a furnace, and after the melting he receives it again in more beautiful form. As thus the dissolving in the furnace was not a destruction, but a renewing of the statue, so the death of our bodies is not a destruction, but a renovation. When, therefore, you see as in a furnace our flesh flowing away to corruption, dwell not on that sight, but wait for the recasting. And advance in your thoughts to a still higher point, for the statuary casting into the furnace a brazen image but makes a brazen one again. God does not thus; but casting in a mortal body formed of clay, He returns you an immortal statue of gold.—*Chrysostom.*

MANSIONS — I understand that the Lord meant by His "Father's house" the whole vast universe; and if so, the point of His comfort to the disciples becomes clear. "In my Father's house," He said, "are many mansions." Do not suppose that this world is all, or that beyond the veil, even the blessedness and joy of this world will not be surpassed. You have found a home here. You have found God here. You have here learned that it is possible to dwell with God. But this is only one mansion and there are many more. You have entered only the first. There are myriads that you have not seen. Do not, therefore, tremble if I leave you. This world is not the whole of the stage on which redemption is to be wrought out. Do not think that death is dissolution to the soul, or that its personal and spiritual relationship to God will be affected by death. If such had been the case I would certainly have told you, and my course of instruction would have been very different. This world is but one place of abode with God. There are innumerably more, and only with these in thought can you realize the worth and promise of a Christian life.—*Purves.*

MEASURED BY THE SOUL—The size of one's Heaven is the exact dimensions of his soul. Happiness is a matter of appetite and capacity. As well prepare dinner for a corpse as Heaven for a soul whose spiritual functions are dead. The problem of the hereafter is not the matter of a celestial climate and a city beautiful. It is the problem of the eternal in man. The kingdom is within him. The greatest concern of a human being therefore should be to feel God's presence, to be stirred by His message, to have faith in the invisible, and to follow aspirations which leap over the boundaries of time and seek satisfaction in the infinite. For to be devoid of all this is to fall a victim to the disease that destroys character, paralyses progress, and forbids happiness.—*Vance.*

Song

When I am dead, my dearest,
　Sing no sad songs for me;
Plant thou no roses at my head,
　Nor shady cypress-tree;
Be the green grass above me
　With showers and dewdrops wet;
And if thou wilt, remember,
　And if thou wilt, forget.

I shall not see the shadows,
　I shall not feel the rain;
I shall not hear the nightingale
　Sing on, as if in pain;
And dreaming through the twilight
　That doth not rise nor set,
Haply I may remember,
　And haply may forget.
　　　　—*Christina G. Rossetti.*

99

XVIII. MEMORY

WHAT TO FORGET — If you would increase your happiness and prolong your life, forget your neighbor's faults. Forget all the slander you have ever heard. Forget the temptations. Forget the fault finding, and give a little thought to the cause which provoked it. Forget the peculiarities of your friends, and only remember the good points which make you fond of them. Forget all personal quarrels or histories you may have heard by accident, and which, if repeated, would seem a thousand times worse than they are. Blot out as far as possible all the disagreeables of life; they will come, but will only grow larger when you remember them, and the constant thought of the acts of meanness, or, worse still, malice, will only tend to make you more familiar with them. Obliterate everything disagreeable from yesterday; write upon today's clean sheet those things lovely and loveable.

THE SCENT OF THE ROSES

Let Fate do her worst; there are relics
    of joy,
Bright dreams of the past, which she
    cannot destroy;
Which come in the night-time of sor-
    row and care,
And bring back the features that joy
    used to wear.
Long, long be my heart with such
    memories filled,
Like the vase in which roses have once
    been distilled—
You may break, you may shatter the
    vase if you will,
But the scent of the roses will hang
    round it still.

—THOMAS MOORE.

REJOICE

Grave on thy heart each past "red-letter
    day"!
Forget not all the sunshine of the way
By which the Lord hath led thee; answer-
    ed prayers,
And joys unasked, strange blessings, lifted
    cares,
Grand promise-echoes! Thus thy life shall
    be
One record of His love and faithfulness
    to thee.

—F. R. Havergal.

THEY SAY—Die when I may, I want it said of me by those who knew me best, that I always plucked a thistle and planted a flower where I thought a flower would grow.—Abraham Lincoln.

REMEMBER

Remember me when I am gone away,
    Gone far away into the silent land;
    When you can no more hold me by
        the hand,
Nor I half turn to go yet turning stay.
Remember me when no more, day by day,
    You tell me of our future that you
        planned:
    Only remember me; you understand
It will be late to counsel then or pray.
Yet if you should forget me for a while
    And afterwards remember, do not
        grieve;
    For if the darkness and corruption
        leave
    A vestige of the thoughts that once I
        had,
Better by far you should forget and smile
    Than that you should remember and
        be sad.

—Christina G. Rossetti.

FORGET

It is better to forget the things that hurt us,
And to live each day and take whatever
    comes,
With the hope that by tomorrow
There will come a balm for sorrow
And help to master life's important sums!
There's a strength comes to us every time
    we suffer,
And our will grows stronger every time
    we fight,
Let us then be doubly grateful
For the things that disappoint us;
They only come to lead us to the light!
    —*Helen Mocksett Stork.*

MEMORABILIA

My mind lets go a thousand things
Like dates of wars and deaths of kings,
And yet recalls the very hour—
'Twas noon by yonder village tower,
And on the last blue noon in May,—
The wind came briskly up this way,
Crisping the brook beside the road;
Then, pausing here, set down its load
Of pine-scents, and shook listlessly
Two petals from that wild-rose tree.
    —*Thomas Bailey Aldrich.*

SAINTED

He loved the House of God;
His dearest wish to be
A minister within her walls
In service full and free.

Beautifully he lived,
We who well loved him know,
Blessing with kindly hands our dead,
Softening death's cruel blow.

Beautifully he died—
The temple floors he trod,
To pass to his reward within
The altar of his God!
    —*Estella Shields Fahringer.*

REMEMBER—The value of time.
The success of perseverance.
The pleasure of working.
The dignity of simplicity.
The worth of character.
The power of kindness.
The influence of example.
The obligation of duty.
The wisdom of economy.
The virtue of patience.
The improvement of talent.
The joy of originating.
    —*Bulletin.*

THE COIN

Into my heart's treasury
    I slipped a coin,
That time cannot rust
    Nor a thief purloin;
Oh, better than the minting
    Of a gold-crowned king
Is the safe-kept memory
    Of a lovely thing.
    —*Sara Teasdale.*

From THE COLLECTED POEMS of Sara Teasdale.
By permission of The Macmillan Company, publishers.

FORGET IT

Forget the slander you have heard.
Forget the hasty, unkind word;
Forget the quarrel and the cause,
Forget the whole affair, because
Forgetting is the only way.
Forget the storm of yesterday,
Forget the chap whose sour face
Forgets to smile in any place.
Forget you're not a millionaire,
Forget the gray streaks in your hair.
Forget the coffee when it's cold,
Forget to kick, forget to scold,
Forget the plumber's awful charge,
Forget the iceman's bill is large;
Forget the coalman and his ways,
Forget the winter's blustery days.
    —*Anonymous.*

THINK ON THESE THINGS — Psychologists tell us that the vividness of our memory depends on the stress of attention. Therefore, says St. Paul, "if there be any virtue, if there be any praise, *think on these things.*"

YOU

Deep in the heart of me,
Nothing but You!
See through the art of me—
Deep in the heart of me
Find the best part of me,
Changeless and true.
Deep in the heart of me
Nothing but You!
—*Ruth Guthrie Harding.*

THINK ON THESE THINGS —

What to remember,—what to forget,— that is the question.

It seems to me that the good things, the heavenly guidance, the help that other men have given us to keep the right path, are the things to remember.

The mistakes, the false leads, the devilish influences, are the things to forget.

LOVE CAN NEVER LOSE ITS OWN

Yet Love will dream and Faith will trust
(Since He who knows our need is just)
That somehow, somewhere, meet we must.
Alas for him who never sees
The stars shine through his cypress trees!
Who, hopeless, lays his dead away,
Nor looks to see the breaking day
Across the mournful marbles play!
Who hath not learned, in hours of faith,
The truth to flesh and sense unknown
That Life is ever lord of Death,
And Love can never lose its own!
—*John Greenleaf Whittier.*

HIM—Dr. S. D. Gordon tells of an old Christian woman whose age began to tell on her memory. She had once known much of the Bible by heart. Eventually only one precious bit stayed with her, "I know whom I have believed, and am persuaded that He is able to keep that which I have committed unto Him against that day." By and by part of that slipped its hold, and she would quietly repeat, "That which I have committed unto Him." At last as she hovered on the borderland between this and the spirit world, her loved ones noticed her lips moving. They bent down to see if she needed anything. She was repeating over and over again to herself the one word of the text, "Him—Him—Him." She had lost the whole Bible but one word. But she had the whole Bible in that one word.

BECAUSE

Because of your strong faith I kept the track
Whose sharp-set stones my strength had well-nigh spent.
I could not meet your eyes if I turned back;
So on I went.

Because you would not yield belief in me,
The threatening crags that rose my way to bar,
I conquered inch by crumbling inch—to see
The goal afar.

And though I struggle toward it through hard years,
Or flinch, or falter blindly, yet within,
"You can!" unwavering my spirit hears
And I shall win.

KEEP ON—Before you give up hope, turn back and read the attacks that were made upon Lincoln.—*Bruce Barton.*

THERE IS A REMEMBRANCE of the dead, to which we turn even from the charms of the living. This we would not exchange for the song of pleasure or the bursts of revelry.—*Washington Irving.*

SAFETY ZONES—In great crisis, the memory of the word of some wise and gracious teacher often comes to our rescue, and the new and bewildering experience in which we stand assumes a familiar and orderly aspect. We are set free from fear and panic and enabled to act with sanity and wisdom. For those whose memory is full of the words of Christ, there is strength in all life's emergencies.

JOY'S RECOLLECTION is no longer joy, while sorrow's memory is sorrow still.—*Byron.*

ROADSIDE MEETINGS

A little more tired at close of day,
A little less anxious to have our way;
A little less ready to scold and blame;
A little more care for a brother's name—
And so we are nearing the journey's end,
Where time and eternity meet and blend.
The book is closed and the prayers are
    said,
And we are a part of the countless dead.
Thrice happy then if some soul can say
"I live because he has passed this way."
          —*Stephen Crane.*

MEMORY IS NOT WISDOM; idiots can by rote repeat volumes.—Yet what is wisdom without memory?
          —*Tupper.*

THE TRUE ART of memory is the art of attention.—*Johnson.*

DEFINED—Memory is the cabinet of imagination, the treasury of reason, the registry of conscience, and the council chamber of thought.—*Basil.*

COMPENSATION — If the memory is more flexible in childhood, it is more tenacious in mature age; if childhood has sometimes the memory of words, old age has that of things, which impress themselves according to the clearness of the conception of the thought which we wish to retain.—*Bonstetten.*

BOOK OF JUDGMENT — That memory is the book of judgment, I can well believe. I have, indeed, seen the same thing asserted in modern books, and accompanied by a remark which I am convinced is true, namely: that the dread book of account, which the Scriptures speak of is, in fact, the mind itself of each individual. Of this, at least, I feel assured —that there is no such thing as forgetting, possible to the mind; a thousand accidents may and will interpose a veil between our present consciousness and the secret inscriptions on the mind; accidents of the same sort will also rend away this veil; but whether veiled or unveiled, the inscription remains forever; just as the stars seem to withdraw before the common light of day; whereas, in fact, we know that it is the light which is drawn over them as a veil, and that they are waiting to be revealed, when the obscuring daylight shall have withdrawn.
          —*De Quincey.*

A JOY FOREVER—A memory without blot or contamination must be an exquisite treasure, an inexhaustible source of pure refreshment.—*Charlotte Bronte.*

XIX. MYSTICISM

SPIRITUAL VALUES—And now comes the new day in which we live—a day of social reconstruction and spiritual awakening. The typical Christian of this new day will be the practical mystic. He will be a mystic—sensitive to the spiritual values of life and its deepest music; but he will also be a man of practical power, facing the social problems of the age and contributing to their solution.—*Albert W. Parker.*

GUIDANCE—In the daily events of our life we mistake the Divine for the human. You may cross a street, and not know the reason why, and in that very crossing you may unconsciously be obeying a Divine suggestion. You may hold over the letter box a letter, and suddenly you may say, "I'll not send it by this post," and your not sending it may occasion you a blessing that you never thought of. You cannot account for these things. You say, "I thought just at the last moment I would not do so;" but that is a fool's explanation of life. I rather believe that God's angels are just overhead, or just by our side, and that we do things by Divine impulse without always knowing what we are in reality doing. You say, "Yes, but don't let us be superstitious." I answer, I am more afraid of people losing veneration than I am afraid of their becoming superstitious; and it is a poor life that does not begin in veneration, and continue in worship to the end.—*J. Parker.*

The Mystery

He came and took me by the hand
    Up to a red rose tree,
He kept His meaning to Himself,
    But gave a rose to me.

I did not pray Him to lay bare
    The mystery to me;
Enough the rose was heaven to smell,
    And His own face to see.

—*Ralph Hodgson.*

From POEMS. By permission of The Macmillan Company, publishers.

SEARCH FOR GOD

I sought His love in lore of books,
    In charts of science's skill;
They left me orphaned as before—
    His love eluded still;
Then in despair I breathed a prayer;
The Lord of Love was standing there!

I sought His love in sun and stars,
    And where the wild seas roll,
And found it not. As mute I stood,
    Fear overwhelmed my soul;
But when I gave to one in need,
I found the Lord of Love indeed.

—THOMAS CURTIS CLARK.

A Prayer

Soul of Christ, sanctify me!
    Body of Christ, save me!
Blood of Christ, inebriate me.
Water from the side of Christ, cleanse me.
    Passion of Christ, strengthen me!
        O good Jesus, hear me!
    Within Thy wounds, hear me!
Suffer me never to be separated from Thee!
From the malicious enemy defend me!
    At the hour of my death call me!
        And bid me come to Thee!
That with Thy saints I may praise Thee!
    For ever and ever!
        Amen.

—*St. Ignatius.*

Immortality

Immortality is the
glorious discovery
of Christianity.

— *Channing.*

SONG OF THE MYSTIC

I walk down the Valley of Silence
Down the dim, voiceless valley—alone!
And I hear not the fall of a footstep
Around me, save God's and my own;
And the hush of my heart is as holy
As havens where angels have flown.

Long ago was I weary of voices
Whose music my heart could not win,
Long ago was I weary of noises
That fretted my soul with their din,
Long ago was I weary of places
Where I met but the human—and sin.

And I toiled on, heart-tired of the Human,
And I moaned midst the mazes of men
Till I knelt, long ago, at an altar
And I heard a voice call me. Since then
I walk down the Valley of Silence
That lies far beyond human ken.

Do you ask what I found in the Valley?
Tis my trysting place with the Divine,
And I fell at the feet of the Holy
And above me, a voice said: "Be mine."
And there rose from the depths of my
    spirit
An echo: "My heart shall be thine."

Do you ask me the place of the Valley,
Ye hearts that are harrowed by Care?
It lieth afar between mountains,
And God and His angels are there:
And one is the dark mount of Sorrow,
And one the bright mountain of Prayer.
                    —Abram J. Ryan.

REFLECTIONS — The world is a
looking-glass, and gives back to every man
the reflection of his own face. Frown at it,
and it in turn will look sourly upon you;
laugh at it and with it, and it is a jolly,
kind companion.
            —William Makepeace Thackeray.

THE MYSTIC'S PRAYER

Lay me to sleep in sheltering flame
    O Master of the Hidden Fire!
Wash pure my heart, and cleanse for me
    My soul's desire.

In flame of sunrise bathe my mind,
    O Master of the Hidden Fire,
That, when I wake, clear-eyed may be
    My soul's desire.
                    —William Sharp

THE ESSENCE OF RELIGION—

The efficacy of religion lies precisely in
that which is not rational, philosophic,
nor external; its efficacy lies in the unfore-
seen, the miraculous, the extraordinary.
Thus religion attracts more devotion in
proportion as it demands more faith—
that is to say, as it becomes more incred-
ible to the profane mind. The philosopher
aspires to explain away all mysteries, to
dissolve them into light. It is mystery, on
the other hand, which religious instinct
demands and pursues; it is mystery which
constitutes the essence of worship . . .
No positive religion can survive the supernatural element, which is the reason for
its existence.

                    —Henri-Frederic Amiel.

THE UNKNOWN GOD

Far up the dim twilight fluttered
    Moth wings of vapour and flame:
The lights danced over the mountains,
    Star after star they came.

The lights grew thicker unheeded,
    For silent and still were we;
Our hearts were drunk with a beauty
    Our eyes could never see.
            —A.E. (George William Russell)

From SELECTED POEMS of AE. By permission of
The Macmillan Company, publishers.

THE OLD KENT ROAD

The weary tavern yawns, so to confess
The dissipation of the night before
And lack of interest in the crowds that
    pour
Along the street; and therefore none
    would guess
That, deep beneath its morning conscious-
    ness,
Lie buried holy memories a score
Of how, where recent ale-slops foul its
    floor,
The soil received a martyr's selfishness!
Small room for thoughts like this amidst
    the din
Of traffic: few seem able to afford
The time to gather heavenly treasures in
When hunger drives, or Mammon is
    abroad.
But lo! through haunts of care and ways
    of sin
Moves some one with the Body of the
    Lord!

—*Leo Rowlands.*

THE GLORY OF COMMUNION
—Father Dalgairns declared, "The human heart is incurably mystical. . ."

Cardinal Manning, in his blessed little classic, *The Eternal Priesthood,* says, "The priest stands every morning upon the shores of the eternal world." We catch glimpses of the Supernal. As we speak the mystic words of the Mass, the thin, ethereal curtain between the two worlds is blown aside for a moment and we see at least briefly and dimly what the Mass really means. When we come away from the altar, returning so to speak from the other world to this, it is our duty and our privilege to convey, or at least to try to convey to the people what we have seen and heard. We shall do it with the help of the sacred words in which the mystery of the Mass is en-shrined, by means of the ritual and the liturgy, the combination of word and action that makes the Mass. In whatever proportion we succeed in imparting to the people a realization of the Mass, not as a poem, a form of beautiful words expressing profound thought; not as a drama, impressive, fascinating like the Passion Play, but as at once Poem, Drama, Fact, Reality, a Reality from the other world strangely taking place in this world; in proportion as we make the people see that the Mass is the Only Genuine Reality we shall teach them to love the Mass and cling to the Mass, even though like so many martyrs in Rome, in England, in Ireland, in Russia, in China, in Japan, they shall have to die for the Mass.—*James M. Gillis.*

THE VIRGIN

Mother, whose virgin bosom was uncrost
With the least shade of thought to sin
    allied;
Woman, above all women glorified,
Our tainted nature's solitary boast;
Purer than foam on central ocean tost,
Brighter than eastern skies at daybreak
    strewn
With fancied roses, than the unblem-
    ished moon
Before her wane begins on heaven's blue
    coast,
Thy image falls to earth. Yet some, I ween,
Not unforgiven the suppliant knee might
    bend
As to a visible form in which did blend
All that was mixed and reconciled in
    thee
Of mother's love with maiden purity,
Of high with low, celestial with terrene.

—*William Wordsworth.*

WHEN men cease to wonder, God's secrets remain unrevealed.

ENOUGH FOR THE PRESENT—

"Religion is full of questions that we cannot answer," declared Dr. James McCosh in an address to his students at Princeton University, "because we only know in part,"—a long pause, then with thrilling emphasis,—*"but we know!"*

There are things of which we may be positively certain though we cannot comprehend all their connections and relations. We know that our souls exist as truly as our bodies. We know that there is a God, who is not blind force, but a spirit who answers the souls who seek peace and joy. Evil brings discord and death to the soul. We know that Jesus Christ is absolutely good, the perfect union of the Divine and the human spirits. We know through Him that love is the source of power, and that life continues after death.

Beyond our ken lie the mysteries unexplored. But we have light enough to steer by, if we will. We know as much as we need. If we live by it we shall know more, some day.

SYMBOL

My faith is all a doubtful thing,
  Wove on a doubtful loom,—
Until there comes, each showery spring,
  A cheery tree in bloom.

And Christ who died upon the tree
  That death had stricken bare,
Comes beautifully back to me,
  In blossoms, everywhere.
                    —*David Morton.*

DISCOVERY — It is not when I am going to meet Him, but when I am just turning away and leaving Him, that I discover that God is.—*Thoreau.*

IMMANENT—The most real fact in this universe is God. The whole creation bears witness to His presence. The sunlight that floods the earth, the glories of the firmament, night and day, winter and spring, all declare that the Creator is everywhere in His world. The rose that was blooming one morning in my garden, with colors more delicate than the brush of a Turner could paint, told me that the great Artist was there. The laughter of little children, the love of friends, the upward march of the races of men proclaim that God is about us and within us richly imparting His grace. The unsatisfied aspiration of the heart, its pain, its joy, its penitence, its thoughts too deep for words tell us how near God is.

WHAT SHADOWS we are, and what shadows we pursue!—*Burke.*

ACCEPTANCE

I cannot think or reason,
I only know he came
With hands and feet of healing
And wild heart all aflame.

With eyes that dimmed and softened
At all the things he saw,
And in his pillared singing
I read the marching Law.

I only know he loves me,
Enfolds and understands—
And oh, his heart that holds me,
And oh, his certain hands!
                    —*Willard Wattles.*

I WOULD FAIN KNOW ALL that I need, and all that I may.—I leave God's secrets to Himself.—It is happy for me that God makes me of His court, and not of His council.—*Joseph Hall.*

WHERE THE SEARCH ENDS — "I searched the world over for God and found Him in my heart," said Augustine. In the heart of the believer a still small voice speaks in clearest accents, bearing "witness with our spirits that we are the children of God." Nothing on earth is so heavenly as that—so like "the voice of angels singing in the silence." It is as clear as bells at eventime. It is assuring like the familiar voice of a friend beloved. The Holy Spirit speaking in the secret chambers of the heart is the climax of God's revelation to us!

EACH PARTICLE of matter is an immensity; each leaf a world; each insect an inexplicable compendium.—*Lavater.*

MYSTERY is but another name for our ignorance; if we were omniscient, all would be perfectly plain.
—*Tryon Edwards.*

MORTAL — When Anaxagoras was told of the death of his son, he only said, "I knew he was mortal." So we in all casualties of life should say, "I knew my riches were uncertain, that my friend was just a man." Such considerations would soon pacify us, because all our troubles proceed from their being unexpected.
—*Plutarch.*

USE IT—While reason is puzzling itself about mystery, faith is turning it to daily bread, and feeding on it thankfully in her heart of hearts.—*F. D. Huntington.*

EVANESCENT—Man must be prepared for every event of life, for there is nothing that is durable.—*Menander.*

I DO NOT KNOW HOW the great loving Father will bring out light at last, but He knows, and He will do it.
—*David Livingstone.*

STAY ON YOUR LEVEL—Happy is the man who is content to traverse this ocean to the haven of rest, without going into the wretched diving-bells of his own fancies.—There are depths; but depths are for God.—*Evans.*

A RELIGION without mystery must be a religion without God.

BEYOND REASON — It has been well said that a thing is not necessarily against reason, because it happens to be above it.—*Colton.*

SPECULATE NOT TOO MUCH on the mysteries of truth or providence.— The effort to explain everything, sometimes may endanger faith.—Many things God reserves to Himself, and many are reserved for the unfolding of the future life.—*Tryon Edwards.*

WHICH?—The idea of philosophy is truth; the idea of religion is life.
—*Peter Bayne.*

OUR LORD has written the promise of the resurrection, not in books alone, but in every leaf in springtime.
—*Martin Luther.*

NONE BUT GOD can satisfy the longing of the immortal soul; as the heart was made for Him, He only can fill it.
—*Trench.*

XX. NATURE

GOD'S THOUGHTS—The mountains are God's thoughts piled up. The ocean is God's thoughts spread out. The flowers are God's thoughts in bloom. The dew drops are God's thoughts in pearls.—*Sam Jones.*

On Every Rose

I see His blood upon the rose
  And in the stars the glory of His eyes,
His body gleams amid eternal snows
  His tears fall from the skies.

I see His face in every flower;
  The thunder and the surging of the
    birds
Are but His voice—and carven by His
    power
  Rocks are His written words.

All pathways by His feet are worn,
  His strong heart stirs the ever-beating
    sea,
His crown of thorns is twined with every
    thorn
  His cross is every tree.
                    —*Joseph Mary Plunkett.*

FLOWERS—I do not believe a child, brought up under my ministry in this Church, will ever see flowers till he dies without having some thought of religion, of the sanctuary, and of the inspiration of flowers. So, flowers at our service have a meaning. They are not in any special way a symbolization; they simply bring things common into higher relations on a principle of association; and having them on the platform, besides affording pleasure, to a certain extent interprets a part of my idea of the Christian ministry.
                    —*Beecher.*

COMMONPLACE

"A commonplace life," we say, and we
    sigh,
But why should we sigh as we say?
The commonplace sun in the common-
    place sky
Makes up the commonplace day;
The moon and the stars are common-
    place things,
And the flower that blooms, and the bird
    that sings;
But dark were the world, and sad our lot,
If the flowers failed, and the sun shone
    not;
And God, who studies each separate soul,
Out of commonplace lives makes His
    beautiful whole.
                    —*"Susan Coolidge."*

From A FEW MORE VERSES, by Susan Coolidge. By permission of Little, Brown & Company, Publishers.

A BALLAD OF TREES AND THE MASTER

Into the woods my Master went,
Clean forspent, forspent.
Into the woods my Master came,
Forspent with love and shame.
But the olives they were not blind to
    Him;
The little gray leaves were kind to Him;
The thorn-tree had a mind to Him
When into the woods He came.

Out of the woods my Master went,
And He was well content.
Out of the woods my Master came,
Content with death and shame.
When death and shame would woo
    Him last,
From under the trees they drew Him
    last:
'Twas on a tree they slew Him—last
When out of the woods He came.
                    —SIDNEY LANIER.
By permission of Charles Scribner's Sons, Publishers.

TEACHERS

"The eye—it cannot choose but see;
We cannot bid the ear be still;
Our bodies feel, where'er they be,
Against and with our will.

"Nor less I deem that there are Powers
Which of themselves our minds impress;
That we can feed this mind of ours
In a wise passiveness."

One impulse from a vernal wood
May teach you more of man,
Of moral evil and of good,
Than all the sages can.
—*William Wordsworth.*

TRANSCENDENT

Dear heart, perhaps you can not find
  God's hand
Or see His face through some hour of
  despair.
Do not be grieved, go seek the good,
  clean land,
And you will find Him there.

He is a part of every wind that sweeps
Across the furrows, down their upturned
  length.
Breathe deeply of it—here is where God
  keeps
Stored healing and stored strength.

Wander awhile down some still wooded
  way;
Stoop to the lichen, dig through the
  mossy sod.
Stir in the leafmold—and the feathery
  spray
Of a fern can show you God.

You can touch Him as you touch the bark
  of a tree;
You can hear His voice in the voice of the
  singing birds.
Dear God, may we listen—God, may we
  look and see
Thy face, and hear Thy words.

MAN was made last because he was
worthiest. The soul was inspired last,
because yet more noble. No air, no earth,
no water was here used to give help to
this work; Thou, that breathest upon man
and gavest him the Holy Spirit, didst also
breathe upon the body and gavest it a
living spirit; we are beholden to nothing
but Thee for our soul. Our flesh is from
flesh, our spirit is from the God of spirits.
—*Joseph Hall.*

THE BIRTH OF THE FLOWERS

God spoke! and from the arid scene
Sprang rich and verdant bowers,
Till all the earth was soft with green,—
He smiled; and there were flowers.
—*Mary McNeil Fenolloso.*

OUT IN THE FIELDS WITH GOD

The little cares that fretted me
  I lost them yesterday,
Among the fields above the sea,
  Among the winds at play,
Among the lowing of the herds,
  The rustling of the trees,
Among the singing of the birds,
  The humming of the bees.

The foolish fears of what might happen,
  I cast them all away
Among the clover-scented grass,
  Among the new-mown hay,
Among the husking of the corn,
  Where drowsy poppies nod
Where ill thoughts die and good are
  born—
Out in the fields with God.
—*Louise Imogen Guiney.*

REALITY—Nature forever puts a premium on reality. What is done for effect,
is seen to be done for effect; what is done
for love, is felt to be done for love.

BE STILL WITH GOD.—To be idle sometimes is the part of wisdom. It is the needful rest and relaxation which Christ invited His disciples to share with Him when they were overstrained and worn out with labour. The best way to enjoy it is to get away from the crowd into some quiet place where the heart can be still with God in the open air. It is most sweet when it is shared by true friends.

Such idleness may be very fruitful. It reaps

"The harvest of a quiet eye
That broods and sleeps on His own
heart."

OVERTONES

I heard a bird at break of day
Sing from the autumn trees
A song so mystical and calm,
So full of certainties,
No man, I think, could listen long
Except upon his knees.
Yet this was but a simple bird,
Alone, among dead trees.
—*William Alexander Percy.*

TOGETHER.—Lyman Abbott says: I pluck an acorn and hold it to my ear, and this is what it says to me: "By and by the birds will come and nest in me. By and by I will furnish shade for the cattle. By and by I will provide warmth for the home. By and by I will be shelter from the storm to those who have gone under the roof. By and by I will be the strong ribs of a great vessel, and the tempest will beat against me in vain, while I carry men across the Atlantic." "O foolish little acorn, wilt thou be all this?" I ask. And the acorn answers, "Yes, God and I."

THE GATES.— The man who can really, in living union of the mind and heart, converse with God through nature, finds in the material forms around him a source of power and happiness inexhaustible and like the life of angels.— The highest life and glory of man is to be alive unto God; and when this grandeur of sensibility to Him, and this power of communion with Him is carried, as the habit of the soul, into the forms of nature, then the walls of our world are as the gates of Heaven.—*G. B. Cheever.*

MARVEL.—The ignorant man marvels at the exceptional; the wise man marvels at the common; the greatest wonder of all is the regularity of nature.
—*G. D. Boardman.*

STOREHOUSE.—A man finds in the productions of nature an inexhaustible stock of material on which he can employ himself, without any temptation to envy or malevolence, and has always a certain prospect of discovering new reasons for adoring the sovereign author of the universe.—*Johnson.*

PANACEA.— It were happy if we studied nature more in natural things; and acted according to nature, whose rules are few, plain, and most reasonable.
—*Penn.*

WELLSPRING.— Nature is the armoury of genius. Cities serve it poorly, books and colleges at second hand; the eye craves the spectacle of the horizon; of mountain, ocean, river and plain, the clouds and stars; actual contact with the elements, sympathy with the seasons as they rise and roll.—*A. B. Alcott.*

THE LAWS OF NATURE are just, but terrible. There is no weak mercy in them. Cause and consequence are inseparable and inevitable. The elements have no forbearance. The fire burns, the water drowns, the air consumes, the earth buries. And perhaps it would be well for our race if the punishment of crimes against the law of man were as inevitable as the punishment of crimes against the laws of nature,—were man as unerring in his judgment as nature.—*Longfellow.*

SYMPATHY WITH NATURE is a part of the good man's religion.
—*F. H. Hedge.*

NATURE
The day before April
  Alone, alone,
I walked to the woods
  And I sat on a stone.

I sat on a broad stone
  And sang to the birds.
The tune was God's making
  But I made the words.
—*Mary Carolyn Davies.*

NATURE AND WISDOM always say the same.—*Juvenal.*

THE BEST PEDAGOGUE—Nature is man's teacher. She unfolds her treasures to his search, unseals his eye, illumes his mind, and purifies his heart; an influence breathes from all the sights and sounds of her existence.—*Street.*

EVEN THE LEAST — Nature hath nothing made so base, but can read some instruction to the wisest man.—*C. Aleyn.*

NATURE is commanded by obeying her.—*Bacon.*

CLOAK — Nature is the time-vesture of God that reveals Him to the wise, and hides Him from the foolish.—*Carlyle.*

ALL SUNSHINE makes the desert.
—*Arabian Proverb.*

PROSECUTOR—There is no witness so terrible—no accuser so powerful as conscience which dwells within us.
—*Sophocles.*

IGNORANCE AND FAITH — In dwelling on divine mysteries, keep thy heart humble, thy thoughts reverent, thy soul holy. Let not philosophy be ashamed to be confuted, nor logic to be confounded, nor reason to be surpassed. What thou canst not prove, approve; what thou canst not comprehend, believe; what thou canst believe, admire and love and obey. So shall thine ignorance be satisfied in thy faith, and thy doubt be swallowed up in thy reverence, and thy faith be as influential as sight. Put out thine own candle, and then shalt thou see clearly the sun of righteousness.—*Jeremy Taylor.*

STUDY NATURE as the countenance of God.—*Kingsley.*

NATURE is but a name for an effect whose cause is God.

LOOK THROUGH nature up to nature's God—*Pope.*

XXI. OPPORTUNITY

OPTIMISM—I have told you of the Spaniard who always put on his spectacles when about to eat cherries, that they might look bigger and more tempting. In like manner, I make the most of my enjoyments, and pack away my troubles in as small a compass as I can.—*Robert Southey.*

CIVILIZATION itself is simply a granary into which society has swept all the rich harvests of the mind. Now ten-talent men are few. Thus far philosophers have found five men whose genius is of the first order, and whose work has been epic-making and revolutionary. But the dizzy space that separates these men from the rudest savage is not so great as the space that separates earth's five greatest intellects from this divine carpenter, whose achievements for home and friendship, for law and liberty, for learning and religion, make His forehead to strike against the stars.—*Hillis.*

LUCK—Luck is an ignis fatuus. You may follow it to ruin, but not to success. —*James A. Garfield.*

IT is not the position but the disposition that makes men and women happy.

Circumstances may make a man, but circumstances never made a man out of unprepared material.

About the only exercise some folks take is jumping at conclusions.

Make a man believe he is worthless, and he will act worthlessly.

Good clothes on some folks remind you of pretty labels on empty bottles.

Character stands for all that this moral demanding century wants.—*Dinger-isms.*

THE GREAT CONQUEROR—Jesus of Nazareth, without money and arms, conquered more millions than Alexander, Caesar, Mahomet, and Napoleon; without science and learning, He shed more light on things human and Divine than all philosophers and scholars combined; without the eloquence of schools, He spoke words of life as never were spoken before or since, and produced effects which lie beyond the reach of orator or poet; without writing a single line, He has set more pens in motion, and furnished themes for more sermons, orations, discussions, learned volumes, works of art, and sweet songs of praise, than the whole army of great men of ancient and modern times. Born in a manger, and crucified as a malefactor, He now controls the destinies of the civilized world, and rules a spiritual empire which embraces one-third of the inhabitants of the globe. There never was in this world a life so unpretending, modest, and lowly in its outward form and condition, and yet producing such extraordinary effects upon all ages, nations, and classes of men. The annals of history produce no other example of such complete and astonishing success in spite of the absence of those material, social, literary, and artistic powers and influences which are indispensable to success for a mere man. —*Schaff.*

THE SAYING OF OMAR IBN, AL HALIF, THE SECOND CALIPH

Four things come not back:
The spoken word;
The sped arrow;
Time past;
The neglected opportunity.

OBSCURING TRUTH — I cannot think but that the world would be better and brighter if our teachers would dwell on the Duty of Happiness as well as the Happiness of Duty.—*John Lubbock.*

Every duty we omit obscures some truth we should have known.—*Ruskin.*

RENEWAL—There is one illustration of the value of the constant renewal of society from the bottom that has always interested me profoundly. The only reason why government did not suffer dry rot in the Middle Ages under the aristocratic system which then prevailed was that so many of the men who were efficient instruments of government were drawn from the church,—from that great religious body which was then the only church, that body which we now distinguish from other religious bodies as the Roman Catholic Church. The Roman Catholic Church was then, as it is now, a great democracy. There was no peasant so humble that he might not become a priest, and no priest so obscure that he might not become Pope of Christendom; and every chancellery in Europe, every court in Europe, was ruled by these learned, trained and accomplished men, —the priesthood of that great and dominant body. What kept government alive in the Middle Ages was this constant rise of the sap from the bottom, from the rank and file of the great body of the people through the open channels of the priesthood.—*Woodrow Wilson.*

SPECIAL PROVIDENCES—People talk about special providences. I believe in the providences, but not in the specialty. I do not believe that God lets the thread of my affairs go for six days, and on the seventh evening takes it up for a moment.—*George Macdonald.*

RESOURCES — No man is blamed for being a fourteen-foot catboat instead of a steam yacht or an Atlantic liner. It is only required of him that he heave up whatever sail he carries and be headed right. This simplifies the whole matter and makes the path of duty plain. How much energy and wisdom, how much goodness and spiritual efficiency have you? "Not much," you say. No matter, bring it along! As you live in the spirit of Christian devotion your life will unfold in faith, in hope, and in love until men will say of your Master, "This of a truth is that prophet that should come into the world."

There is a false self-distrust which denies the worth of its own talent. It is not humility—it is petty pride, withholding its simple gifts from the hands of Christ because they are not more pretentious. There are men who would endow colleges, they say, if they were millionaires. They would help in the work of Bible study if they were as gifted as Henry Drummond. They would strive to lead their associates into the Christian life if they had the gifts of Dwight L. Moody. But they are not ready to give what they have and do what they can and be as it has pleased God to make them, in His service—and that is their condemnation.
—*Charles Reynolds Brown.*

TALENT—It is your duty to use your talents. Remember if you do not use you will lose. It is reported of Charles Darwin that when he had finished his scientific work, he settled down to enjoy life. He thought that he would now enjoy poetry, music and art. Sad to say he soon discovered that these things did not strike a response in his being. Later he said, "It is too late now because I have allowed these parts of my being to atrophy."
—*Zollars.*

USE WHAT YOU HAVE—A ship lost at sea for many days suddenly sighted a friendly vessel. From the mast of the unfortunate vessel was seen the signal: "Water, water; we die of thirst!" The answer from the friendly vessel at once came back: "Cast down your bucket where you are." A second and a third time the signal, "Water, water, send us water!" ran up from the distressed vessel, and was answered: "Cast down your bucket where you are." . . . The captain of the distressed vessel at last heeding the injunction, cast down his bucket, and it came up full of fresh, sparkling water from the mouth of the Amazon River. To those of my race who depend on bettering their condition I would say: "Cast down your bucket where you are—cast it down in making friends in every manly way of the people of all the race by whom we are surrounded."

We shall prosper in proportion as we learn to dignify and glorify common labor and put brains and skill into the common occupations of life; shall prosper in proportion as we learn to draw the line between the superficial and the substantial, the ornamental gewgaws of life and the useful. No race can prosper till it learns that there is as much dignity in tilling a field as in writing a poem. It is at the bottom of life we must begin, and not at the top.—*Booker T. Washington.*

HITCH HIKERS—If you want to succeed in the world, you must make your own opportunities as you go on. The man who waits for some seventh wave to toss him on dry land will find that the seventh wave is a long time a-coming. You can commit no greater folly than to sit by the roadside until some one comes along and invites you to ride with him to wealth and influence.—*John B. Gough.*

WHAT LUCK MEANS — Luck means the hardships and privations which you have not hesitated to endure; the long nights you have devoted to work. Luck means the appointments you have never failed to keep; the trains you have never failed to catch.—*Max O'Rell.*

CLOSED DOORS — When God shuts a door He opens a window.

EXTRAORDINARY—The true calling of a Christian is not to do extraordinary things, but to do ordinary things in an extraordinary way.—*Dean Stanley.*

INDIVIDUALITY — Whoso would be a man must be a nonconformist. He who would gather immortal palms must not be hindered by the name of goodness, but must explore if it be goodness. Nothing is at last sacred but the integrity of your own mind. . .

What I must do is all that concerns me, not what the people think . . . It is easy to live after our own; but the great man is he who in the midst of the crowd keeps with perfect sweetness the independence of solitude . . .

A foolish consistency is the hobgoblin of little minds, adored by little statesmen and philosophers and divines. With consistency a great soul has simply nothing to do.—*Ralph Waldo Emerson.*

SELF-MADE MEN — I am tired of hearing about self-made men. There is not a self-made man in the world. The so-called self-made man is the man who has seized his opportunities, and those given him by circumstances, and has made use of them.—*Lucius Tuttle.*

SUI GENERIS — All truly wise thoughts have been thought already thousands of times; but to make them really ours we must think them over again honestly, till they take firm root in our personal experience.—*Goethe.*

GREAT QUALITIES—It is not sufficient to have great qualities; we must be able to make proper use of them.
—*La Rochefoucauld.*

FUTILE—One does not gain much by mere cleverness.—*Vauvenargues.*

PERSONALITY—As the world was plastic and fluid in the hands of God, so it is ever to so much of His attributes as we bring to it. To ignorance and sin, it is flint . . . The great man makes the great thing. Wherever Macdonald sits, there is the head of the table . . . The day is always his who works in it the serenity and great aims.
—*Ralph Waldo Emerson.*

MAKING THE BEST—My business is not to remake myself, but to make the absolute best of what God made.
—*Robert Browning.*

DUTY — All higher motives, ideals, conceptions, sentiments in a man are of no account if they do not come forward to strengthen him for the better discharge of the duties which devolve upon him in the ordinary affairs of life.
—*Henry Ward Beecher.*

ORIGINALITY — To do easily what is difficult for others is the mark of talent. To do what is impossible for talent is the mark of genius.—*Henri-Frederic Amiel.*

DISCOURAGEMENT — Never let us be discouraged with ourselves; it is not when we are conscious of our faults that we are the most wicked; on the contrary, we are less so. We see by a brighter light; and let us remember, for our consolation, that we never perceive our sins till we begin to cure them.
—*Francois de la Mothe Fenelon.*

COMPLAINING—You are never to complain of your birth, your training, your employments, your hardships; never to fancy that you could be something if only you had a different lot and sphere assigned you. God understands His own plan, and He knows what you want a great deal better than you do. The very things that you most deprecate, as fatal limitations or obstructions, are probably what you most want. What you call hindrances, obstacles, discouragements, are probably God's opportunities. Bring down your soul, or rather, bring it up to receive God's will and do His work, in your lot, in your sphere, under your cloud of obscurity, against your temptations, and then you shall find that your condition is never opposed to your good, but really consistent with it.—*H. Bushnell.*

EVEN THE POOREST—There has been no man of pure genius; as there has been none wholly destitute of genius.
—*Thoreau.*

FAIRY GOLD — Of all good gifts which ever came out of the wallet of the Fairy Godmother, the gift of natural gladness is the greatest and best. It is to the soul what health is to the body, what sanity is to the mind, the test of normality.
—*Bliss Carman.*

116

XXII. OTHERS

INFLUENCE — Alice Freeman Palmer, the second president of Wellesley College, was happiest when she was doing most for others. When she left the college she gave herself so unweariedly to her self-imposed task of lightening the burdens of the unfortunate, that her husband, a Harvard professor, expostulated. He thought she should give her time and strength to writing books that would make her still more famous. "You are building no monument," he said. "When you are gone people will ask who you are, and no one will be able to say." "Well, why should they?" was the answer. "I am trying to make girls happier and wiser. Books don't help much toward that. It is people that count. You want to put yourself into people; they touch other people; these, others still, and so you go on working forever."

—*John T. Faris.*

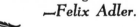

THE TORCH BEARER—The hero is one who kindles a great light in the world, who sets up blazing torches in the dark streets of life for men to see by. The saint is the man who walks through the dark paths of the world, himself a light.

—*Felix Adler.*

THE SPEECH OF ANGELS—Music is well said to be the speech of angels; in fact, nothing among the utterances allowed to man, is felt to be so Divine. It brings us near to the Infinite; we look for moments across the cloudy elements into the eternal light, when song leads and inspires us. Serious nations, all nations that can listen to the mandate of nature, have prized song and music as a vehicle for worship, for prophecy, and for whatsoever in them was Divine.—*Carlyle.*

UNSELFISHNESS—There is nothing like putting the shine on another's face to put the shine on our own. Nine-tenths of all loneliness, sensitiveness, despondency, moroseness, are connected with personal interests. Turn more of these selfish interests into unselfish ones, and by so much we change opportunities for disheartenment into their opposite.

—*W. C. Gannett.*

NEIGHBOR—Love your neighbor for God's sake, and God for your own sake, who created all things for your sake, and redeemed you for His mercy's sake. If your love hath any other motive, it is false love; if your motive hath any other end, it is self-love. If you neglect your love to your neighbor, in vain you profess your love of God; for by your love of God, your love to your neighbor is acquired; and by your love to your neighbor, your love of God is nourished.

—*The Beauties of Thought.*

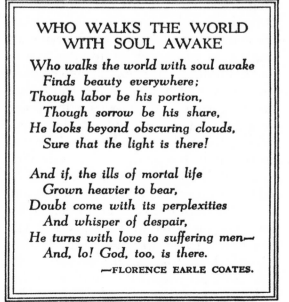

WHO WALKS THE WORLD WITH SOUL AWAKE

Who walks the world with soul awake
  Finds beauty everywhere;
Though labor be his portion,
  Though sorrow be his share,
He looks beyond obscuring clouds,
  Sure that the light is there!

And if, the ills of mortal life
  Grown heavier to bear,
Doubt come with its perplexities
  And whisper of despair,
He turns with love to suffering men—
  And, lo! God, too, is there.

—FLORENCE EARLE COATES.

INFLUENCE—The least may influence the greatest. It was St. Andrew that influenced St. Peter to "come and see" Jesus. One least spoken of among the apostles influenced the one who took the foremost place among them as if to show that such power is independent of personal superiority. It is not the great and gifted alone who exercise this mysterious power of influence. It is a universal law of life. These personal influences, first of Jesus on Andrew, then of Andrew on Peter, were the beginning of the conversion of the world.—*T. T. Carter.*

HELPFULNESS — "Did you know Dr. Osler?" someone asked another. "Yes," was the answer, "intimately, but I only saw him once. It was late twilight; the city square was almost deserted when a woman carrying a heavy child came slowly up the square and sat down to rest on the coping bordering the pavement. The child's heavy head was pressed against her bosom and she seemed all in. I started to speak to her when up the square came jauntily a man in full evening dress, top coat, silk hat, flower in his buttonhole, light gloves in one hand and his can swinging in the other, evidently singing. In an instant he saw the woman and her burden. He stopped, made a playful dive with his cane at the child, then throwing cane and gloves on the grass, he gently lifted the child into his arms, holding its head against his own breast as he talked to the mother. Then whistling to a little boy who chanced in sight he said: 'Get a cab as quick as you can and if you are back in five minutes, riches! for you!' and he patted his breast pocket. The boy flew off and was back quickly with the cab. Dr. Osler put the woman in the cab, carefully placed the child on her lap —then he wrote on a card, 'This is Mrs.

Osler's youngest. See that he is well taken care of until I come tomorrow night. He read what he had written aloud to the woman, winked his eye at me, gave the driver his fare, told him to drive at once to the Hopkins Hospital, see that the woman and boy were safely attended to—then pressed a five dollar bill in the woman's hand, said: 'Your laddie will be well looked after at the hospital. I will see him tomorrow.' Then he slammed the door of the cab and was off. All done while I was trying to say, 'Can I help you?' "
—*Edith G. Reid.*

OBEDIENCE—The man who would lift others must be uplifted himself, and he who would command others must learn to obey.—*Charles K. Ober.*

MARCHING TOGETHER—In the Roman army of old the soldier carried a large oblong shield on his left arm. When a city was beseiged the men in close rank locked their shields together over their heads and then marched in safety to the gate. So is it, in an organization where brotherhood prevails. We lock our shields over our heads as we march against the vicissitudes, the trials and temptations of life, and not over our own heads alone, but others are sheltered beneath them. A comrade falls, but our locked shields ward off hardship and penury from his widow and her little ones. A companion is prostrated with sickness, but he is cared for and the wants of both him and his are supplied.

SELF-POISON — Bad temper is its own scourge. Few things are bitterer than to feel bitter. A man's venom poisons himself more than his victim.
—*Charles Buxton.*

A SOLDIER OF THE COMMON GOOD—A life without love in it is like a heap of ashes upon a deserted hearth—with the fire dead, the laughter stilled, and the light extinguished. It is like a winter landscape—with the sun hidden, the flowers frozen, and the wind whispering through the withered leaves. God knows we need all the unselfish love that can come to us. For love is seldom unselfish. There is usually the motive and the price. Do you remember William Morris, and how his life was lived, his fortune spent, his hands busied—in the service of others? He was the father of the settlement movement, of cooperative homes for working people, and of the arts and crafts revival, in our day. He was a "soldier of the common good." After he was gone—his life began to grow in radiance and power, like a beacon set high upon a dangerous shore. In the twilight of his days he wrote what I like to think was his creed —and mine: "I am going your way, so let us go hand in hand. You help me and I'll help you. We shall not be here very long, for soon death, the kind old nurse, will come back and rock us all to sleep. Let us help one another while we may."

—*Frank P. Tebbetts.*

FOLLY — Consider how few things are worthy of anger, and thou wilt wonder that any fools should be wroth.

—*Robert Dodsley.*

KINGDOM—The kingdom of God is a society of the best men, working for the best ends, according to the best methods. Its law is one word—loyalty; its gospel one message—love. If you know anything better, live for it; if not, in the name of God and of humanity, carry out Christ's plan.

—*Henry Drummond.*

TRAVELING HOMEWARD — **To** be strong and true; to be generous in praise and appreciation of others; to impute worthy motives even to enemies; to give without expectation of return; to practise humility, tolerance, and self-restraint; to make the best use of time and opportunity; to keep the mind pure and the judgment charitable; to extend intelligent sympathy to those in distress; to cultivate quietness and non-resistance; to seek truth and righteousness; to work, love, pray, and serve daily, to aspire greatly, labor cheerfully, and take God at His word—this is to travel heavenward.

—*Grenville Kleiser*

SOULS

My soul goes clad in gorgeous things,
  Scarlet and gold and blue;
And at her shoulder sudden wings
  Like long flames flicker through.

And she is wallow-fleet, and free
  From mortal bonds and bars.
She laughs, because Eternity
  Blossoms for her with stars!

O folk who scorn my stiff gray gown,
  My dull and foolish face,—
Can ye not see my Soul flash down,
  A singing flame through space?

And folk, whose earth-stained looks I
    hate,
Why may I not divine
Your Souls, that must be passionate,
  Shining and swift, as mine!

—*Fannie Stearns Davis*

BREAKING BARRIERS — **This,** then, is Christianity: to smash the barriers and get next to your fellowman.

—*John T. Faris*

THE MOST POWERFUL MO-
TIVE—The sense of somebody's need is,
I believe, the most powerful motive in the
world, one that appeals to the largest
number of people of every age, race, and
kind. It wakes up the whole nature, the
powers that learn as well as those that
perform; it generates the vigor of interest
that submerges selfishness and cowardice;
it rouses the inventiveness and ingenuity
that slumber so soundly in students' class-
rooms. For many of us . . . work that is
service taps a great reservoir of power,
sets free some of our caged and leashed
energy.—*Richard C. Cabot.*

KEEP THEM TO YOURSELF —
What right have I to make every one in
the house miserable because I am miserable? Troubles must come to all, but
troubles need not be wicked, and it is
wicked to be a destroyer of happiness.
—*Amelia E. Barr.*

SECOND CHANGES—We all have
to learn, in one way or another, that neither men nor boys get *second* chances in this
world. We all get *new* chances till the end
of our lives, but not second chances in the
same set of circumstances; and the great
difference between one person and another is, how he takes hold of and uses his
first chance, and how he takes his fall if
it is scored against him.—*Thomas Hughes.*

CHURCH

A reading church is an informed church;
An informed church is an interested
    church;
An interested church is an acting church;
An acting church is a serving church;
A serving church is a Christian church.
—*Selected.*

SINS OF SOCIETY—Some one has
said that the seven deadly sins of society
are these: Policies without principles;
wealth without work; pleasure without
conscience; knowledge without character;
commerce and industry without morality;
science without humanity; worship without sacrifice.—*Observer.*

WHEN A MAN COMES TO HIM-
SELF—Surely a man has come to himself only when he has found the best that
is in him, and has satisfied his heart with
the highest achievement he is fit for. It is
only then that he knows of what he is capable and what his heart demands. And,
assuredly, no thoughtful man ever came
to the end of his life, and had time and a
little space of calm from which to look
back upon it, who did not know and acknowledge that it was what he had done
unselfishly and for others, and nothing
else, that satisfied him in the retrospect,
and made him feel that he had played
the man. And so men grow by having responsibility laid upon them, the burden
of other people's business. Their powers
are put out at interest, and they get usury
in kind. They are like men multiplied.
Each counts manifold. Men who live with
an eye only upon what is their own are
dwarfed beside them—seem fractions
while they are integers. The trustworthi-
ness of men trusted seems often to grow
with the trust.—*Woodrow Wilson.*

SACRIFICE—There can be no real
and abiding happiness without sacrifice.
Our greatest joys do not result from our
efforts toward self-gratification, but from
a loving and spontaneous service to other
lives. Joy comes not to him who seeks it
for himself, but to him who seeks it for
other people.—*H. W. Sylvester.*

TUNING-UP — Every morning compose your soul for a tranquil day, and all through it be careful often to recall your resolution, and bring yourself back to it, so to say. If something discomposes you, do not be upset, or troubled; but having discovered the fact, humble yourself gently before God, and try to bring your mind into a quiet attitude. Say to yourself, "Well, I have made a false step; now I must go more carefully and watchfully." Do this each time, however frequently you fall. When you are at peace use it profitably, making constant acts of meekness, and seeking to be calm even in the most trifling things. Above all, do not be discouraged; be patient; wait; strive to attain a calm, gentle spirit.

—*St. Francois de Sales.*

GOODNESS — You can only make others better by being good yourself.

—*Hugh R. Hawies.*

ICH DIEN — The crest of the Prince of Wales bears the simple watchword, "I serve," and no more princely motto can be found.

We cannot determine whether our faces shall be beautiful or ugly, our bodies graceful or deformed. But the shaping of our life is in our own hands. We make that great or small, noble or mean, as we will.

The motto, "I serve," always betokens real power and lasting authority. More, it is a truly Christian motto and proclaims eternal kinship with the highest.

—*George Henry Hubbard.*

COOPERATION — Never one thing and seldom one person can make for a success. It takes a number of them merging into one perfect whole.—*Marie Dressler.*

DEPENDENCE — We can't play alone in the game of life. We're dependent, my friend, on others; we cannot "get by" in the struggle and strife, except for the help of our brothers! Whatever we plan, or whatever we do, whatever we give of our best, is meant to include all our fellow men too, and add to the joy of the rest.

REWARD — Service to a just cause rewards the worker with more real happiness and satisfaction than any other venture of life.—*Carrie Chapman Catt.*

For Those Who Love Me

I live for those who love me,
For those who know me true,
For the Heaven that smiles above me,
  And awaits my coming too;
For the cause that lacks assistance,
For the wrong that needs resistance,
For the future in the distance,
  And the good that I can do.

—*G. Linnaeus Banks.*

BURNING BRIDGES—He who can not forgive others breaks the bridge over which he must pass himself.

—*George Herbert.*

ROBBING ONESELF — Of all the passions that are incident to a man, there is none so impetuous, or that produceth so terrible effect as anger; for besides that intrinsical mischief which it works in a man's own heart, in regard whereof Hugo said well, "Pride robs me of God, envy of my neighbor, anger of myself." What bloody tragedies doth this passion act every day in the world, making the whole earth nothing but either an amphitheatre for fight or a shambles for slaughter.

—*Joseph Hall.*

TEAMWORK — We may call it by this name, or call it by that—"teamwork" or "cooperation;" together we stand, by ourselves we fall flat; together, my friend, we're the Nation! Whatever we do, or whatever we plan—we can't stand alone, e'en the best of us; but must share of our gifts with our good fellowman—for we're only a part of the rest of us!

FELLOWSHIP — We are told that William Penn, clad in simple garb, stood in the center of a company of Indian chieftains and said, "My friends, we have met on the broad pathway of good faith. We are all one flesh and blood. Being brethren, no advantage shall be taken on either side. Between us there shall be nothing but openness and love." Jumping to their feet these Indian chiefs replied, "While the rivers run and the sun shines, we shall live in peace with the children of William Penn." Although no record of this treaty was made on parchment, yet the war whoop of the Indian was not heard again in Pennsylvania for more than seventy years.—*Selected.*

GIFTS

He gives nothing but worthless gold
  Who gives from a sense of duty;
But he who gives but a slender mite,
And gives to that which is out of sight,
  That thread of the all-sustaining
    Beauty
Which runs through all and doth all
    unite,—
The hand cannot grasp the whole of his
  alms,
The heart outstretches its eager palms,
For a god goes with it and makes it store
To the soul that was starving in darkness
  before.
      —*James Russell Lowell.*

PURGE—Out of every heart the lurking grudge. Give us the grace and strength to forebear and to persevere. Offenders, give us the grace to accept and to forgive offenders. Forgetful ourselves, help us to bear cheerfully the forgetfulness of others. Give us courage and gaiety and the quiet mind. Spare to us our friends, soften to us our enemies. Bless us, if it may be, in all our innocent endeavors. If it may not, give us the strength to encounter that which is to come, that we be brave in peril, constant in tribulation, temperate in wrath, and in all changes of fortune, and down to the gates of death, loyal and loving one to another.
    —*Robert Louis Stevenson.*

A TEST — A cobbler at Leyden, who used to attend the public disputations held at the academy, was once asked if he understood Latin. "No," replied the mechanic; "but I know who is in the wrong in the argument by seeing who is angry first.

TOGETHER—These seven "togethers" are seven links of a chain which bind us indissolubly to Christ: Crucified together; quickened together; raised together; seated together in Heavenly places; sufferers together; heirs together; and glorified together with Christ. They indicate the everlasting purpose of God in our redemption, and His plan in effecting that purpose.

COURTESY is not the creation of effort, it is the product of grace; it is born, not made. Paul was born of grace, and therefore he was gracious, and instinctively his courtesy fitted itself to all the changing requirements of the day . . . Grace is the bountiful mother of all the graces.—*J. H. Jowett.*

SELF-PRESERVATION — The use of anger is to stir us up to self preservation, and to put us upon our guard against injuries. When it has done this, it has performed all that belongs to it; for what measures we may take to effect this, how we may secure ourselves, and how we should behave towards those who offend us—these are the points concerning which we must not consult our passions, but our reason, which was given us to moderate our passions, and to prescribe laws for our actions.—*Jortin.*

TEMPER—If religion has done nothing for your temper, it has done nothing for your soul.—*Clayton.*

VAIN REGRET
My mind was ruffled with small cares today,
And I said pettish words, and did not keep
Long-suffering patience well, and now how deep
My trouble for this sin! in vain I weep
For foolish words I never can unsay.
—*H. S. Sutton.*

TASTE—If I had my life to live over again, I would have made a rule to read some poetry and listen to some music at least once a week: for perhaps the parts of my brain now atrophied would thus have been kept active through use.

The loss of these tastes is a loss of happiness, and may possibly be injurious to the intellect, and more probably to the moral character, by enfeebling the emotional part of our nature.—*Darwin.*

IT TAKES TWO—Labor and trouble one can always get through alone, but it takes two to be glad.—*Ibsen.*

UNCONSCIOUS GROWTH—Art creates an atmosphere in which the proprieties, the amenities, and the virtues unconsciously grow.—*Robert G. Ingersoll.*

CALMNESS — We often forget this, most of us; but it is true. Noise, anger, explosive tones, superlatives, exaggerations of passion, add nothing to the force of what we say, but rather rob our words of the power that belongs to them. But the utterance that shows a spirit subdued by truth and mastered by wisdom is the utterance that sweeps away opposition, that persuades and overcomes. Go into a heated political convention, and you will find that it is not the men who get angry and storm and swear who carry the day. But the men who never lose their tempers and never raise their voices; who keep talking quietly and placidly as if they were discussing the weather. This is a truth that all of us who seek to influence our fellow beings, in the family, in the church, in the school, in society, in politics, anywhere, must lay to heart. We are prone to forget it; but we make a great mistake when we do forget it. The soft tongue breaketh the bone. The tamed tongue subdues the adversary.—*Gladden.*

DISSATISFACTION with our condition is often due to the false idea we have of the happiness of others.—*Churchman.*

THIS is the final test of a gentleman: His respect for those who can be of no possible service to him.
—*William Lyon Phelps.*

MANY HANDS — By many hands the work of God is done.
—*Richard Le Gallienne.*

CHRISTMAS SPIRIT — I am the Christmas spirit!

I enter the home of poverty, causing palefaced children to open their eyes wide, in pleased wonder.

I cause the miser's clutched hand to relax, and thus paint a bright spot on his soul.

I cause the aged to renew their youth and to laugh in the old, glad way.

I keep romance alive in the heart of childhood, and brighten sleep with dreams woven of magic.

I cause eager feet to climb dark stairways with filled baskets, leaving behind hearts amazed at the goodness of the world.

I cause the prodigal to pause a moment on his wild, wasteful way, and send to anxious love some little token that releases glad tears—tears which wash away the hard lines of sorrow.

I enter dark prison cells, reminding scarred manhood of what might have been, and pointing forward to good days yet to be.

I come softly into the still, white home of pain, and lips that are too weak to speak just tremble in silent, eloquent gratitude.

In a thousand ways I cause the weary world to look up into the face of God, and for a little moment forget the things that are small and wretched.

I am the Christmas spirit!

—*E. C. Baird.*

ARRANGEMENT — A child, desirous of presenting his father with a bouquet, goes into the garden and gathers a lapful of flowers and weeds, all mixed together. His mother selects, arranges, and binds the flowers, and makes the gift acceptable. So Christ makes ever our poor services acceptable to God as a sweet-smelling savor.—*Ambrose.*

MUSIC is nature's high-water mark. It is when the brook is full and goes with strong pulsing current toward the sea that it sings sweet music. When the writer of the book of Job would give us the noblest idea of beauty and harmony in the universe, he declares that in creation's dawn "The morning stars sang together." When God would give the most glorious prelude to the birth of Jesus, angels sang together on the plains of Bethlehem.

—*Gordon.*

Who Is Brother?

He who understands your silence.

He who will be a balance in the seasaw of life.

He who considers your needs before your deservings.

He who to himself is true and therefore must be so to you.

He who, when he reaches the top of the ladder, does not forget you if you are at the bottom.

He who is the same today when prosperity smiles upon you, and tomorrow when adversity and sorrows come.

He who cheerfully comes in when all the world has gone out; who weeps with you when the laughing is away.

He who guards your interests as his own, neither flatters nor deceives, gives just praise to your good deeds, and equally condemns your bad acts.

He who is the same to you in the society of the wealthy and proud, as in the solitude of poverty; whose cheerful smile sheds sunshine in every company.

—*Lodge Record.*

HAVING AND GETTING—There is no happiness in having and getting, but only in giving. Half the world is on the wrong scent in the pursuit of happiness.—*F. W. Gunsaulus.*

COURTESY—Some friends of mine, motoring in winter over the Spanish Guadarramas, stuck in a deep snowdrift and asked a passing muleteer if he would be kind enough to drag their car to the top of the pass. He agreed, and at the top they offered him a tip which must have seemed to him a small fortune. But he waved it aside with an apologetic smile, as if unwilling to hurt their feelings, saying: "All that the poor can offer is favors."

—*Howard of Penrith.*

Outwitted

He drew a circle that shut me out—
Heretic, rebel, a thing to flout.
But love and I had the wit to win:
We drew a circle that took him in.
—*Edwin Markham.*
Reprinted by permission.

LOVE is the medicine of all moral evil. By it the world is to be cured of sin. Love is the wine of existence. When you have taken that, you have taken the most precious drop that there is in the cluster. Love is the seraph, and faith and hope are but the wings by which it flies. The nature of the highest love is to be exquisitely sensitive to the act of forcing itself unbidden and unwelcomed upon another. The finer, the stronger, the higher love is, the more it is conditioned upon reciprocation. No man can afford to invest his being in anything lower than faith, hope, love—these three, the greatest of which is love.

—*Henry Ward Beecher.*

I WILL NOT FOLLOW where the path may lead, but I will go where there is no path, and I will leave a trail.

—*Muriel Strode.*

RICH men have built our hospitals, endowed our colleges, founded our orphan homes, assisted the scientists in combating disease, and they have in a thousand ways blessed this old world. Let us be fair. We have no right to pick out a few who have worshipped the dollar and lived for self at the expense of human life and judge all by them. The world is full of good men and women who have accumulated wealth and who are blessing the world in which they live. Every man and woman to their task: Ability, Labor and Capital must each make its contribution to civilization and prosperity. Prosperity is a granary that can be filled to overflowing only when all workers unite in bringing in their contributions, large and small.

—*Public Speakers Library.*

BACKWARD — By putting his best foot forward, many a man pulls his worst foot back. —*Ralph W. Sockman.*

Hold Out a Light

Hold out a light,
    The way is dark,
No ray to guide
    Yon struggling bark.
Rough rocks are near,
    And wild waves roar;
Hold out a light
    To show the shore.

Hold out a light;
    Your brother may
Win back to land
    With your small ray;
New courage find
    Life's storms to face
With strengthened faith
    To win the race.
—*Addison Howard Gibson.*

GOOD NATURE—A cheerful temper, joined with innocence, will make beauty attractive, knowledge delightful, and wit good-natured. It will lighten sickness, poverty, and affliction; convert ignorance into an amiable simplicity, and render deformity itself agreeable.

—*Addison.*

Via Crucis

If thou wouldst follow Me upon the way,
Take up My cross where I have laid it
down.
Cast off thy life of luxury and ease,
Take to thy heart My hyssop and My
crown.

Tread where I trod, each step a thing of
pain,
Meeting nor help nor succor on the road.
Strengthen thine ears to listen to the gibes
Flung at thee as thou fallest 'neath thy
load.

Thy friends will be the sad at heart and
poor,
Those who are burdened with a life of
shame,
Those sufferers who are the halt andd
blind,
Those to whom Beauty is a distant name.

Take up My cross where I have laid it
down,
My mantle wrap about thee and My pain,
Give of My love to all thy fellow-men—
This being done, I'll not have died in vain!
—*Hesper Le Gallienne.*

SELF-DENIAL — Our superfluities should be given up for the convenience of others. Our conveniences should give place to the necessities of others. And even our necessities give way to the extremities of the poor.—*John Howard.*

PATIENCE — We have need of patience with ourselves and with others; with those below, and those above us, and with our own equals; with those who love us and those who love us not; for the greatest things and for the least; against sudden inroads of trouble, and under daily burdens; disappointments as to the weather, or the breaking of the heart; in the weariness of the body, or the wearing of the soul; in our own failure of duty; or others' failure toward us; in every-day wants, or in the aching of sickness or the decay of old age; in disappointment, bereavement, losses, injuries, reproaches; in heaviness of the heart; or its sickness amid delayed hopes. In all these things, from childhood's little troubles to the martyr's sufferings, patience is the grace of God, whereby we endure evil for the love of God—*E. B. Pusey.*

Liberality

He is dead whose hand is not open wide
To help the need of a human brother;
He doubles the length of his lifelong ride
Who gives his hand to another.
And a thousand million lives are his
Who carries the world in his sympathies.
To give is to live. To deny is to die.
—*Selected.*

LAYMEN—Preachers and laymen are each rowing different oars, but they are both in the same boat. When only one oar is being pulled, there is a lot of splash but no progress. Let us see that both oars are being pulled. We are facing great problems and must work them out together, each with confidence in the other, each with love for the other, and each unselfishly thinking of the generations to come, with less thought for ourselves.
—*Roger Babson.*

BROTHERHOOD—There is an old legend of a general who found his troops disheartened. He believed it was owing to the fact that they did not realize how close they were to the other divisions of the same army on account of a dense growth of small trees and shrubbery. Orders therefore were given to "Burn the underbrush." It was done and they saw they were not isolated, as they had supposed, but were part of one great army. The result was that their courage revived, and they went forward in triumph. So let us burn the brushwood between the workingman and the church—the brushwood of prejudice, mistrust and separation. We all have far more in common than we think. We are all under the same great Captain. Let the brushwood be burned away in the glow of united song, and in the enthusiasm of common worship.—*Messenger.*

YOU WANT to double your wealth without gambling or stock-jobbing. Share it. Whether it be material or intellectual, its rapid increase will amaze you. What would the sun have been had he folded himself up in darkness? Surely he would have gone out. So would Socrates.
—*J. C. Hare.*

RIGHT

The world is a difficult world indeed,
　And the people are hard to suit,
And the man who plays on the violin
　Is a bore to the man with a flute.
And I myself have often thought,
　How very much better 'twould be
If every one of the folks that I know
　Would only agree with me.
But since they will not, the very best way
　To make the world look bright,
Is never to mind what others say,
　But do what you think is right.
　　　　—Light and Life Evangel.

SUNSHINY — Have you ever had your day suddenly turn sunshiny because of a cheerful word? Have you ever wondered if this could be the same world, because someone had been unexpectedly kind to you? You can make today the same for somebody. It is only a question of a little imagination, a little time and trouble. Think now, "What can I do today to make someone happy?"—old persons, children, servants—even a bone for the dog, or sugar for the bird! Why not?—*Babcock.*

ENEMIES—Ye have enemies; for who can live on this earth without them? Take heed to yourselves; love them. In no way can thy enemy so hurt thee by his violence as thou dost hurt thyself if thou love him not. And let it not seem to you impossible to love him. Believe first that it can be done, and pray that the will of God may be done in you. For what good can thy neighbor's ill do to thee? If he had no ill, he would not even be thine enemy. Wish him well, then, that he may end his ill, and he will be thine enemy no longer. For it is not the human nature in him that is at enmity with thee, but his sin. . . . Let thy prayer be against the malice of thine enemy, that it may die, and he may live. For if thine enemy were dead, thou hast lost, it might seem, an enemy, yet has thou not found a friend. But if his malice die, thou hast at once lost an enemy and found a friend.
　　　　—St. Augustine.

TWINS

Devotion borrows Music's tone,
And Music took Devotion's wing;
And like the bird that hails the sun,
They soar to heaven, and soaring, sing.
　　—The Hermit of St. Clement's Wall.

SELF-CONTROL—Self-Control implies command of temper, command of feeling, coolness of judgment, and the power to restrain the imagination and curb the will. It means such thorough mastery over self as Robert Ainsworth, the lexicographer, possessed, who, when his wife, in a fit of passion, committed his voluminous manuscript to the flames, calmly turned to his desk, and recommenced his labors.

—W. H. Davenport Adams.

Measure of Success

When sunset falls upon your day
And fades from out the west,
When business cares are put away
And you lie down to rest,
The measure of the day's success
Or failure may be told
In terms of human happiness
And not in terms of gold.

Is there beside some hearth tonight
More joy because you wrought?
Does some one face the bitter fight
With courage you have taught?
Is something added to the store
Of human happiness?
If so, the day that now is o'er
Has been a real success.

—Selected

CHIVALRY—Some say that the age of chivalry is past. The age of chivalry is never past, so long as there is a wrong left unredressed on earth, or a man or woman left to say, "I will redress that wrong, or spend my life in the attempt." The age of chivalry is never past, so long as we have faith enough to say, "God will help me to redress that wrong; or, if not me, He will help those that come after me, for His eternal Will is to overcome evil with good."—Kingsley.

HARMONIUM — Besides Theology, music is the only art capable of affording peace and joy of the heart like that induced by the study of the science of Divinity. The proof of this is that the Devil, the originator of sorrowful anxieties and restless troubles, flees before the sound of music almost as much as he does before the Word of God. This is why the prophets preferred music before all the other arts, proclaiming the Word in psalms and hymns.

My heart, which is full of overflowing, has often been solaced and refreshed by music when sick and weary.

—Martin Luther.

A CHALLENGING FACT—Brotherhood is no longer simply a religious ideal, but a challenging material fact; for there is no peace but universal peace, no enduring prosperity that does not comprehend all mankind. It was Dante who said seven centuries ago that no soul could ever be quite happy in Heaven while it was conscious of a single suffering soul in Hell.—Edgar White Burrill.

ENEMIES—If we would read the secret history of our enemies, we would find in each man's life sorrow and suffering enough to disarm all hostility.

—Longfellow.

True

He's true to God who's true to man: wherever wrong is done
To the humblest and the weakest, neath the all-beholding sun,
That wrong is also done to us; and they are slaves most base
Whose love of right is for themselves and not for all their race.

—James Russell Lowell.

PREACHING — Every problem that the preacher faces leads back to one basic question: how well does he understand the thoughts and lives of his people? That he should know his gospel goes without saying, but he may know it ever so well and yet fail to get it within reaching distance of anybody unless he intimately understands people and cares more than he cares for anything else what is happening inside of them. Preaching is wrestling with individuals over questions of life and death, and until that idea of it commands a preacher's mind and method, eloquence will avail him little and theology not at all.
—*Harry Emerson Fosdick.*

BENEVOLENCE — God is positive. Evil is merely primitive, not absolute. It is like cold, which is the privation of heat. All evil is so much death to nonentity. Benevolence is absolute and real. So much benevolence as a man hath, so much life hath he; for all things proceed out of this same spirit, which is differently named love, justice, temperance, in its different applications, just as the ocean receives different names on the several shores which it washes.—*Emerson.*

RECOMMENDATION — The memorial tablet to Dr. Geddie, at Aneitum, New Hebrides, bears the words: "When he landed in 1840, there were no Christians here; when he left in 1872, there were no heathen." These words are more suggestive than hundreds of pages of history. They are the best that can be said about any Christian worker. It is the nullification of self and the exaltation of the Master that are more eloquent than words or deeds. As John said, "He must increase but I must decrease." It is "Christ in us, the hope of glory." It is not what we say, but what we are.

MEASURING RODS—At the close of life the question will be not, how much have you got, but how much have you given; not how much have you won, but how much have you done; not how much have you saved, but how much have you sacrificed; how much have you loved and served, not how much were you honored.—*Nathan C. Schaeffer.*

JUSTICE is the paying universally what we owe. St. Paul explains this, and at the same time shows the profound connection between love and justice when he says, "Owe no man anything, but to love one another;" for "he that loveth another hath fulfilled the law." Here love is the eternal debt of righteousness, which justice must be forever paying. Now charity does not suppress righteousness either in God or in man; in us, it is the strength by which the debt is paid, as well as the watchful requital of the debt itself. The Christian ethics of justice are deeply affected by the supremacy of love.
—*W. B. Pope.*

INVISIBILITY—No man can wrap his cloak about him and say that he will stand alone, that his life shall not influence nor be influenced by other lives. Even the mountain that lifts its snow-capped summit to the clouds is enclosed around with influences that constantly change its characteristics, the sun, the mighty king of day, melts its ice-bound top, and the rain plows furrows in its gigantic sides. So these different organizations throw around human lives, sunshine of friendship and rain drops of charity and love, protecting the living, soothing the dying, holding in fond remembrance the dead, assisting with tender care the loved ones who remain.—*Brotherhood.*

THE REAL TEST—Society affects to estimate men by their talents, but really feels and knows them by their character. —*Thoreau.*

SELF-SACRIFICE—Shortly after the death of Phillips Brooks, his oldest brother said to Dr. McVicker, "Phillips might have saved himself, and so prolonged his life. Others do; but he was always giving himself to any who wanted him." Dr. McVickers answered: "Yes, indeed, he might have saved himself, but in so doing he would not have been Phillips Brooks. The glory of his life was that he did not save himself." Ah! the glory of any life is that it does not save itself. Like Mary, Bishop Brooks gave the best he had to God and humanity, and that is why the fragrance of his life has filled two continents with its sweetness.—*Tidings.*

GIVING—Never be afraid of giving up your best, and God will give you His better.—*Hinton.*

PEACEABLE—A peaceable disposition is a distinguishing mark of Christian character, and the want of it is a serious defect in the character of any one "that nameth the name of Christ." Upon all who claim to be His followers it is enjoined, in the words of an inspired apostle: "If it be possible, as much as lieth in you, live peaceably with all men." —*The Watchman.*

I HAVE SOMEWHERE MET with the epitaph on a charitable man which has pleased me very much. I cannot recollect the words, but here is the sense of it: "What I spent I lost; what I possessed is left to others; what I gave away remains with me."—*Addison.*

ENVY is called a passion; and means suffering. Envy is a mysterious and terrible disease. The nerves of sensation within the man are attached by some unseen hand to his neighborhood all around him, so that every step of advancement which they make tears the fibres that lie next his heart. The wretch enjoys a moment's relief when the mystic chord is temporarily slackened by a neighbor's fall; but his agony immediately begins again, for he anticipates another twitch as soon as the fallen is restored to prosperity.—*W. Arnot.*

REPRESENTATIVES—We are here to represent Christ—to present Him again, to re-present Him.—*Babcock.*

EXAMPLE—We reprove each other unconsciously by our own behavior. Our very carriage and demeanor in the streets should be a reprimand that will go to the conscience of every beholder. An infusion of love from a great soul gives a color to our faults which will discover them as lunar caustic detects impurities in water. —*Thoreau.*

DEPORTMENT — Godliness is that outward deportment which characterizes a heavenly temper.—*G. Crabb.*

BENEVOLENCE—He that lays out for God, God lays up for him. But, alas! God's credit runs low in the world; few care to trust Him. Give and spend, and be sure that God will send; for only in giving and spending do you fullfill the object of His sending.—*J. G. Holland.*

TAPERS—If you have knowledge, let others light their candles at it.

CONSIDERATENESS — One imbued with this high quality never sees deformity or blemish. A lame man could easily classify his friends, as to their breeding, by drawing a line between those who ask how it happened, and those who refrain from all questions. The gentleman will not talk to the beggar of his rags, nor boast of his health before the sick, nor speak of his wealth among the poor; he will not seem to be fortunate among the hapless, nor make any show of his virtue before the vicious. He will avoid all painful contrast, always looking at the thing in question from the standpoint of the other person.—*T. T. Munger.*

Uprightness

Who serves his country best?
  Not he who guides her senates in debate,
And makes the laws which are her prop and stay;
  Not he who wears the poet's purple vest,
  And sings her songs of love and grief and fate;
    There is a better way.

He serves his country best
  Who lives pure life, and doeth righteous deed,
And walks straight paths, however others stray,
And leaves his sons as uttermost bequest
  A stainless record which all may read;
    This is a better way.
          —Selected.

PUNCTUALITY — Punctuality preserves peace and good temper in a family or a business; it gives calmness of mind; it gives weight to character; it is contagious, and thus leads to a general saving of time and temper and money.
          —Adams.

INFLUENCE — Every human being has influence. It is inseparable from existence. Its effects are as penetrating as ointment. Its presence is as manifest in every life as the leaven that swells the meal.

Each moral action and utterance is linked to a chain of sequences no mortal can foretell. Each is a vast whispering gallery, where words and actions live on and ring on forever.

Scientists tell us that the words spoken by Abraham and Elijah are still influencing the air; that the atmosphere is a mighty library, on whose pages human actions and utterances have all been impressed. Influence is born with us like fire in the flint. It walks with us, flashes from the eyes and radiates from us like light from the sun. Influence is posthumous; and of an evil man, like the fallen Abel, it may be said, "He being dead, yet speaketh!"—*Morgan.*

Charity

Knowledge shall fail, and prophecy shall cease:
Yea, constant faith and holy hope shall die,
One lost in certainty, and one in joy;
While thou, more happy power, fair Charity,
Triumphant sister, greatest of the three,
Thy office and thy nature still the same,
Lasting thy lamp, and unconsumed thy flame,
Still shalt survive;
Shalt stand before the host of heaven confest,
For ever blessing, and for ever blest!
          —Prior.

CHARACTER—Keep clear of a man who does not value his own character.

LIMITLESS—The Church must grope her way into the alleys, and courts, and purlieus of the city, and up the broken staircase, and into the bare room, and beside the loathsome sufferer; she must go down into the pit with the miner, into the forecastle with the sailor, into the tent with the soldier, into the shop with the mechanic, into the factory with the operative, into the field with the farmer, into the countingroom with the merchant. Like the air, the Church must press equally on all the surfaces of society; like the sea, flow into every nook of the shore line of humanity; and like the sun, shine on things foul and low as well as fair and high, for she was organized, commissioned, and equipped for the moral renovation of the whole world.—*Simpson.*

HATE — I will tell you what to hate. Hate hypocrisy, hate cant, hate intolerance, oppression, injustice; hate pharisaism; hate them as Christ hated them— with a deep, living, godlike hatred.
—*F. W. Robertson.*

Parable of the Rhone
Erstwhile, beside the placid river Rhone,
Paused I and pondered as I stood alone,
And marveled at the beauty of the scene.
The massive stream flows on its great
  course,
So wide and deep, yet noiseless in its glee,
Still rushes mad-like with tremendous
  force,
As on it wends its way towards the sea.
From this majestic memory, oft I scan
The field of effort shown in human skill.
See how true merit in the life of man
Runs broad and deep, to execute his will,
How, like a river, man in varied poise,
The greater be the life, the less the noise.
—*Octave F. Ursenbach.*

EMPTINESS — Do, and it shall be done. Do with another, that it may be done with thee; for thou aboundest and thou lackest. Thou aboundest in things temporal, thou lackest things eternal. A beggar is at thy gate, thou art thyself a beggar at God's gate. Thou art sought, and thou seekest. As thou dealest with thy seeker, even so God will deal with His. Thou art both empty and full. Fill thou the empty out of thy fulness, that out of the fulness of God thine emptiness may be filled.—*St. Augustine.*

The Bridge Builder
An old man traveling a lone highway,
Came at the evening cold and gray,
To a chasm vast and deep and wide,
Through which was flowing a sullen tide.
The old man crossed in the twilight dim,
The sullen stream held no fears for him;
But he turned when safe on the other side,
And builded a bridge to span the tide.

"Old man," cried a fellow pilgrim near,
"You're wasting your time in building
  here.
Your journey will end with the closing
  day;
You never again will pass this way.
You have crossed the chasm deep and
  wide,
Why build you this bridge at even-tide?"

The builder lifted his old gray head:
"Good friend, in the path I have come,"
  he said,
"There followeth after me today
A youth whose feet must pass this way.
This stream which has been as naught
  to me,
To that fair-haired youth may pitfall be;
He, too, must cross in the twilight dim—
Good friend, I am building this bridge
  for him." —*Will Allen Dromgoole.*

AMIABLE — How shall a man cultivate an amiable temper, and exhibit a becoming example? Why, by adopting the following rules:

Reflect upon and deliberately weigh the peculiar advantages resulting from such a temper and conduct. To an individual this will bring serenity, peace, and joy; to a family, comfort, harmony, and help.

Carefully guard against such things as have the least tendency to disturb the mind and awaken uneasy tempers.

Assiduously avoid being ruffled or moved by little events. Neglect of this maxim has been the source of most little animosities.—*Evangelical Magazine.*

HELPFULNESS — Mark how the hand comes to the defense of the eye in its weakness; and how the eye with its sight, and from its elevated position, keeps watch for the welfare of the lowly, blind, but laborious and useful foot. The mutual helpfulness of these members is absolutely perfect. Such should be the charity between brother and brother of God's family on earth.—*W. Arnot.*

GOODNESS conditions usefulness. A grimy hand may do a gracious deed, but a bad heart cannot. What a man says and what a man is must stand together, —must consist. His life can ruin his lips or fill them with power. It is what men see that gives value to what we say. Being comes before saying or doing. Well may we pray, "Search me, O God! Reveal me to myself. Cleanse me from secret faults, that those who are acquainted with me, who know my downsittings and my uprisings, may not see in me the evil way that gives the lie to my words."
—*Babcock.*

FORGIVENESS — How great is the contrast between that forgiveness to which we lay claim from God towards us, and our temper towards others! God, we expect, will forgive us great offences—offences many times repeated; and will forgive them freely, liberally, and from the heart. But we are offended at our neighbor, perhaps, for the merest trifles, and for an injury only once offered; and we are but half reconciled when we seem to forgive. Even an uncertain humor, an ambiguous word, or a suspected look, will inflame our anger; and hardly any persuasion will induce us for a long time to relent.—*H. Thornton.*

SO IT HAS ALWAYS BEEN—they come to Christ, the brainiest come to the manger. Who was the greatest metaphysician this country ever has produced? Jonathan Edward, the Christian. Who was the greatest poet ever produced? John Milton, the Christian. Why is it that every college and university in the land has a chapel? They must have a place for the wise men to worship.—*Scoville.*

MIRACLES — Some skeptics say, "Oh, the miracles, I can't accept miracles." One may drop a brown seed in the black soil and up comes a green shoot. You let it grow and by and by you pull up its root and you find it red. You cut the red root and find it has a white heart. Can any one tell how this comes about—how brown cast into black results in green and then in red and white? Yet you eat your radish without troubling your mind over miracles. Men are not distressed by miracles in the dining room; they reserve them all for religion!
—*Bryan.*

XXIII. PERSEVERANCE

FAILURES—Scarcely a great man can be named who has not failed the first time. In such defeat no shame lies; the shame consists in one's not retrieving it. Lord Beaconsfield made, as everybody knows, a signal failure in his maiden speech in the House of Commons. But he was not cowed by the derisive laughter which greeted him. With astonishing self-control, and no less astonishing self-knowledge, he exclaimed, "I have begun several times many things, and have succeeded in them at last. I shall sit down now; but the time will come when you will hear me." The command of temper, the mastery over self, which these words displayed, is almost sublime. The late Lord Lytton made many failures. His first novel was a failure; so was his first play; so was his first poem. But he would not yield to disappointment. He subdued his mortification, and resumed his pen, to earn the eventual distinction of a foremost place among our foremost novelists, and to contribute to the modern stage two of its most popular dramas. We should be disposed to define genius as the capacity of surviving failure; in self-control, at all events, it finds a powerful auxiliary and agent.—*Lucas.*

SAILING — To reach the port of Heaven we must sail sometimes with the wind and sometimes against it. But we must sail, and not drift nor lie at anchor.
—*Oliver Wendell Holmes.*

HABIT — We are spinning our own fates, good or evil, never to be undone. Every smallest stroke of virtue or vice leaves its ever-so-little scar. The drunken Rip Van Winkle, in Jefferson's play, excuses himself for every fresh dereliction by saying, "I won't count this time!" Well, he may not count it, and a kind Heaven may not count it; but it is being counted none the less. Down among his nerve-cells and fibers the molecules are counting it, registering and storing it up to be used against him when the next temptation comes. Nothing we ever do is, in strict scientific literalness, wiped out.
—*William James.*

HAND IN HAND — The greatest work has always gone hand in hand with the most fervent moral purpose.
—*Sidney Lanier.*

HOW DID YOU DIE?

*Did you tackle that trouble that came
      your way,
   With a resolute heart and cheerful?
Or hide your face from the light of day
   With a craven soul and fearful?
Oh, a trouble's a ton, or a trouble's an
      ounce,
   Or a trouble is what you make it,
And it isn't the fact that you're hurt
      that counts,
   But only how did you take it?*

*And though you be done to the death,
      what then?
   If you battled the best you could,
If you played your part in the world
      of men,
   Why, the critic will call you good.
Death comes with a crawl or comes
      with a pounce,
   And whether he's slow or spry,
It isn't the fact that you're dead that
      counts,
   But only how did you die?*

—EDMUND VANCE COOKE.

LIFE'S HARD TASKS — Among some skaters was a boy so small and so evidently a beginner that his frequent mishaps awakened the pity of a tender-hearted, if not wise, spectator. "Why, sonny, you are getting all bumped up," she said. "I wouldn't stay on the ice and keep falling down so; I'd just come off and watch the others." The tears of the last down fall were still rolling over the rosy cheeks, but the child looked from his adviser to the shining steel on his feet, and answered, half-indignantly, "I didn't get some new skates to give up with; I got them to learn how with." The whole philosophy of earthly discipline was in the reply. Life's hard tasks are never sent for us "to give up with;" they are always intended to awaken strength, skill, and courage in learning how to master them.
—*Forward.*

GROWTH—To have failed is to have striven, to have striven is to have grown.
—*Maltbie D. Babcock.*

STRUGGLE—There is no royal road to the temple of melody, where St. Cecilia dwells. There is no short cut to the temple of the beautiful, where Apollo reigns as lord of the arts of color, form, and music. The eager aspirant for eloquence, or wealth, or wisdom, begins a long, long way from the excellence that crowns one's life-work. Every morning Mother Nature whispers to the youth, "Strive, struggle." Every night her last message is, "Sleep to waken again to new struggles, wrestlings, and achievements." In the realms of conscience and character man must work out his own salvation through ceaseless struggling, toiling long, hard, and patiently. And just in proportion as he goes toward excellence does the work become difficult.—*Newell Dwight Hillis.*

DISCONTENT—There are two kinds of discontent in this world; the discontent that works, and the discontent that wrings its hands. The first gets what it wants, and the second loses what it has. There's no cure for the first but success; and there's no cure at all for the second.
—*Gordon Graham.*

DO IT BETTER—When the first volume of Thomas Carlyle's *French Revolution* had been completed with tremendous travail, Carlyle entrusted the manuscript to John Stuart Mill for critical reading. It was a black night in Mill's life when, white-faced and trembling, he was obliged to return with the news that except for a few stray sheets, the manuscript had gone up in smoke. The chambermaid had found it handy to start a fire!

When the door finally closed behind their distraught visitor, leaving them to the privacy of their despair, Carlyle said to his wife: "Well, Mill, poor fellow, is terribly cut up. We must endeavor to hide from him how very serious this business is to us." Serious, because they were penniless. Above all, serious because he had written at white heat and, when each chapter was finished, had triumphantly torn up his notes as plaguy and toilsome things which he would never need or wish to see again.

Next day all the Scotch Presbyterian blood in his veins bade him order a fresh supply of paper and make in his diary this entry: "It is as if my invisible school master had torn my copybook when I showed it and said, 'No, boy, thou must write it better'."—*Alexander Woollcott.*

POWER — People do not lack strength; they lack will.—*Victor Hugo.*

DETERMINATION — The longer I live, the more I am certain that the great difference between men — between the feeble and the powerful, the great and the insignificant—is energy, invincible determination—a purpose once fixed, and then death or victory. That quality will do anything that can be done in this world, and no talents, no circumstances, no opportunities, will make a two-legged creature a man without it. There are hindrances without and within, but the outer hindrances could effect nothing if there were no inner surrender to them. Fear of opinion, timidity, dread of change, love of ease, indolence, unfaithfulness, are the great hindrances. Optimism is believing that you can eat the rooster that scratches over your grave.—Sam Jones.

MAN-MAKING

We all are blind until we see
That in the human plan
Nothing is worth the making if
It does not make the man.

Why build these cities glorious
If man unbuilded goes?
In vain we build the world, unless
The builder also grows.
—*Edwin Markham.*
Reprinted by permission.

BEGIN GREATLY—A life without a purpose is a languid, drifting thing.— Every day we ought to renew our purpose, saying to ourselves: This day let us make a sound beginning, for what we have hitherto done is nought.—Our improvement is in proportion to our purpose.—We hardly ever manage to get completely rid even of one fault, and do not set our hearts on daily improvement. —Always place a definite purpose before thee.—*Thomas a' Kempis.*

A MASTER INFLUENCE — Perseverance is the master impulse of the firmest souls; the discipline of the noblest virtues; and the guarantee of acquisitions the most invigorating in their use and inestimable in their worth.—*E. L. Magoon.*

Perpetual pushing and assurance put a difficulty out of countenance, and make a seeming impossibility give away.
—*Jeremy Collier.*

CAFETERIA — Life is a cafeteria. There are no waiters to bring success to you. Help yourself. Paul evidently felt that there was no standstill to human life. He was a part of a great procession and must keep step with alert and eager tread. It will be well if we can catch his spirit. Of all the Apostles, Paul attained the sublimest heights. He had greater capacities to begin with, perhaps, and he bent all the energies of his great soul to the end to which he had consecrated himself completely. Great men have purposes; others have wishes.
—*Public Speakers Library.*

LITTLE BY LITTLE—No great work is ever done in a hurry. To develop a great scientific discovery, to paint a great picture, to write an immortal poem, to become a minister, or a famous general—to do anything great requires time, patience, and perseverance. These things are done by degrees, "Little by Little." Milton did not write "Paradise Lost" at a sitting, nor did Shakespeare compose "Hamlet" in a day. The greatest writers must begin with the alphabet, the most famous musicians once picked out their notes laboriously; a child must learn to draw a straight line before he can develop into a Titian or a Michael Angelo.
—*W. J. Wilmont Buxton.*

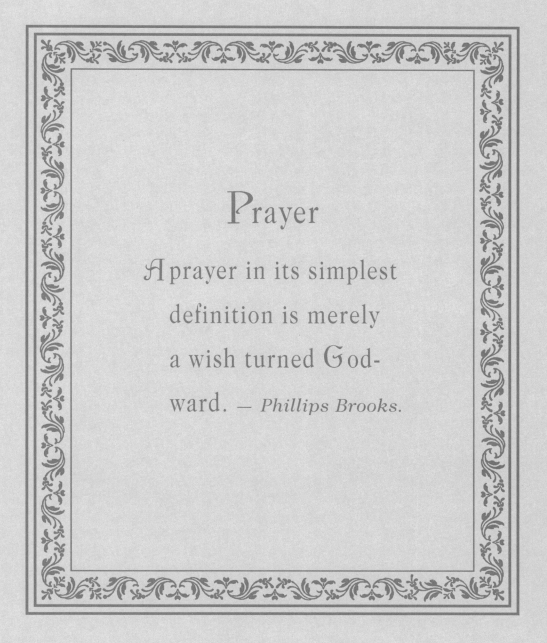

Prayer

A prayer in its simplest
definition is merely
a wish turned God-
ward. — *Phillips Brooks.*

WILL—Our bodies are our gardens, to the which our wills are gardeners; so that if we will plant nettles or sow lettuce, set hyssop and weed up thyme, supply it with one gender of herbs or distract it with many, either to have it sterile with idleness or manured with industry—why, the power and incorrigible authority of this, lies in our wills.—*Shakespeare.*

In the moral world there is nothing impossible if we can bring a thorough will to it. Man can do everything with himself, but he must not attempt to do too much with others.
—*Wilhelm von Humboldt.*

A character is a perfectly formed will.
—*Novalis.*

PERSEVERANCE gives power to weakness, and opens to poverty the world's wealth. It spreads fertility over the barren landscape, and bids the choicest flowers and fruits spring up and flourish in the desert abode of thorns and briars.
—*S. G. Goodrich.*

PATIENCE — Let it be remembered that "steadfast application to a fixed aim" is the law of a well-spent life. When Giardini was asked how long it would take to learn the violin, he replied, "Twelve hours a day for twenty years together." Alas, too many of us think to play our fiddles by a species of inspiration! The Leotards and Blondins whose gymnastic achievements attract such admiring crowds—what labor must they have undergone; what "painful diligence" must they have exhibited! The same energy, the same adherence to a settled purpose, might assuredly have made them benefactors of mankind, had they been animated by a nobler impulse.

WILLING SERVICE—A musician is not recommended for playing long, but for playing well; it is obeying God willingly, that is accepted; the Lord hates that which is forced, it is rather a tax than an offering. Cain served God grudgingly; he brought his sacrifice, not his heart. To obey God's commandments unwillingly is like the devils who came out of the man possessed, at Christ's command, but with reluctancy and against their will. Good duties must not be pressed and beaten out of us, as the waters came out of the rock when Moses smote it with his rod; but must freely drop from us, as myrrh from the tree, or honey from the comb. If a willing mind be wanting, there wants that flower which should perfume our obedience, and make it a sweet-smelling savor unto God.—*T. Watson.*

Will

One ship drives east, and another west
With the self-same winds that blow;
'Tis the set of the sails
And not the gales,
Which decides the way to go.

Like the winds of the sea are the ways
    of fate;
As the voyage along through life;
'Tis the will of the soul
That decides its goal,
And not the calm or the strife.
—*Ella Wheeler Wilcox.*

MAXIMS VERIFIED—For the conduct of life, habits are more important than maxims, because a habit is a maxim verified. To take a new set of maxims for one's guide is no more than to change the title of a book; but to change one's habits is to change one's life. Life is only a tissue of habits.—*Amiel.*

A TASK—To be honest, to be kind, to earn a little, and to spend a little less, to make upon the whole a family happier for his presence, to renounce when that shall be necessary and not to be embittered, to keep a few friends, but these without capitulation; above all, on the same condition, to keep friends with himself; here is a task for all a man has of fortitude and delicacy.—*Robert Louis Stevenson.*

LITTLE STROKES — Jacob Riis, in his drive against slums, never allowed a chance to pass of telling the people of New York what they were harboring. But it took a lot of telling, and he sometimes grew discouraged. "But," he said, "when nothing seems to help I go and look at a stonecutter hammering away at his rock perhaps 100 times without as much as a crack showing in it. Yet at the 101st blow it will split in two, and I know it was not that blow that did it, but all that had gone before."

"THIS ONE THING I DO."—The power of a man increases steadily by continuance in one direction. He becomes acquainted with the resistance and with his own tools; increases his skill and strength and learns the favorable moments and favorable accidents. He is his own apprentice, and more time gives a a great addition of power, just as a falling body acquires momentum with every foot of the fall.—*Emerson.*

Perseverance, dear my lord, keeps honor bright. To have none, is to hang quite out of fashion, like a rusty nail in monumental mockery.—*Shakespeare.*

Great works are performed not by strength, but by perseverance.
—*Book of Reflections.*

FORTITUDE — In November, 1915, the papers told of the death, at Saranac Lake, New York, of Dr. Edward L. Trudeau, who was not different from many another young man until after his physician told him he must die of tuberculosis. But he did not lose courage. He went to the Adirondack wilderness, not because he thought the air would help him, but because he longed for the joy of the out-of-doors life. The air and the exposure were what he needed. As he began to recover his strength he thought of other sufferers whom he might help. During the next forty years he became one of the world leaders in investigations as to the cause and cure of tuberculosis, and he succeeded in building up a great sanitarium for sufferers from the disease, from which thousands have gone with new hope— the first of hundreds of similar institutions, whose builders took their inspiration from him. The secret of his success was optimism, which with him was another name for faith in God. Because of his faith he was able to work with joy, in spite of the slow but steady progress of his disease.—*John T. Faris.*

THE WAY BACK

To keep my health . . . To do my work . . .
   To live!
To see to it I grow, and gain, and give.
Never to look behind me for an hour.
To wait in meekness and to walk in
   power.
But always fronting onward toward the
   right;
Always and always facing toward the
   light.
Robbed, starved, defeated, fallen, wide
   astray,—
On with what strength I have, back to the
   Way!
     —*Charlotte Perkins Gilman.*

XXIV. PERSPECTIVE

VIEW POINTS—There is a story of two Greek sculptors who competed for the placing of a statue on a pillar in the public square. And one worked skilfully and well, until the features of his figure were smoothed and polished to look as if living. But the other left his block of marble crude and jagged and uncouth, so that one could hardly tell if indeed it were a human being at all. And they put the statue of the first up on the pillar, where all might see; but high up on the pillar it was blurred by distance, and it could not be seen clearly from any angle. So they took it down, and put up the other's, and, behold, that which had not seemed true to life was now in its right perspective, and became life-like and beautiful, true to the imagination.
—*Edgar White Burrill.*

FAIRY TALES—Every man's life is a fairy tale written by God's fingers.
—*Hans Christian Andersen.*

NOBILITY—King Philip with a large company of soldiers in splendid array, went to visit Socrates. When the grand procession reached the city where Socrates lived a part of the time, they learned that Socrates was out in the country. The king was astonished! He exclaimed, "Socrates, come with me, I will let you reign over a part of my kingdom." Socrates said, "Then I would be like King Philip?" "Yes." "Well," replied Socrates, "I can see how Socrates could be made like King Philip, but I do not see how King Philip could be made like Socrates." King Philip is buried in the tomb of forgetfulness. Socrates lives on, linked with the harbingers of Christ.

FAITHFULNESS — When Pompeii was destroyed, there were very many buried in the ruins of it, who were afterwards found in very different situations. There were some found who were in the streets, as if they had been attempting to make their escape. There were some found in deep vaults, as if they had gone thither for security. There were some found in lofty chambers; but where did they find the Roman sentinel? They found him standing at the city gate, with his hand still grasping the war weapon, where he had been placed by his captain; and there, while the Heaven threatened him; there, while the earth shook beneath him; there, while the lava stream rolled, he had stood at his post; and there, after a thousand years had passed away, was he found. So let Christians stand to their duty, in the post at which their Captain has placed them.—*Evangelist.*

PESSIMISM—If it wasn't for the optimist, the pessimist would never know how happy he wasn't.

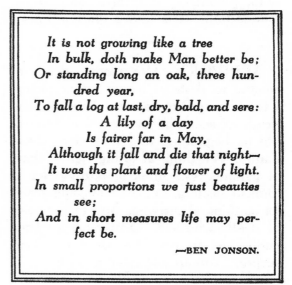

It is not growing like a tree
In bulk, doth make Man better be;
Or standing long an oak, three hundred year,
To fall a log at last, dry, bald, and sere:
A lily of a day
Is fairer far in May,
Although it fall and die that night—
It was the plant and flower of light.
In small proportions we just beauties see;
And in short measures life may perfect be.
—BEN JONSON.

ADAPTATIONS — In "The Natural Law in the Spiritual World," Prof. Henry Drummond has a striking passage, in which he describes "the wonderful adaptation of each organism to its surroundings—of the fish to the water, of the eagle to the air, of the insect to the forest bed; and of each part of every organism—the fish's swim-bladder, the eagle's eye, the insect's breathing tubes." All these, he says, inspire us with a sense of the boundless resources and skill of nature in perfecting her arrangements for the individual life. "Down in the last details the world is made for what is in it; and by whatever process things are as they are, all organisms find in surrounding nature the ample complements of themselves."

All this holds as one ascends the scale of being. Man finds every want met and need answered. It is as true of his mental as of his physical make-up. When we reach the apex of the pyramid of being we must hold that the same law obtains. Faith must have realities adjusted to its varying needs. For faith, the supernatural is the natural. It is faith's medium, its native air. Therefore, the incomprehensible, instead of destroying or preventing faith, permits it. It creates faith. It demands faith. It is faith's glory.—*Brooks.*

ARRIVING — We picture death as coming to destroy; let us rather picture Christ as coming to save. We think of death as sending; let us rather think of life as beginning, and that more abundantly. We think of losing; let us think of gaining. We think of parting; let us think of meeting. We think of going away; let us think of arriving. And as the voice of death whispers, "You must go from earth," let us hear the voice of Christ saying, "You are but coming to Me!"
—Norman Macleod.

IMITATION—To be in Christ, is to live in His ideas, character, spirit, as the atmosphere of being. Men everywhere are living in the ideas and characters of others. He who lives in the spirit of Raphael, becomes a painter; he who lives in the spirit of Milton, becomes a poet; he who lives in the spirit of Bacon, becomes a philosopher; he who lives in the spirit of Caesar, becomes a warrior; he who lives in the spirit of Christ, becomes a man.—*Anonymous.*

STEWARDSHIP

I bought gasoline; I went to the show;
I bought some new tubes for my radio;
I bought candy and peanuts, nut bars and ice cream;
While my salary lasted, life sure was a scream.

It takes careful spending to make money go round;
One's methods of finance must always be sound.
With habits quite costly, it's real hard to save;
My wife spent ten "bucks" on a permanent wave.

The church came round begging. It sure made me sore!
If they'd let me alone, I'd give a lot more.
They have plenty of nerve! They forgot all the past!
I gave them a quarter the year before last.
—Lookout.

VIRTUE— Chinamen wear five buttons only on their coats, that they may keep in sight something to remind them of the five principal moral virtues which Confucius recommended. These are: Humility, Justice, Order, Prudence, and Rectitude.

GOOD—Live for something. Do good and leave behind you a monument of virtue that the storm of time can never destroy. Write your name in kindness, love, and mercy on the hearts of thousands you come in contact with year by year; you will never be forgotten. No, your name, your deeds will be as legible on the hearts you leave behind as the stars on the brow of evening. Good deeds will shine as the stars of heaven. —*Chalmers.*

WORTH LIVING

Is life worth living? Yes, so long
  As there is wrong to right,
Wail of the weak against the strong,
  Or tyranny to fight;
Long as there lingers gloom to chase,
  Or streaming tear to dry,
One kindred woe, one sorrowing face
  That smiles as we draw nigh;
Long as a tale of anguish swells
  The heart, and lids grow wet
And at the sound of Christmas bells
  We pardon and forget;
So long as faith with Freedom reigns,
  And loyal hope survives;
And gracious charity remains
  To leaven lowly lives;
While there is one untrodden tract
  For intellect or will,
And men are free to think and act
  Life is worth living still.
        —*Alfred Austin.*

PEBBLES ON THE SHORE—I do not know what I may appear to the world, but to myself I seem to have been only like a boy playing on the seashore, and diverting myself in now and then finding a prettier shell or a smoother pebble than ordinary, whilst the great ocean of truth lay all undiscovered before me.
        —*Isaac Newton.*

FIRST—When Leonardo da Vinci resolved to paint the Last Supper, he threw all his energies into the work. He labored early and late. No pains were spared by him. He pondered devoutly those pages of the New Testament which record the first sacramental feast, in order that he might do his best to realize and reproduce the memorable scene. At length his task was done. Having given the finishing stroke, he invited a few confidential friends to a private inspection. They gazed attentively, and various remarks were made. An observation from one of them, however, led, as will be seen, to unexpected results. He spoke with great admiration of a golden chalice represented as being on the table at which our Lord and His disciples sat. Its shape, color, size, were all that could be desired. "That," exclaimed the critic, "is the most beautiful object in the picture." Hearing what was said, the artist took up a brush, and dipping it in black paint, deliberately smeared it over the whole canvas. He soon explained it—"If," said he, "what you tell me is true, then my picture is a failure, for I meant my Master's face to be the chief and most beautiful object."

All are artists; a good or bad picture each of us is painting—the picture of life. Too often, alas! men make inferior things the most conspicuous objects on the canvas of their daily history, bestowing rich colors and careful handicraft upon trifles. But the Saviour should be the grand center of our souls, and should have our chief and first attention.—*T. Stevenson.*

TEMPERANCE — There is no difference between knowledge and temperance; for he who knows what is good and embraces it, who knows what is bad and avoids it, is learned and temperate.
        —*Socrates.*

MISTAKES — There are six mistakes of life that many of us make, said a famous writer, and then he gave the following list:

The delusion that individual advancement is made by crushing others down.

The tendency to worry about things that can not be changed or corrected.

Insisting that a thing is impossible because we ourselves can not accomplish it.

Refusing to set aside trivial preferences in order that important things may be accomplished.

Neglecting development and refinement.

The failure to establish the habit of saving money.—*Southern Bulletin.*

MANY-SIDEDNESS—I tell you that Jesus challenges the attention of this world by His many-sidedness. He meets the needs of all classes and conditions of men. As deep answereth unto deep, so does He respond to the movings of each soul of men. Call the roll of the world's workers and ask, "What think ye of Christ?" Their answers amaze us! To the artist, He is the One altogether lovely. To the architect, He is the Chief Corner Stone. To the astronomer, He is the Sun of Righteousness. To the baker, He is the living Bread. To the biologist, He is Life. To the builder, He is the Sure Foundation. To the carpenter, He is the Door. To the doctor, He is the Great Physician. To the educator, He is the Great Teacher. To the farmer, He is the Sower. To the florist, He is the Rose of Sharon. To the geologist, He is the Rock of Ages. To the philanthropist, He is the Unspeakable Gift. To the servant, He is the Good Master. What is He to you? —*Selected.*

THE FOOTPATH TO PEACE—
A Thought for the Opening Year
To be glad of life, because it gives you the chance to love and to work and to play and to look up at the stars; to be satisfied with your possessions, but not contented with yourself until you have made the best of them; to despise nothing in the world except falsehood and meanness, and to fear nothing except cowardice; to be governed by your admirations rather than by your disgusts; to covet nothing that is your neighbor's except his kindness of heart and gentleness of manners; to think seldom of your enemies, often of your friends and every day of Christ; and to spend as much time as you can with body and with spirit, in God's out-of-doors—these are little guideposts on the footpath of peace.
—*Henry Van Dyke.*

LIFE IS EARNEST—Live as though life was earnest, and life will be so.
—*Owen Meredith.*

Voiceless

Vain is the chiming of forgotten bells
That the wind sways above a ruined shrine.
Vainer his voice in whom no longer dwells
Hunger that craves immortal Bread and Wine.

Light songs we breathe that perish with our breath
Out of our lips that have not kissed the rod.
They shall not live who have not tasted death.
They only sing who are struck dumb by God.

—*Joyce Kilmer.*

GUIDE—A man's conscience may be mistaken; but still, after all, it is the only light that he has got which will enlighten him in each separate case where he has a choice of conduct. A man's conscience may be mistaken; but if so, obedience to it is a mistake and not a sin, and we know that mistakes are very different from sins. If our conscience be mistaken because we have not taken due trouble to enlighten it, then for that neglect of cultivating our conscience we are responsible. But even then the conscience claims our obedience, and if to obey it is a mistake, to disobey is a sin. All other authorities speak to men in general; this voice speaks to the very soul that hears it, and to none other. All other authorities speak of the general rules by which we must live; this voice speaks of what is to be done now, here, in these circumstances. Now, no one can help feeling that a command given to him personally to do, or not to do, a given act at the moment, must have more weight than a general command given to all men, given for all times. It is as if God Himself had interfered for our guidance, and had thereby superseded all other guidance. And though the messenger who thus comes direct from God may after all be mistaken, yet surely we can do nothing but obey him, and pray God to guard him against mistakes.

—*John Foster.*

COMRADES

I walked with poets in my youth,
  Because the world they drew
Was beautiful and glorious
  Beyond the world I knew.

The poets are my comrades still,
  But dearer than in youth,
For now I know that they alone
  Picture the world of truth.

—*William Roscoe Thayer.*

LIFE'S LESSONS—We've all got to go to school, I expect, and we don't all get the same lesson to learn, but the one we do get is our'n, 'taint nobody else's, and if it's real hard, why, it shows the teacher thinks we're capable.

—*Rose Terry Cooke.*

FORGETTING GOD—No man can be without his god. If he have not the true God to bless and sustain him, he will have some false god to delude and to betray him. The Psalmist knew this, and therefore he joined so closely forgetting the name of our God and holding up our hands to some strange god. For every man has something in which he hopes, on which he leans, to which he retreats and retires, with which he fills up his thoughts in empty spaces of time; when he is alone, when he lies sleepless on his bed, when he is not pressed with other thoughts; to which he betakes himself in sorrow or trouble, as that from which he shall draw comfort and strength—his fortress, his citadel, his defence; and has not this good right to be called his god? Man was made to lean on the Creator; but if not on Him, then he leans on the creature in one shape or another. The ivy cannot grow alone; it must twine round some support or other; if not the goodly oak, then the ragged thorn; round any dead stick whatever, rather than have no stay nor support at all. It is even so with the heart and affections of man; if they do not twine around God, they must twine around some meaner thing.

—*Trench.*

CREATING SYMPHONIES — We can read poetry, and recite poetry, but to *live* poetry—is the symphony of life.

—*S. Frances Foote.*

SELF RELIANCE—Napoleon, when he was only a boy in years, spread out his future before his uncle. His uncle shook his head and said, "Dreams!" Napoleon stepped quickly to the window, and pointing up into the noonday sky, said, "Do you see that star?" "No," was the reply. "I do," he answered, and that star led him to the summit of human renown. Faith is one condition of greatness, and no man ever yet held the confidence of his fellows who did not believe in himself. The story goes that Colonel Roosevelt went to Heaven. Going up to Saint Peter, he asked if he could have ten thousand soprano singers. The reply was in the affirmative. He then asked for ten thousand alto singers and was told he could have those. Next he asked for ten thousand tenor singers and Saint Peter replied that he could have those. Roosevelt thanked him and started to turn away. Saint Peter stopped him with: "What about bass singers?" "Oh, I am going to sing bass myself."—*Fowler.*

Per Aspera

Thank God, a man can grow!
He is not bound
With earthward gaze to creep along the
    ground:
Though his beginnings be but poor and
    low,
Thank God, a man can grow!
The fire upon his altars may burn dim,
    The torch he lighted may in darkness
      fail,
    And nothing to rekindle it avail,—
Yet high beyond his dull horizon's rim,
Arcturus and the Pleiades beckon him.
        —*Florence Earle Coates.*

HE WHO IS FIRM in will, moulds the world to himself.—*Goethe.*

BETTER—We have read of the young artist, wearied and discouraged, who slept by the picture which he had done his best to complete. The master quietly entered the room and bending over the sleeping pupil, placed on the canvas with his own skilful hand the beauty which the worn artist had striven in vain to portray. And when we, tired and spent, lay down earth's toil, our own great Master will make perfect our picture for the Father's many mansioned house. From our service He will remove every stain, every blemish, and every failure. To our service He will give the brightest luster and highest honor. Shall we not bring ourselves to the One who can make us better?—*Public Speakers Library.*

PROGRESS, in the sense of acquisition, is something; but progress in the sense of being is a great deal more. To grow higher, deeper, wider, as the years go on; to conquer difficulties, and acquire more and more power; to feel all one's faculties unfolding, and truth descending into the soul—this makes life worth living.
        —*J. F. Clarke.*

TEMPTATION—No man was ever lost in a straight road. This famous saying which is attributed to the Emperor Akbar, is worthy of a place among the proverbs of Solomon. It is worthy, too, of a place in the memory of every Christian who would walk worthily of his holy profession, and would keep off forbidden ground. Going on pilgrimage to Heaven in the days of John Bunyan, was not always an easy business, nor is it in our days. Then the chief hindrance arose in the form of violent opposition and persecution; now the danger comes from alluring temptations.—*Cuyler.*

INVICTUS—The soul of perseverance cannot be beaten; imprison it and you get Pilgrim's Progress; blind it, and you get Paradise Lost; deafen it, and you get a wizard in electricity; put it into a log cabin, and it will work its way to the White House; commit to the frozen seas of the Arctic regions, and it finds the north pole; return its poems three score and ten times, and you get a poet for the nation's homes.

THE PROSPECT

Methinks we do as fretful children do,
Leaning their faces on the windowpane
To sigh the glass dim with their own
    breath's stain,
And shut the sky and landscape from their
    view;
And thus, alas! since God the maker
    drew
A mystic separation 'twixt those twain,—
The life beyond us and our souls in
    pain,—
We miss the prospect which we are call-
    ed unto
By grief we are fools to use. Be still and
    strong,
O man, my brother! hold thy sobbing
    breath,
And keep thy soul's large window free
    from wrong
That so, as life's appointment issueth,
Thy vision may be clear to watch along
The sunset consummation-lights of death.
    —*Elizabeth Barrett Browning.*

NEW YEAR—1. Face the New Year with the Old Book.

2. Face the New Needs with the Old Promises.

3. Face the New Problems with the Old Gospel.

4. Face the New Life with the Old Remedies.—*Selected.*

CHRISTIANITY — The Christian life is an enlistment for the whole man and for life. The call of Christ is a call to detach ourselves from many things that we may attach ourselves to one thing.—*Tyler.*

VERBS — No one really knows what it is to live until he can truly say these eleven great verbs of life: I am, I think, I know, I feel, I wonder, I see, I believe, I can, I ought, I will, I serve. Life is but the process of learning through daily experience the meaning of these eleven wonderful little verbs of life and acquiring the personal power of each:

I AM: the power of self-knowledge.

I THINK: the power to investigate.

I KNOW: the power to master facts.

I FEEL: the power to appreciate, to value and to love.

I WONDER: the power of reverence, curiosity, worship.

I SEE: the power of insight, imagination, vision.

I BELIEVE: the power of adventurous faith.

I CAN: power to act and skill to accomplish.

I OUGHT: the power of conscience, the moral imperative.

I WILL: will power, loyalty to duty, consecration.

I SERVE: power to be useful, devotion to a cause.

    —*George Walter Fiske.*

LIFE'S LOYALTIES — I am not bound to win, but I am bound to be true. I am not bound to succeed, but I am bound to live by the light that I have. I must stand with anybody that stands right, stand with him while he is right, and part with him when he goes wrong.

    —*Abraham Lincoln.*

RECIPE FOR A HAPPY NEW YEAR — Take twelve, fine, full-grown months, see that these are thoroughly free from all old memories of bitterness, rancor, hate and jealousy; cleanse them completely from every clinging spite; pick off all specks of pettiness and littleness; in short, see that these months are freed from all the past—have them as fresh and clean as when they first came from the great storehouse of Time.

Cut these months into thirty or thirty-one equal parts. This batch will keep for just one year. Do not attempt to make up the whole batch at one time (so many persons spoil the entire lot in this way), but prepare one day at a time, as follows:

Into each day put twelve parts of faith, eleven of patience, ten of courage, nine of work (some people omit this ingredient and so spoil the flavor of the rest), eight of hope, seven of fidelity, six of liberality, five of kindness, four of rest (leaving this out is like leaving the oil out of the salad —don't do it), three of prayer, two of meditation, and one well selected resolution. If you have no conscientious scruples, put in about a teaspoonful of good spirits, a dash of fun, a pinch of folly, a sprinkling of play, and a heaping cupful of good humor.

Pour into the whole love *ad libitum* and mix with a vim. Cook thoroughly in a fervent heat; garnish with a few smiles and a sprig of joy; then serve with quietness, unselfishness, and cheerfulness, and a Happy New Year is a certainty.

—H. M. S.

IMAGINATION — There are two worlds: the world that we can measure with line and rule, and the world that we feel with our hearts and imagination.

—Leigh Hunt.

PROGRESS—Our business in life is not to get ahead of other people, but to get ahead of ourselves. To break our own record, to outstrip our yesterdays by to-days, to bear our trials more beautifully than we ever dreamed we could, to whip the tempter inside and out as we never whipped him before, to give as we never have given, to do our work with more force and a finer finish than ever,—this is the true ideal—to get ahead of ourselves. To beat some one else in a game, or to be beaten, may mean much or little. To beat our own game means a great deal. Whether we win or not, we are playing better than we ever did before, and that's the point after all—to play a better game of life.—*Evangelist.*

I have a rendezvous with Life,
In days I hope will come,
Ere youth has sped and strength of mind,
Ere voices sweet grow dumb.
I have a rendezvous with Life,
When Spring's first heralds hum.

Sure some would cry it better far
To crown their days with sleep,
Than face the wind, the road, the rain,
To heed the falling deep.
Though wet, nor blow, nor space I fear,
Yet fear I deeply too,
Lest Death should greet and claim me ere
I keep Life's rendezvous.

—Countee Cullen.

"I Have a Rendezvous With Life" is from COLOR, by Countee Cullen. Copyright, 1925, by Harper & Brothers.

GREATNESS—It is great—and there is no other greatness—to make one nook of God's creation more fruitful, better, more worthy of God; to make some human heart a little wiser, manlier, happier, more blessed, less accursed.—*Carlyle.*

XXV. POSSESSIONS

VAIN GLORY—A little while ago, I stood by the grave of the old Napoleon—a magnificent tomb of gilt and gold, fit almost for a dead deity—and gazed upon the sarcophagus of rare and nameless marble, where rest at last the ashes of that restless man. I leaned over the balustrade and thought about the career of the greatest soldier of the modern world.

I saw him walking upon the banks of the Seine, contemplating suicide. I saw him at Toulon—I saw him putting down the mob in the streets of Paris—I saw him at the head of the army of Italy—I saw him crossing the bridge of Lodi with the tricolor in his hand—I saw him in Egypt in the shadows of the pyramids—I saw him conquer the Alps and mingle the eagle of France with the eagles of the crags. I saw him at Marengo—at Ulm and Austerlitz.

I saw him in Russia, where the infantry of the snow and the cavalry of the wild blast scattered his legions like winter's withered leaves. I saw him at Leipsic in defeat and disaster—driven by a million bayonets back upon Paris—clutched like a wild beast—banished to Elba. I saw him escape and retake an empire by the force of his genius. I saw him upon the frightful field of Waterloo, where Chance and Fate combined to wreck the fortunes of their former king. And I saw him at St. Helena, with his hands crossed behind him, gazing out upon the sad and solemn sea.

I thought of the orphans and widows he had made—of the tears that had been shed for his glory, and of the only woman who ever loved him, pushed from his heart by the cold hand of ambition. And I said I would rather have been a French peasant and worn wooden shoes. I would rather have lived in a hut with a vine growing over the door, and the grapes growing purple in the kisses of the autumn sun. I would rather have been that poor peasant with my loving wife by my side, knitting as the day died out of the sky—with my children upon my knees and their arms about me—I would rather have been that man and gone down to the tongueless silence of the dreamless dust, than to have been that imperial impersonation of force and murder, known as "Napoleon the Great."—*Robert G. Ingersoll.*

MONEY — Luther used to say that each one needed a three-fold conversion, that of his heart, his head and his pocketbook. Some one has said that the book with the seven seals that no one could open was the pocketbook. We need to feel that every dollar in our keeping belongs to God and must be used so as to best promote the interests of His kingdom. The greatest thing you can do for God and yourself today, is to consecrate everything to the Lord.

TREASURE

I am rich today, a baby ran to meet me,
And put her tiny hand within my own
And smiled, her rosy lips a flower,
The light within her eyes, from heaven
  shone.
And when I crossed the fields the
  birds were singing,
A golden blossom in my pathway lay,
It wasn't much; but, oh, the joy there's
  in it,
To have a baby smile at you
  In just that way.
        —MARGUERITE A. GUTSCHOW.

SANDALPHON

Have you read in the Talmud of old,
In the Legends the Rabbins have told
   Of the limitless realms of the air,
Have you read it,—the marvelous story
Of Sandalphon, the Angel of Glory,
   Sandalphon, the Angel of Prayer?

How, erect, at the outermost gates
Of the City Celestial he waits,
   With his feet on the ladder of light,
That, crowded with angels unnumbered,
By Jacob was seen as he slumbered
   Alone in the desert at night?

But serene in the rapturous throng,
Unmoved by the rush of the song,
   With eyes unimpassioned and slow,
Among the dead angels, the deathless
Sandalphon stands listening breathless
   To sounds that ascend from below;—

And he gathers the prayers as he stands,
And they change into flowers in his
   hands,
   Into garlands of purple and red;
And beneath the great arch of the portal,
Through the streets of the City Immortal
   Is wafted the fragrance they shed.

When I look from my window at night,
And the welkin above is all white,
   All throbbing and panting with stars,
Among them majestic is standing
Sandalphon the angel, expanding
   His pinions in nebulous bars.

And the legend, I feel, is a part
Of the hunger and thirst of the heart,
   The frenzy and fire of the brain,
That grasps at the fruitage forbidden,
The golden pomegranates of Eden,
   To quiet its fever and pain.
       —*Henry Wadsworth Longfellow.*

THRIFT—"My other piece of advice," said Mr. Micawber, "you know. Annual income twenty pounds, annual expenditure nineteen six, result happiness. Annual income twenty pounds, annual expenditure twenty pounds ought and six, result misery. The blossom is blighted, the leaf is withered, the god of day goes down upon the dreary scene, and—and in short, you are forever floored. As I am."
—*Dickens—"David Copperfield."*

UTILITARIANISM — Whatever strengthens and purifies the affections, enlarges the imagination, and adds spirit to sense, is useful.—*Shelley.*

WHAT MONEY CAN'T BUY—It's good to have money and the things that money can buy, but it's good, too, to check up once in a while and make sure you haven't lost the things that money can't buy.—*George Horace Lorimer.*

VIEWPOINT — One day a rich but miserly Chassid came to a Rabbi. The Rabbi led him to the window. "Look out there," he said, "and tell me what you see."

"People," answered the rich man.

Then the Rabbi led him to a mirror. "What do you see now?" he asked.

"I see myself," answered the Chassid.

Then the Rabbi said, "Behold—in the window there is glass and in the mirror there is glass. But the glass of the mirror is covered with a little silver, and no sooner is a little silver added than you cease to see others and see only yourself."—*S. Ansky.*

WITHIN—Joy is not in things; it is in us.—*Wagner.*

TREASURE—A happy man or woman is a better thing to find than a five-pound note. He or she is a radiating focus of good-will; and their entrance into a room is as though another candle had been lighted. We need not care whether they could prove the forty-seventh proposition; they do a better thing than that—they practically demonstrate the great Theorem of the Livableness of Life.

—*Robert Louis Stevenson.*

REWARD—I made courtiers; I never pretended to make friends, said Napoleon . . . On a rocky little island he fretted away the last years of his life—alone.

—*Bruce Barton.*

HONEY — My Dear Robert, — One passage in your letter a little displeased me * * * You say that "this world to you seems drained of all its sweets!" At first I had hoped you only meant to insinuate the high price of Sugar! but I am afraid you meant more. O Robert, I don't know what you call sweet. Honey and the honeycomb, roses and violets, are yet in the earth. The sun and moon yet reign in Heaven, and the lesser lights keep up their pretty twinklings. Meats and drinks, sweet sights and sweet smells, a country walk, spring and autumn, follies and repentance, quarrels and reconcilements, have all a sweetness by turns. So good humor and good nature, friends at home that love you, and friends abroad that miss you—you possess all these things, and more innumerable; and these are all sweet things. You may extract honey from everything; do not go a-gathering after gall * * * I assure you I find this world a very pretty place.

—*Charles Lamb to Robert Lloyd.*

PRIDE—The man who has not anything to boast of but his illustrious ancestors is like a potato—the only good belonging to him is underground.

—*Thomas Overbury.*

GAIN — What is gain? The worldly man says money: the Word of God says godliness. What can money do? Can it cure an aching head? Can it ease an aching heart? Can it scare away disease? Can it restore health to the sickly frame, or hope to the hopeless heart? Ah, no! It may purchase a softer pillow to nurse the pain; it may secure a more experienced physician to battle with the disease; it may find a sunnier clime, in which the wasted frame may pine and languish till it be laid to rest in its long home: but there the power of money ends. How is it with godliness? It cannot purchase the softer pillow. Yes, it can. It can place the aching head, the aching heart, on the pillow—the soft, the downy pillow of contentment. "Father, not my will, but Thine be done." It can secure the services of the Great Physician and the balm of Gilead —the hand that heals both soul and body. It can waft the wearied heart, that feels the pangs of suffering, the inroads of disease, or the approach of death—that heart it can waft into the sunnier regions of eternal day; and, while the wasted body pines, the brightening spirit, hovering on the outskirts of Heaven, tastes a peace that passeth all understanding, a joy unspeakable and full of glory.

—*R. B. Nichol.*

Superfluous wealth can buy superfluities only. Money is not required to buy one necessary of the soul.—*Thoreau.*

Goodness is the only investment that never fails.—*Thoreau.*

OVER-EQUIPPED—David was not the first, nor is he the last man to find himself handicapped by too much equipment. Many a man's native skill is restrained by the heavy armour laid on him by foolish friends or by his silly self.

Preachers keep themselves from preaching the Gospel because they desire to make a great display of their learning.

Churches fail to win the allegiance of men because they devote too much time to material equipment. Colleges and schools provide the latest things in dormitories and class-rooms and laboratories, but take too much for granted the teaching and studying that is supposed to justify them.

Parents spend huge sums of money on the clothing of their children, their external manners and appearance and in preparing the positions in life which they are to occupy. But like as not the poor youths will rattle around in it all like dry peas in a pod.

The finest equipment is sometimes only a handicap.

CHRIST

He is a path, if any be misled;
   He is a robe, if any naked be;
If any chance to hunger, He is bread;
   If any be a bondman He is free;
   If any be but weak, how strong is He!
To dead men life He is, to sick men health;
To blind men sight, and to the needy
      wealth;
A pleasure without loss, a treasure without stealth.

—*Giles Fletcher.*

COMPENSATION — Fortune, to show us her power, and abate our presumption, seeing she could not make fools wise, has made them fortunate.

—*Montaigne.*

THE GOLDEN AGE—Over a doorway in an old Dutch banking house is this inscription in French:

"The Golden Age is the age in which gold does not rule."

The value of money lies in its control by spiritual purpose. To desire it for its own sake is to destroy all human values.

CHOKING WEEDS—I knew a boy whose education was stifled because his father gave him two automobiles and a motorboat.

I knew a man who could never accomplish anything seriously worthwhile because he was always tinkering with trifles. I knew another man whose house was so full of rare and costly bric-a-brac that he was a slave to the care of his collections.

Unless we know the difference between flowers and weeds we are not fit to take care of a garden.

It is not enough to have truth planted in our minds. We must learn and labor to keep the ground clear of thorns and briars, follies and perversities, which have a wicked propensity to choke the word of life.

THREE WAYS — There are three things a man can do with himself and his possessions. He may selfishly hoard them; he may lavishly waste them; he may intelligently spend them.

The temporary nature of earthly strength and riches is plain to all men who think.

Only he who spends it freely and gladly for the purposes of his soul may experience the full meaning of life and say at the end:

"Glad did I live and gladly die,
   And I laid me down with a will."

GET RID OF THE WEEDS — An old Vermont farmer was talking with a young neighbor. The young man was complaining because the devil's paintbrush (that bright but destructive weed) was ruining his hay crop. "Fertilize your land, my boy, fertilize your land," said the old man, "I've noticed that the devil's paintbrush is like lots of folks. It can't stand prosperity."

BOOKS—I would rather be a poor man in a garret with plenty of books than a king who did not love reading.

—*Macauley.*

CHECKMATE — In life, as in chess, one's own pawns block one's way. A man's very wealth, ease, leisure, children, books, which should help him to win, more often checkmate him.

—*Charles Buxton.*

TRUE OWNERSHIP—One's own—what a charm there is in the words! how long it takes boy and man to find out their worth! how fast most of us hold on to them! faster and more jealously, the nearer we are to the general home into which we can take nothing, but must go naked as we came into the world. When shall we learn that he who multiplieth possessions multiplieth troubles, and that the one single use of things which we call our own, is that they may be his who hath need of them?—*Hughes.*

FALSE GOD—Worldly wealth is the devil's bait; and those whose minds feed upon riches, recede in general from real happiness, in proportion as their stores increase; as the moon, when she is fullest of light, is farthest from the sun.—*Burton.*

THE GREATEST HUMBUG in the world is the idea that money can make a man happy. I never had any satisfaction with mine until I began to do good with it.—*C. Pratt.*

WHY DEPRESSIONS — Everything in the world can be endured, except continual prosperity.—*Goethe.*

A SMOOTH SEA never made a skilful mariner; neither do uninterrupted prosperity and success qualify men for usefulness and happiness.

COUNT THE COSTS—No man is prosperous whose immortality is forfeited.—No man is rich to whom the grave brings eternal bankruptcy.—No man is happy upon whose path there rests but a momentary glimmer of light, shining out between clouds that are closing over him in darkness forever.—*H. W. Beecher.*

VIEWPOINT — He is not poor that has little, but he that deserves much.

—*Daniel.*

POVERTY is no disgrace to a man but it is confoundedly inconvenient.

—*Sydney Smith.*

OF ALL THE ADVANTAGES which come to any young man, I believe it to be demonstrably true that poverty is the greatest.—*J. G. Holland.*

HELPLESS—In a terrible crisis there is only one element more helpless than the poor, and that is the rich.

—*Clarence Darrow.*

XXVI. PRAYER

AS THOU WILT—O Lord, Thou knowest what is best for us; let this or that be done, as Thou shalt please. Give what Thou wilt, and how much Thou wilt, and when Thou wilt. Deal with me as Thou thinkest good. Set me where Thou wilt, and deal with me in all things just as Thou wilt. Behold, I am Thy servant, prepared for all things: for I desire not to live unto myself, but unto Thee! and oh, that I could do it worthily and perfectly!—*Thomas a' Kempis.*

Lord, what a change within us one short hour
Spent in Thy presence will avail to make!
What heavy burdens from our bosoms take!
What parched grounds refresh as with a shower!
We kneel, and all around us seem to lower;
We rise, and all, the distant and the near,
Stands forth in sunny outline, brave and clear;
We kneel, how weak; we rise, how full of power!
Why, therefore, should we do ourselves this wrong,
Or others—that we are not always strong—
That we are sometimes overborne with care—
That we should ever weak or heartless be,
Anxious or troubled—when with us is prayer,
And joy and strength and courage are with Thee?

—RICHARD C. TRENCH.

HEART—Pray Him to give you what Scripture calls "an honest and good heart," or "a perfect heart;" and, without waiting, begin at once to obey Him with the best heart you have. Any obedience is better than none. You have to seek His face; obedience is the only way of seeing Him. All your duties are obediences. To do what He bids is to obey Him, and to obey Him is to approach Him. Every act of obedience is an approach—an approach to Him who is not far off, though He seems so, but close behind this visible screen of things which hides Him from us.—*J. H. Newman.*

FACULTIES — If we stand in the openings of the present moment, with all the length and breadth of our faculties unselfishly adjusted to what it reveals, we are in the best condition to receive what God is always ready to communicate.—*T. C. Upham.*

CONFIDING — Lord, I know not what I ought to ask of Thee; Thou only knowest what I need; Thou lovest me better than I know how to love myself. O Father! give to Thy child that which he himself knows not how to ask. I dare not ask either for crosses or consolations; I simply present myself before Thee; I open my heart to Thee. Behold my needs which I know not myself; see, and do according to Thy tender mercy. Smite, or heal; depress me, or raise me up; I adore all Thy purposes without knowing them; I am silent; I offer myself in sacrifice; I yield myself to Thee! I would have no other desire than to accomplish Thy will. Teach me to pray; pray Thyself in me.

—Selected.

THREE DEGREES — Poor, broken-winded things our prayers are, like a wounded bird fluttering along the ground, rising like an arrow shot from a child's hand, going a little way to the sky, and then dropping down again. I am afraid most of us have three degrees of temperature in regard to our prayers or our desires. The highest is for temporal wants for ourselves; medium, spiritual good for ourselves; the most tepid of them all for the progress of Christ's kingdom. It takes a man with a spirit to pray, "Thy will be done in earth as it is in Heaven," as it ought to be prayed.—*Maclaren.*

Prayer at Early Mass

Deep in the east the dawn is white,
Pale like Thy Face beneath the thorn.
High in the east the dawn is red,
Red like the Heart a lance had torn.
Deep in the east the dawn is white,
Pale like the Bread You bid us break.
High in the east the dawn is red,
Red like the Wine You bid us take.
Uplifted Host! Uplifted Cup of Wine
Cry within this morning! And the sweet
Sweet pleading comes again that once
    was Thine
Upon a hill whereon no sun would shine!
O Lord, I know not if Thy Paradise
Shall keep such moment for the wakened
    dead,
Nor any dawn to flame it in their skies,
But if the beauty that the east has worn
Be gathered still and still be white and
    red,
Then in my heart a single prayer is born:
Lord, let me be, wherever it is morn.
                    —*John W. Lynch.*

UNANSWERED — I have lived to thank God that all my prayers have not been answered.—*Jean Ingelow.*

HELP—God brings no man into the conflicts of life to desert him. Every man has a Friend in Heaven whose resources are unlimited; and on Him he may call at any hour and find sympathy and assistance.—*Morris.*

Asking

1. "Ask ye of the Lord." (Zec. 10:1). "My God shall supply all your need."
2. "Ask and it shall be given you." (Matt. 7:7). "The testimony of the Lord is sure."
3. "Ask in a prayer." (Matt. 21:22). There must be prayerful dependence.
4. "Ask in faith." (James 1:6). "He that cometh to God must believe."
5. "Ask what I shall give thee." (1 Kings 3:5). "His ears are open unto our prayers." (2 Chron. 1:7).
6. "Ask diligently." (Deut. 13:14). "Abound in faith and all diligence."

PRIVATE PRAYER is our refuge from troubles. High above the beating waves, and near Heaven, it is our fortress. What sometimes would become of us, if we might not shut the door upon mankind, and find repose in our Father's bosom? The afflicted Christian, entering his citadel, says, like persecuted David, "I give myself unto prayer." Thou, who knowest all, and changest never, art on my side. If I grieve any, I would not grieve Thee. I would not make Thee my enemy, I would retain Thy favor. Oh my Almighty Friend, "say unto my soul, I am thy salvation." Heavenly Father, Thy smile invigorates me. I am glad and safe when I hear Thy voice.—*Robinson.*

REPOSE — Thou hast made us for Thyself, O Lord; and our heart is restless until it rests in Thee.—*St. Augustine.*

LOVE—We sometimes fear to bring our troubles to God, because they must seem so small to Him who sitteth on the circle of the earth. But if they are large enough to vex and endanger our welfare, they are large enough to touch His heart of love. For love does not measure by a merchant's scales, nor with a surveyor's chain. It hath a delicacy which is unknown in any handling of material substances.—*Torrey.*

FAITH—During the Civil War fourteen inmates of Andersonville Prison, on August 20, 1864, bowed in prayer to the Almighty that he would send them water; and a spring broke out on the outside of the wall and ran through the prison. The people there were unanimous in their belief that it was of divine origin, the water in the nearby stream being fearfully unwholesome. The spring is reported to be still flowing.—*Christian Endeavor World.*

SORROWS — Learn to entwine with your prayers the small cares, the trifling sorrows, the little wants of daily life. Whatever affects you be it a changed look, an altered tone, an unkind word, a wrong, a wound, a demand you cannot meet, a change you cannot notice, a sorrow you cannot disclose—turn it into prayer, and send it up to God. Disclosures you may not make to man you can make to the Lord. Man may be too little for your great matters: God is not too great for your small ones. Only give yourself to prayer, whatever be the occasion that calls for it.—*Winslow.*

PROVISION — Good prayers never come creeping home. I am sure I shall receive either what I ask or what I should ask.—*Joseph Hall.*

THE EXPRESSION OF THE SOUL—Prayer is not necessarily in fluency of speech; it is not in painted imagery; it is not in deep thoughts; it is not in burning words; it is not in the length and breadth and fulness of petition. Prayer is something more: it is the wish of the heart—the expression of the soul.—*Dear.*

PRAYER has been defined to be a wish referred to God; and if we could keep this thought before us, it would help us to acquire the habit of prayer by making us refer each wish, as it comes into our minds, to God, for His assistance in furtherance or frustration.—*J. R. Illingworth.*

The Kneeling Camel

The camel, at the close of day
    Kneels down upon the sandy plain
To have his burden lifted off
    And rest to gain.

My soul, thou too shouldst to thy knees
    When the daylight draweth to a close,
And let thy Master lift thy load
    And grant repose:

Else how canst thou tomorrow meet,
    With all tomorrow's work to do,
If thou thy burden all the night
    Dost carry through?

The camel kneels at break of day
    To have his guide replace his load,
Then rises up again to take
    The desert road.

So thou shouldst kneel at morning's dawn
    That God may give thee daily care,
Assured that He no load too great
    Will make thee bear.
                    —*Anna Temple.*

APPEAL TO AUTHORITY—Prayer is the application of want to Him who alone can relieve it, the voice of sin to Him who alone can pardon it. It is the urgency of poverty, the prostration of humility, the fervency of penitence, the confidence of trust. It is not eloquence, but earnestness; not figures of speech, but compunction of soul. It is the "Lord, save, I perish" of drowning Peter. . . . It is not a mere conception of the mind nor an effort of the intellect, nor an act of the memory, but an elevation of the soul towards its Maker. It is the devout breathing of a creature struck with a sense of its own misery and of the infinite holiness of Him whom it is addressing, experimentally convinced of its own emptiness and of the abundant fulness of God, of His readiness to hear, of His power to help, of His willingness to save . . . Prayer is right in itself as the most powerful means of resisting sin and advancing in holiness. It is above all might, as everything is, which has the authority of Scripture, the command of God, and the example of Christ.—*Hannah More.*

SURRENDER

O Father, grant Thy love divine,
To make these mystic temples Thine
When wasting age and weary strife
Have sapped the leaning walls of life.
When darkness gathers over all
And the last tottering pillars fall,
Take the poor dust Thy mercy warms,
And mould it into heavenly forms.
                    —Selected.

SUBMISSION — May our Lord's sweet hand square us and hammer us, and strike off all kinds of pride, self-love, world-worship, and infidelity, so that He can make us stones and pillars in His Father's house.—*Samuel Rutherford.*

ABOVE — A Jewish legend tells us that during the famine in Canaan, Joseph ordered his officers to throw wheat and chaff upon the waters of the Nile that the people below might see that there was plenty above. God puts upon the River of Life wheat from the heavenly fields in order that we may seek things that are above.—*Torrey.*

THE SUM OF ALL—All subjects for thought are represented in this prayer which begins with God, comprehends Heaven and earth, and terminates in eternity.—*W. N. Percival.*

If you run over and through all the words of all holy prayers, you will find nothing which this prayer of the Lord doth not comprehend and contain.
                    —St. Augustine.

For like as the law of love is the sum and abridgment of the other laws, so this prayer is the sum and abridgment of all other prayers; all the other prayers are contained in this prayer; yea, whatsoever mankind hath need of to soul and body, that same is contained in this prayer.

Any clause of it might suffice a whole day as a fountain of pious thought, a base of manifold petition, a medium of rich communication with the Father.
                    —Robinson.

REMEMBERING — We talk about God's remembering us, as if it were a special effort. But if we could only know how truly we belong to God, it would be different. God's remembrance of us is the natural claiming of our life by Him as true part of His own.—*Phillips Brooks.*

THE ABLEST MEN in all walks of modern life are men of faith. Most of them have much more faith than they themselves realize.—*Bruce Barton.*

THE MODEL — In one of Carlyle's letters to an old-time Scottish friend, a few years ago, he said:—"Our Father which art in Heaven, hallowed be Thy name, Thy will be done." What else can we say? The other night, in my sleepless tossings about, which were growing more and more miserable, these words, that brief and grand prayer, came strangely into my mind, with an altogether new emphasis; as if written and shining for me in mild, pure splendor, on the black bosom of the night there; when I, as it were, read them word by word—with a sudden check to my imperfect wanderings, with a sudden softness of composure which was much unexpected. Not for perhaps thirty or forty years had I once formally repeated that prayer. Nay, I never felt before how intensely the voice of man's soul it is; the inmost aspiration of all that is high and pious in poor human nature; right worthy to be recommended with an "After this manner pray ye."

BRIEF LET ME BE — The fewer words the better prayer.—*Luther.*

HE WHO RUNS from God in the morning will scarcely find him the rest of the day.—*Bunyan.*

PREFATORY—Prayer is the preface to the book of Christian living; the text of the new life sermon; the girding on of the armor for battle; the pilgrim's preparation for his journey. It must be supplemented by action or it amounts to nothing.—*A. Phelps.*

PRAYER BOOK—Open thy heart to God; if He be there, the outspread world will be thy book of prayer.—*Tholuck.*

THE LORD'S PRAYER contains the sum total of religion and morals.
—*Wellington.*

THY WILL

To know Thy will, Lord of the seeking
    mind,
To learn Thy way for me, Thy purpose
    kind,
Thy path to follow and Thy guide find—
    For this I pray.
To do Thy will, Lord of the eager soul,
To bring my restlessness 'neath Thy con-
    trol,
To give Thee, not a part, but all—the
    whole—
    For this I pray.
To love Thy will, Lord of the ardent heart,
To bid all selfishness, all sloth depart,
To share with gladness all Thou dost and
    art—
    For this I pray.
           —*Alice M. Kyle.*

ANY HEART turned God-ward, feels more joy in one short hour of prayer, than e'er was raised by all the feasts on earth since its foundation.—*Bailey.*

WHEN TO PRAY — Prayer, as the first, second, and third element of the Christian life, should open, prolong, and conclude each day. The first act of the soul in early morning should be a draught at the heavenly fountain. It will sweeten the taste for the day. A few moments with God at that calm and tranquil season, are of more value than much fine gold. And if you tarry long so sweetly at the throne, you will come out of the closet as the high priest of Israel came from the awful ministry at the altar of incense, suffused all over with the heavenly fragrance of that communion.—*H. W. Beecher.*

XXVII. SPEECH

KIND WORDS — Cold words freeze people, and hot words scorch them, and bitter words make them bitter, and wrathful words make them wrathful. Kind words also produce their own image on men's souls; and a beautiful image it is. They smooth, and quiet, and comfort the hearer.

—*Pascal.*

POWER OF THE PULPIT — The power of preaching is not gone, says C. J. Brown, D.D., of Edinburgh. But, he adds, "I will tell you, though, what is gone. The power of a neat little manuscript, carried to the pulpit and prettily read, that is gone. If such a practice is to continue, the pulpit cannot indeed compete with the press. We shall be miserably beaten in the competition. But carry to the pulpit a different thing altogether; carry to it well-digested thoughts with suitable words to express them, written in your inmost soul; thoughts and words wherewith to stir the souls of your hearers to their inmost depths, wherewith to hold living intercourse with them; tell them, indeed, what God has been telling you, and both you and they shall find that the pulpit still wields a power altogether its own."

PREPARATION — A celebrated preacher being asked, "How long does it take you to prepare an address?" replied, "If I am only to speak for fifteen or twenty minutes, it requires at least a week's preparation and prayerful thought beforehand; if I may occupy thirty or forty minutes, two or three days' preparation will do; but if I may speak for an hour, a few minutes forethought will be sufficient."

ORATORY — "And the common people heard Him gladly," for "He taught them as one having authority." These sentences reveal the very heart of effective speaking. Considered from the human viewpoint alone, the Son of Mary was the prince of speakers. He alone has delivered a perfect address—the Sermon on the Mount. The two other speeches that approach it are Paul's appeal to the Athenians on Mars Hill and the speech of Abraham Lincoln at Gettysburg. These have no tricks, no devices, no tinsel gilt. They do not attempt to "split the ears of the groundlings," and yet they are addressed to the commonest of the world's common people.—*Beveridge.*

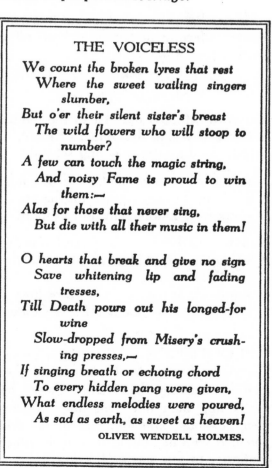

THE VOICELESS

We count the broken lyres that rest
  Where the sweet wailing singers
    slumber,
But o'er their silent sister's breast
  The wild flowers who will stoop to
    number?
A few can touch the magic string,
  And noisy Fame is proud to win
    them:—
Alas for those that never sing,
  But die with all their music in them!

O hearts that break and give no sign
  Save whitening lip and fading
    tresses,
Till Death pours out his longed-for
    wine
  Slow-dropped from Misery's crush-
    ing presses,—
If singing breath or echoing chord
  To every hidden pang were given,
What endless melodies were poured,
  As sad as earth, as sweet as heaven!

OLIVER WENDELL HOLMES.

ILLUSTRATIONS — The subject matter of Christian teaching pre-eminently requires illustration. The barrister has, in a new case, that which stimulates attention, while the preacher has an oft-told tale to set before his people.
—*Andrew Fuller.*

The aim of the teacher, who would find his way to the hearts and understandings of his hearers, will never be to keep down the parabolical element in his teaching, but rather to make as much and as frequent use of it as he can.
—*Trench.*

To have one's page alive the author must be alive himself, constantly acquiring fresh thought.
—*Matthews.*

Genius lights its own fire, but it is constantly collecting materials to keep alive the flame.—*Wilmott.*

A Narrow Window

A narrow window may let in the light,
A tiny star dispel the gloom of night,
A little deed a mighty wrong set right.

A rose, abloom, may make a desert fair,
A single cloud may darken all the air,
A spark may kindle ruin and despair.

A smile, and there may be an end to strife;
A look of love, and Hate may sheathe the
    knife;
A word—ah, it may be a word of life!
—*Florence Earle Coates.*

ELOQUENCE — There is no power like that of oratory. Caesar controlled men by exciting their fears, Cicero by captivating their affections and swaying their passions. The influence of the one perished with its author, that of the other continues to this day.—*H. Clay.*

SELF-EXAMINATION — If any speak ill of thee, flee home to thy own conscience, and examine thy heart; if thou be guilty, it is a just correction; if not guilty, it is a fair instruction; make use of both, so shalt thou distill honey out of gall, and out of an open enemy create a secret friend.—*Quarles.*

EXCEPT a living man there is nothing more wonderful than a book! a message to us from the dead—from human souls we never saw, who lived, perhaps, thousands of miles away. And yet these, in those little sheets of paper, speak to us, arouse us, terrify us, teach us, comfort us, open their hearts to us as brothers.
—*Charles Kingsley.*

KIND WORDS are the bright flowers of earthly existence; use them, and especially around the fireside circle. They are jewels beyond price, and powerful to heal the wounded heart and make the weighed-down spirit glad.

Let us use our speech as we should wish we had done when one of us is silent in death. Let us give all the communications, make all the explanations, speak all the loving words ere it is too late.

A genuine word of kindness is often the best lever to raise a depressed spirit to its natural level.

The art of saying appropriate words in a kindly way is one that never goes out of fashion, never ceases to please, and is within the reach of the humblest.

Always say a kind word if you can, if only that it may come in, perhaps, with singular opportuneness, entering some mournful man's darkened room, like a beautiful firefly, whose happy circumvolutions he cannot but watch, forgetting his many troubles.—*Arthur Helps.*

THOUGHT — The three foundations of thought: perspicuity, amplitude, and justness.

The three ornaments of thought: clearness, correctness, and novelty.

The three properties of just thinking: What is possible, what is commendable, and what ought to be—*Catherall.*

~

DIRECTNESS — The ability to state our convictions with clearness and completeness yields two benefits. It makes our convictions respected. There is persuasion in the forceful putting of a thought, and in sentences sharply drawn and well considered. Considerable of what passes as the weightiness of an opinion is no more than the gravity and dignity of its presentation. The effect of words, as of soldiers, can be trebled by their manner of marshaling. A word aptly chosen is an argument, and a phrase judiciously contrived a syllogism. "A word fitly spoken is like apples of gold in pictures of silver." It was the transparent terseness of the man born blind which so inconvenienced the Pharisees. "I was blind, now I see." There was all there that was said, and more beside—a conclusion without its being stated. Here lies the power of proverbs, in their lucid brevity.—*Parkhurst.*

~

GOODNESS—His words had power because they accorded with his thoughts; and his thoughts had reality and depth because they harmonized with the life he had always lived. It was not mere breath that this preacher uttered; they were the words of life, because a life of good deeds and holy love was melted into them. Pearls, pure and rich, had been dissolved into the precious draught.
—*Nathaniel Hawthorne.*

PLAINNESS (*not puerility*)—A style may be lofty yet clear. As a medieval preacher has said, "The stars, clear and distinct as they are, are most lofty; so is a sermon like stars that all can see, yet few measure." True loftiness is shown not in rhetoric so much as in nobility of thought and wealth of experience. Here is the power of some early Puritan sermons that were "studied in a jail, preached under a hedge, printed in a garret, sold at a peddler's stall, bought by a priest's footman, applauded by a bishop and ordered to the press by a procession of gentry."

~

THE POET

Ever I must sing
As poets have;
The old tradition keep,
To laugh or weep
In some forgotten attic
As they have done
Rousing the world from sleep
To laugh or weep.

Ever must I bring
As poets have
The passions of life and truth
From the bosom of youth
That never rouses itself in me
But leaves in its wake
A verse; an ache.
—*Lillian Arline Walbert.*

~

WAKE UP—Sydney Smith, the prince of clerical wit, speaking of a preacher noted for his dull sermons made this remark: "He evidently thought sin was to be taken from man, as Eve was from Adam, by casting him into a deep sleep." A Scotch minister advised a lady who was given to sleeping in church to take some snuff. She replied: "Put more snuff into your sermons."—*Boen.*

The Parson's Prayer

I do not ask
That crowds may throng the temple,
That standing room be priced,
I only ask that as I voice the message,
They may see Christ!

I do not ask
For churchly pomp or pageant,
Or music such as wealth alone can buy.
I only ask that as I voice the message,
He may be nigh!

I do not ask
That men may sound my praises
Or headlines spread my name abroad,
I only pray that as I voice the message,
Hearts may find God!

I do not ask
For earthly place or laurel,
Or of this world's distinctions any part,
I only ask when I have voiced the message,
My Savior's heart!—*Ralph S. Cushman.*

From PRACTISING THE PRESENCE by Ralph S. Cushman. Copyright, 1936. Used by permission of the publisher, Abingdon-Cokesbury Press.

AUTHORS — When Addison had completed the Guardian, he was asked to publish another work, but said, "I must take time to relax and lay in fuel for it." Samuel Johnson declined to be introduced to a popular author, saying that he did not wish to talk with a man who wrote more than he read.

Fuller said that he "guessed good housekeeping, not by the number of chimneys, but by the smoke." Many capacious mental fireplaces lack fuel, and many large libraries lack readers. Only as we get can we give.

"I have two poems, one on the 'Bible' and the other on the 'Ocean,' but cannot find a publisher to take them." "Throw one into the other!" was the wise advice of a sarcastic friend.

LEARNING — The preacher should keep his learning subordinate to his love and respect for men. There are times when it must be crucified, and the preacher must literally "die daily." It may be for him the right eye to be plucked out. Dr. Duff, on his way to India, was shipwrecked near Cape Town. He had purchased a large library to gratify his love for classical literature. All this was lost. Strangely enough, his Bagster's Bible and hymn-book were washed ashore. He accepted this as an intimation that henceforth "human learnings must be to him a means, and not an end."—*E. P. Abbott.*

SERMON—As the preacher goes on (giving living bread, and not "critical" stones), yonder tired mother opens her heart, and is inspired with new hope to go on in her pressed home-life; the business man hears God's voice, and he, too, is encouraged; some word reaches that young man, and he is kept from doing the evil thing he had planned that very night. But no demonstration is made; in some way the burning words of the preacher have lifted the whole congregation Heavenward. Measure that sermon? Yes, if you can measure a sunbeam; yes, if you can measure a mother's love; yes, if you can measure a spiritual uplift by the miserable yardsticks of human measurement! No, no, my friend, the effect of that word given in that service, can only be measured by Him in that day when the final judgment of every man's work is made.—*Parkhurst.*

"LET ME SEE YOUR TONGUE" —One of the first things which a physician says to his patient is, "Let me see your tongue." A spiritual adviser might often do the same.—*N. Adams.*

PROFANITY—It is no mark of a gentleman to swear. The most worthless and vile, the refuse of mankind, the drunkard and the prostitute, swear as well as the best dressed and educated gentleman. No particular endowments are requisite to give a finish to the art of cursing. The basest and meanest of mankind swear with as much tact and skill as the most refined; and he that wishes to degrade himself to the very lowest level of pollution and shame should learn to be a common swearer. Any man has talents enough to learn to curse God, and imprecate perdition on himself and his fellow men. Profane swearing never did any man any good. No man is the richer or wiser or happier for it. It helps no one's education or manners. It commends no one to any society. It is disgusting to the refined, abominable to the good, insulting to those with whom we associate, degrading to the mind, unprofitable, needless, and injurious to society; and wantonly to profane His name, to call His vengeance down, to curse Him, and to invoke His vengeance, is perhaps of all offenses the most awful in the sight of God.—Luther.

BREVITY — That which Guthrie would have spread over an entire page, elaborating every particular with pre-Raphael-like minuteness, Arnot would have given in a sentence; and while the hearer of the former would have said, "What a beautiful illustration!" that of the latter would have exclaimed, "How clear he made it all by that simple figure!"
—W. M. Taylor.

ELOQUENCE — He is an eloquent man who can treat humble subjects with delicacy, lofty things impressively, and moderate things temperately.—Cicero.

BREVITY — The American audience appreciates most of all the story that is brief. Nothing in my experience so well serves to illustrate a point and to make a slight break in the tension, as the story that can be put in half a dozen words.

As an example, perhaps the following will serve: in discussing the low average intelligence of the common people I throw in this thought: "You would be amazed if you knew how many people don't even know that the epistles were not the wives of the apostles." I find that humorous relief does not check the flow of thought, but does serve to revive and reconcentrate upon a technical discourse the flagging attention of an audience.
—Charles Henry Mackintosh.

READING is to the mind what exercise is to the body. As by the one, health is preserved, strengthened and invigorated: by the other, virtue (which is the health of the mind) is kept alive, cherished and confirmed.—Addison.

ORATORY is the greatest art known to man and embraces a number of great arts. In music tradition furnishes the ideas. The poet clothes them in words. The composer sets these to music, and the singer renders them into song. The orator must be able to do all these things. He must furnish the ideas, he must clothe them in words, he must give these a rhythmic arrangement, and he must deliver them with all the care with which a singer sings a song. Each of these elements is of supreme importance. The ideas must be bright and seem alive. The language must be chaste and expressive. The arrangement must be logical, natural and effective. There must be a natural unfolding of the subject matter.—King.

A LOST ANGEL'S SONG — Kind words are the music of the world. They have a power which seems to be beyond natural causes, as if they were some angel's song which had lost its way and come on earth. It seems as if they could almost do what in reality God alone can do—soften the hard and angry hearts of men. No one was ever corrected by a sarcasm—crushed, perhaps, if the sarcasm was clever enough—but drawn nearer to God, never.—*F. W. Faber.*

Speak Gently

Speak gently: It is better far
  To rule by love than fear;
Speak gently: Let no harsh words mar
  The good we might do here.

Speak gently to the little child
  Its love be sure to gain,
Teach it in accents soft and mild
  It may not long remain.

Speak gently to the aged one,
  Grieve not the careworn heart;
The sands of life are nearly run,
  Let such in peace depart.

Speak gently, kindly to the poor;
  Let no harsh tone be heard.
They have enough they must endure
  Without an unkind word.

Speak gently to the erring; know
  They must have toiled in vain;
Perchance unkindness made them so,
  Oh, win them back again.
                    —*David Bates.*

THREE TESTS — When I want to speak let me think first. Is it true? Is it kind? Is it necessary? If not, let it be left unsaid.—*Babcock.*

PLEASANT — God has given us tongues that we may say something pleasant to our fellow-men.—*Heinrich Heine.*

SERMONS — A sermon is too often like Hodge's horse. It is overdone with brasses and bells, harness and harmony, but there is no real strength in it, no life and vigor. It is fine, but not forcible. Now, it strikes everybody that the trappings of a poor old half-starved horse look like mockery. You cannot plough fields with ribbons and bells; you want muscle and sinew; and so there is no moving men's hearts with pretty phrases and musical nothings. What is needed is thought, truth, and sound doctrine, and the Spirit of God. Young men are apt to think less of what to say than of how to say it; but our advice is, think of both in due proportion. Set the matter before the manner; get the horse first, and get a good one, and then harness him. Give the people the grand old Gospel, and plenty of it, and they will not much mind the way in which you bring it forth. A good horse should be decently harnessed, and Divine truth should be fitly spoken; the mischief is that some appear to think that the harness makes the horse, and that a fine style is the main thing in a sermon. Churches and chapels would not so often be empty if ministers would take heed what they preach as well as how they preach.
                    —*Spurgeon.*

DRAMA—To me it seems as if when God conceived the world, that was poetry; He formed it, and that was sculpture; He varied and colored it, and that was painting; and then, crowning all, He peopled it with living beings, and that was the grand divine, eternal drama.
                    —*Charlotte Cushman.*

SPEAKING — Daniel Webster said: "If all my talents and powers were to be taken from me by some inscrutable Providence, and I had my choice of keeping but one, I would unhesitatingly ask to be allowed to keep the Power of Speaking, for through it, I would quickly recover all the rest."

TALES — As a basket of silver filled with apples of gold,
So is the preached word with tales well told.

Always carry with you into the rostrum a sense of the immense consequences which may depend on your full and faithful presentation of the truth.—*R. S. Storrs.*

The orator is thereby an orator that he keeps his feet ever on a fact.
—*Emerson.*

HOW SWEET the words of truth breathed from the lips of love.
—*James Beattie.*

SYCOPHANT — Only experience can show how salt is the savor of another's bread, and how sad a path it is to climb and descend another's stairs.
—*Dante.*

ONE GREAT USE of words is to hide our thoughts.—*Voltaire.*

KIND WORDS cost no more than unkind ones. Kind words produce kind actions, not only on the part of those to whom they are addressed, but on the part of those by whom they are employed; and this not incidentally only, but habitually in virtue of the principle of association.
—*Jeremy Bentham.*

ORNAMENT — It is not to be used for its own sake. Dr. Taylor once suggested to a workman a certain embellishment in making a library case. The man replied, "I could not do that, sir, for it would be contrary to one great rule in art." "What rule?" "That we must never construct ornament, but only ornament construction." "It was quaintly spoken, but it was to me a word in season. I saw in a moment that this principle held as truly in the architecture of a sermon as in that of a cathedral—in the construction of a discourse as in that of a bookcase; and often since, when I have caught myself making ornament for its own sake, I have destroyed what I had written; and I have done so simply from the recollection of that artisan's reproof."

PROUD WORDS

'Tis sweet to hear "I love you"
Beneath a giggling moon;
'Tis fun to hear "You dance well"
To a lilting, swinging tune;
'Tis great to be proposed to
And whisper low, "I do;"
But the sweetest words in all the world,
"I've got a job for you."
—*Margaret Deeney.*

REMINDING—The object of preaching is, constantly to remind mankind of what mankind are constantly forgetting; not to supply the defects of human intelligence, but to fortify the feebleness of human resolutions; to recall mankind from the by-paths where they turn, into that broad path of salvation which all know, but few tread.—*Sydney Smith.*

INDEX — Speech is the index of the mind.—*Seneca.*

BRIEF.—Be brief; for it is with words as with sunbeams—the more they are condensed the deeper they burn.—*Southey.*

PULPIT TEMPTATIONS — The Christian pulpit needs to be on guard against the snare of words. One of the greatest curses that can come to a young preacher is that of a glib tongue. It means almost certain ruin. How futile, no matter how pleasing, are the efforts of a mere ministerial rhetorician! Language was meant to reveal thought, to open up to human minds the vast riches of reality; often, however, words constitute simply a dust storm to conceal every vestige of truth. When a minister ceases to think and study he takes refuge in shibboleths, he shuffles the symbols, and "rings the changes" on old words and phrases, with many an appeal to the "faith of our fathers" and the "good old-time religion." Then straightway he becomes a problem for the bishop and the cabinet, for such a preacher's sole stock in trade is an outfit of moth-eaten verbalisms. He may be saved, of course, if he is willing to begin to buy books, to read, and to study; for in this way, and in this way only, can a speaker put new life into his words and give them meaning and content. After all, the most important thing is to have something to say. If a mind be filled with the abundant resources of thought, the soul of the man will come bursting through into eloquent speech, sometimes crowding even into a commonplace word marvels of beauty and power.
Zion's Herald.

LOVE — What are our lame praises in comparison with His love? Nothing, and less than nothing; but love will stammer rather than be dumb.
—*Robert Leighton.*

RULES FOR SPEAKERS.—Be prepared.
Speak distinctly.
Look your audience in the eyes.
Favor your deep tones.
Speak deliberately.
Cultivate earnestness.
Be logical.
Don'ts for Speakers—
Don't be afraid of your voice.
Don't forget your audience can think.
Don't be ashamed of your own opinion.
Don't cover too much ground.
Don't forget to practice.
First Aid to Speakers—
Be prepared and don't rely on inspiration.
Originality comes from meditation.
Have a definite purpose.
Avoid irrelevancy.
Be sincere, earnest and enthusiastic
Don't hurry into your subject.
Wait for attention.
Begin in a conversational tone but loud enough to be heard.
Don't force gestures.
Cultivate the straight-forward open eye.
Don't walk about while speaking.
Don't be didactic.
Good diction is a passport recognized by everyone.
Let your grammar, vocabulary and pronunciation be the best.
Cultivate a genial manner.
Pauses are of great oratorical value.
Write much and often.
Read aloud and regularly.
The best way to learn to speak is to speak.
—*Walter Robinson.*

POWER.—To have what we want is riches; but to be able to do without is power.—*George Macdonald.*

SAYINGS—The best preaching is uncomfortable preaching.

No church ever saved a community by quarreling among themselves.

I know a lot of people who desecrate Sunday on Saturday night.

Most church quarrels arise over some one's rights, not over some one's prayers.

God loveth a cheerful giver who does not talk too much about it nor expect too much credit for it.

Blessed is the man who does not insist upon talking about his children when I want to talk about mine.

Blessed is the man who appreciates his own time too highly to waste the time of some one else.—*Roy L. Smith.*

FORCE — From the lawyer, the minister may learn to establish his case. The minister usually starts out with a proposition stated in the form of a text, the truth of which he is presumably going to prove. To do this he must present his evidence, marshal his facts, and set them forth in a logical and convincing manner. This the minister often fails to do. It is not required that every sermon shall be an exercise in logic, a sample of argument, but that it will seek to inform, to instruct, and to convince. Our sermons frequently lack facts, convincing facts, moving facts. We are inclined to forget that, "in all our preaching we must preach for verdicts. We must present our case, we must seek a verdict, and we must ask for an immediate execution of the verdict."—*Smith.*

MISOGYNIST — Any time Europe wants us to fall for somepin they got, they tell us they want our moral leadership. We should sympathize with Europe and all that, but we don't have to marry her.
—*Will Rogers.*

MULTUM IN PARVO—The people that throw mud always have dirty hands.

The road to Somewhere is not paved. The paved road passes through Anywhere and stops at Nowhere.

You can't whitewash yourself by blackening others.

Face the sunshine and the shadows will fall behind you.

For every bad habit you give up you automatically contract a good one.

Swear off on talking and see what a good listener you become.

Use the Golden Rule.

Oil your brain occasionally with a good brand of constructive thoughts.

It's a hard job to work with rusty tools.

Every time you frown you vaccinate yourself against happiness.

Keep it up and it is bound to take.

Be patient with the faults of others—they have to be patient with you.

The man who keeps himself and machine under control at all times never becomes angry—or kills anybody.

The pathway of Life is just about like any other congested street. If you don't keep going you get crowded to one side.
—*Charles H. Cowgill.*

BEHAVIOR—Christianity is pre-eminently the religion of the heart. It does not always ask words, but it always wants work. The motives and not the means are the things on which it passes judgment. And the man who shows by his life that he is not ashamed of the Gospel will assuredly one day find that the Gospel is not ashamed of him. There is much more which might be said, but I refrain. Ere I close, you will let me add my emphasis to the fact that it is in our life and conduct that we must show our devotion to Christ. The silent Gospel reaches further than the grandest rhetoric.—*Wilson.*

XXVIII SERIES

A RECIPE — I leave these words with you. It is only a young man's message to young men. The message is simple enough. There's nothing impossible about it to any young man, so long as he bears in mind the salient points: First—What success means; the successful doing, the doing well of whatever he does in whatever position he is. Second—The price of success; hard work, patience, and a few sacrifices.

Then for his keys—In his religious life: A firm, unwavering belief in God and in prayer, and a life consistent with that belief for himself and for others. In his social life: Moderation. In his marriage: Love. And in business: Thoroughness. Not thoroughness alone in large things or what is apparent to the eye; but thoroughness in all things; not slighting small things.—*Edward Bok.*

IMPOSSIBLE — The engineer, when he cannot carry his tunnel across or around a mountain, tunnels through it. "Impossibilities!" cried Lord Chatham, " I trample upon impossibilities! "Impossible!" ex-

claimed Mirabeau, "Talk not to me of that blockhead of a word." If a man's faith in himself and his mission be real and earnest, he cannot fail to gain a certain measure of success. If he does not satisfy the world, he will at least satisfy the voice of conscience. When we look back upon the history of humanity, we see nothing else but a record of what has been achieved by men of strong will. Their will it is that has opened up the way to their fellows. Their enthusiasm of purpose, their fixity of aim, their heroic perseverance—we are all inheritors of what these high qualities have won. "The world is no longer clay," says Emerson, "but rather iron in the hands of its workers, and men have got to hammer out a place for themselves by steady and rugged blows."

HOW TO WIN—Keep up the fires of thought, and all will go well . . . You fail in your thoughts or you prevail in your thoughts alone.—*Thoreau.*

VICTORY—There is a serene Providence which rules the fate of nations, which makes little account of time, little of one generation or race, makes no account of disasters, conquers alike by what is called defeat or by what is called victory, thrusts aside enemy or obstruction, crushes everything immortal as inhuman, and obtains the ultimate triumph of the best race by everything which resists the moral laws of the world.
—*Ralph Waldo Emerson.*

HOME AT LAST

To an open house in the evening,
Home shall men come,
To an older place than Eden,
And a taller town than Rome.
To the end of the way of the wandering star,
To the things that cannot be and that are,
To the place where God was homeless,
And all men are at home.

GILBERT K. CHESTERTON.

TRIUMPH—There never shall be one lost good. *All* we have willed or hoped or dreamed of good shall exist.
—*Robert Browning.*

AN INSPIRATION

However the battle is ended,
  Though proudly the victor comes
With fluttering flags and prancing nags
  And echoing roll of drums,
Still truth proclaims this motto,
  In letters of living light,—
No question is ever settled,
  Until it is settled right.

Though the heel of the strong oppressor
  May grind the weak to dust,
And the voices of fame with one acclaim
  May call him great and just,
Let those who applaud take warning,
  And keep this motto in sight,—
No question is ever settled
  Until it is settled right.

Let those who have failed take courage;
  Tho' the enemy seems to have won,
Tho' his ranks are strong, if he be in the
    wrong
  The battle is not yet done;
For, as sure as the morning follows
  The darkest hour of the night,
No question is ever settled
  Until it is settled right.

O man bowed down with labor!
  O woman, young, yet old!
O heart oppressed in the toiler's breast
  And crushed by the power of gold!
Keep on with your weary battle
  Against triumphant might;
No question is ever settled
  Until it is settled right.
                    —*Ella Wheeler Wilcox.*

RECOLLECTION is the only paradise here on earth from which we cannot be turned out.—*Richter.*

WHATEVER DISUNITES man from God disunites man from man.
                    —*Burke.*

SUCCESS—He has achieved success who has lived well, laughed often and loved much; who has gained the respect of intelligent men and the love of little children; who has filled his niche and accomplished his task; who has left the world better than he found it, whether by an improved poppy, a perfect poem or a rescued soul; who has never lacked appreciation of earth's beauty or failed to express it; who has looked for the best in others and given the best he had; whose life was an inspiration; whose memory is a benediction.—*Mrs. A. J. Stanley.*

TOGETHER

Ho, brother, it's the hand clasp and the
    good word and the smile
That does the most and helps the most
    to make the world worth while!
It's all of us together, or it's only you
    and I—
A ringing song of friendship, and a word
    or two of cheer,
Then all the world is gladder, and the
    bending sky is clear.
It's you and I together—and we're brothers
    one and all
Whenever through good fellowship we
    hear the subtle call,
Whenever in the ruck of things we feel
    the helping hand
Or see the deeper glow that none but we
    may understand—
Then all the world is good to us and all is
    worth the while;
Ho, brother, it's the hand clasp and the
    good word and the smile!

POWER — Responsibility gravitates toward him who gets ready for it, and power flows to him and through him who can use it.—*George Walter Fiske.*

WATCH AND PRAY—Jesus commands both vigilance and supplication, readiness and dependence.

"Pray to God and row to shore," says the proverb of the Russian fishermen. "Pray to God and keep your powder dry," runs the saying of our pioneer forefathers.

There are two sides to man's religious life: his own honest efforts and God's guidance and support. Either without the other is inadequate.

HIDDEN TREASURE

" 'Twas long ago I read the story sweet—
Of how the German mothers, o'er the sea,
Wind in, throughout the yarn their girlies
   knit,
Some trinkets small, and tiny shining
   coins,
That when the little fingers weary grow,
And fain would lay aside the tiresome
   task,
From out the ball will drop the hidden
   gift,
To please and urge them on in search
   for more.
And so, I think, the Father kind above
Winds in and out the skein of life we
   weave,
Through all the years, bright tokens of
   His love,
That when we weary grow and long for
   rest
They help to cheer and urge us on for
   more;
And far adown within the ball we find,
When all the threads of life at last are
   spun,
The grandest gift of all—eternal life."
                              —*Anonymous.*

THINK BACK — Often a retrospect delights the mind.—*Dante.*

STAND YOUR GROUND — The following story is told about Henry Ward Beecher as a boy:

The teacher in the school he attended asked a boy a question which the boy answered. Apparently the teacher was much incensed at the answer and cried testily: Sit down! The abashed boy sat abruptly down. Several boys were asked the same question and gave the same answer and promptly became confused when the teacher voiced his unexplained disapproval.

Finally Beecher was called and gave the same answer as the other boys. Sit down! roared the teacher. But Beecher held his ground and insisted that the answer was correct. For a few moments the teacher stormed at him, but seeing Beecher obdurate and convinced, he smiled and said: Well, boys, you were all correct, but Beecher was the only one sure enough to stand up for it.

It is important not only to give the right answer but to stick to it through thick and thin.

MY WAGE

I bargained with Life for a penny,
   And Life would pay no more,
However I begged at evening
   When I counted my scanty score.

For Life is a just employer,
   He gives you what you ask,
But once you have set the wages,
   Why, you must bear the task.

I worked for a menial's hire,
   Only to learn, dismayed,
That any wage I had asked of Life,
   Life would have paid.
                     —*Jessie B. Rittenhouse.*

From THE DOOR OF DREAMS, by Jessie Belle Rittenhouse. Used by permission of the publishers, Houghton Mifflin Company.

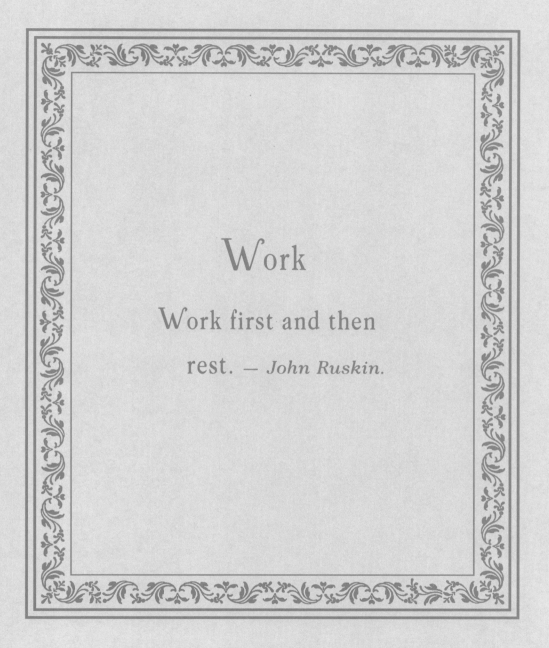

Work

Work first and then

rest. — *John Ruskin.*

THE FOLLY OF IMPATIENCE —
Action taken under the impulse of haste
and impatience is usually foolish. A
superficial glance often seems to justify
a course which a little patience reveals
as the utterest folly.

Impatience accounts for many wild
schemes in days of emergency and creates
many a frightful panic. Action is the
result toward which thought tends, but
impatient action is always the result of
folly.

Can you hope to hit the mark if you
go off at half-cock?

WHOEVER sincerely endeavors to
do all the good he can will probably do
much more than he imagines or will ever
know to the day of judgment when the
secrets of all hearts shall be made manifest.—*Anonymous.*

PREPAREDNESS

For all your days prepare,
    And meet them ever alike:
When you are the anvil, bear;
    When you are the hammer, strike.
                —*Edwin Markham.*
                Reprinted by permission.

I HAVE come to see life, not as a
chase of forever impossible personal
happiness, but as a field for endeavor
toward the happiness of the whole human
family. There is no other success. I know
indeed of nothing more subtly satisfying
and cheering than a knowledge of the
real good will and appreciation of others.
Such happiness does not come with
money; nor does it flow from a fine physical state. It cannot be bought. But it is
the keenest joy, after all, and the toiler's
truest and best reward.
                —*William Dean Howells.*

OVER-CONFIDENCE — Sir James
M. Barrie said: "We are all of us failures
—at least all the best of us are."

The man who is in real danger is the
man who thinks he is perfectly safe.

EFFICIENCY — "Nothing," said
Carlyle, "is more terrible than activity
without insight."

The tragedy of life is not hardship,
labour, suffering; but meaninglessness,
emptiness, effort without objective. The
fever-racked man who aimlessly passes
through the motions of his accustomed
daily conduct is a pitiable object. How
much more so those whose daily conduct
is merely the expression of the fever of life.

Only the man whose activity is directed
by a great purpose can be fundamentally
happy. Life easily degenerates into the
mere dance of death unless it be intelligently directed. Behind the expenditure
of the precious energy of life there must
be the highest degree of wisdom. Otherwise that energy which can never be
recaptured is wasted.

THE HUMAN RACE is in the best
condition when it has the greatest degree
of liberty.—*Dante.*

MAKE YOUR OWN LUCK—If a
man exercises foresight and develops the
strength and courage to include various
contingencies in the scope of his plans,
he puts luck in its proper place as the
minor uncertainty that lends savour to
life. Luck is too much dependent on men
to be a god.

Nansen once said of Amundsen's discovery of the South Pole: "Let no one
come and prate about luck and chance,
Amundsen's luck is that of the strong
man who looks ahead."

XXIX. TODAY

BANISH THE FUTURE—Banish the future; live only for the hour and its allotted work. Think not of the amount to be accomplished, the difficulties to be overcome, but set earnestly at the little task at your elbow, letting that be sufficient for the day; for surely our plain duty is "not to see what lies dimly at a distance, but to do what lies clearly at hand."—*Osler.*

THE MAN-I-YET-MAY-BE — Yesterday I dragged wearily along, passively resigned—the Man-I-Am—between the Man-I-Might-Have-Been and the Man-I-Yet-May-Be. But now, today, I feel that with Christ's help all things are possible to the aspirations, the energy, and courage that are thrilling in me in this beautiful new-born life of today, and the Man-I-Yet-May-Be draws closer to my side.
—*O. F.*

DAYS

Daughters of Time, the hypocritic Days,
Muffled and dumb like barefoot dervishes,
And marching single in an endless file,
Bring diadems and fagots in their hands.
To each they offer gifts after his will,
Bread, kingdoms, stars, and sky that holds them all.
I, in my pleached garden, watched the pomp,
Forgot my morning wishes, hastily
Took a few herbs and apples, and the Day
Turned and departed silent. I, too late,
Under her solemn fillet saw the scorn.
EMERSON.

ONLY ONCE — We live but once. The years of childhood, when once past, are past for ever. It matters not how ardently we may wish to live them over; it avails us nothing. So it is with the other stages of life. The past is no longer ours. It has gone beyond our reach. What we have made it, it shall remain. There is no power in Heaven or on earth that can change it. The record of our past stands forth in bold and ineffaceable characters, open to the all-seeing eye of God. There it stands, and one day we shall give an account of it. The present moment alone is ours. "Now is thy treasure possessed unawares." Today is a day which we never had before, which we shall never have again. It rose from the great ocean of eternity, and again sinks into its unfathomable depths.—*Talmage.*

FEELINGS—For a few brief days the orchards are white with blossoms. They soon turn to fruit, or else float away, useless and wasted, upon the idle breeze. So will it be with present feelings. They must be deepened into decision, or be entirely dissipated by delay.
—*Theodore Cuyler.*

GONE—Lost wealth may be replaced by industry, lost knowledge by study, lost health by temperance, but lost time is gone for ever.—*Smiles.*

THRIFT—Believe me when I tell you that thrift of time will repay you in after-life, with a usury of profit beyond your most sanguine dreams; and that waste of it will make you dwindle alike in intellectual and moral stature, beyond your darkest reckoning.—*W. E. Gladstone.*

FILL THE SPACES—Select a large box, and place in it as many cannon balls as it will hold, and it is, after a fashion, full; but it will hold more if smaller matters be found. Bring a quantity of marbles; very many of these may be packed in the spaces between the larger globes; the box is now full, but still only in a sense; it will contain more yet. There are interstices in abundance, into which you may shake a considerable quantity of small shot, and now the chest is filled beyond all question; but yet there is room. You cannot put in another shot or marble, much less another ball; but you will find that several pounds of sand will slide down between the larger materials, and, even then between the granules of sand, if you empty yonder jug, there will be space for all the water, and for the same quantity several times repeated. Where there is no space for the great, there may be room for the little; where the little cannot enter, the less can make its way; and where the less is shut out, the least of all may find ample room. So, where time is, as we say, fully occupied, there must be stray moments, occasional intervals, and snatches, which might hold a vast amount of little usefulness in the course of months and years. What a wealth of minor good, as we think it to be, might be shaken down into the interstices of ten years' work, which might prove to be as precious in result by the grace of God, as the greater works of the same period.
—*C. H. Spurgeon.*

BUILDING

For Yesterday is but a Dream,
And To-Morrow is only a Vision;
But To-Day, well lived,
Makes every Yesterday
A dream of Happiness,
And every To-Morrow a Vision of Hope.

TOMORROW — Today is the wise man's day; tomorrow is the fool's day. The wise man is the man who, when he sees what ought to be done, does it today. The foolish man is the man who, when he sees what ought to be done, says, "I will do it tomorrow." The men who always do today the thing they see ought to be done today are the men who make a success for time and for eternity. The men and women who put off until tomorrow what ought to be done today are the men and women who make a shipwreck of time and of eternity.—*Banks.*

WELL-EARNED SLEEP — Make a rule, and pray God to help you to keep it, never, if possible, to lie down at night without being able to say, "I have made one human being, at least, a little wiser, a little happier, or a little better this day."
—*Charles Kingsley.*

DO IT NOW—There is no moment like the present. The man who will not execute his resolutions when they are fresh upon him can have no hope from them afterwards: they will be dissipated, lost, and perish in the hurry and scurry of the world, or sunk in the slough of indolence.—*Maria Edgeworth.*

MOMENTS—The small stones which fill up the crevices have almost as much to do with making the fair and firm wall as the great rocks; so the wise use of spare moments contributes not a little to the building up in good proportions a man's mind.—*E. Paxton Hood.*

PROMPTNESS — I owe all my success in life to having been always a quarter of an hour beforehand.—*Lord Nelson.*

WATCH your way then, as a cautious traveler; and don't be gazing at that mountain or river in the distance, and saying, "How shall I ever get over them?" but keep to the present little inch that is before you, and accomplish that in the little moment that belongs to it. The mountain and the river can only be passed in the same way; and when you come to them, you will come to the light and strength that belong to them.

—*M. A. Kelty.*

PUPIL—Today is yesterday's pupil.
—*Franklin.*

WAYFARERS — I expect to pass through this world but once. Any good thing, therefore, that I can do or any kindness I can show to any fellow human being let me do it now. Let me not defer nor neglect it, for I shall not pass this way again.—*Stephen Grellet.*

INDECISION—The sun rose; it rose upon no sadder sight than the man of good abilities, and good emotions, incapable of their directed exercise, incapable of his own help and his own happiness, sensible of the blight upon him, and resigning himself to let it eat him away.
—*Dickens—"Tale of Two Cities."*

HELPFULNESS—Today is your day and mine, the only day we have, the day in which we play our part. What our part may signify in the great whole we may not understand; but we are here to play it, and now is our time. This we know: it is a part of action, not of whining. It is a part of love, not cynicism. It is for us to express love in terms of human helpfulness.—*David Starr Jordan.*

DAY-BREAK — The morning, which is the most memorable season of the day, is the awakening hour . . . Little is to be expected of that day, if it can be called a day, to which we are not awakened by our Genius. . . All memorable events, I should say, transpire in morning time and in a morning atmosphere . . . To him whose elastic and vigorous thought keeps pace with the sun, the day is a perpetual morning . . . Morning is when I am awake and there is a dawn in me. . .
—*Thoreau—"Walden."*

The Time Is Brief

Because the longest life is brief
I must be swift in keeping
The little trysts with kindliness,
Before the time of sleeping!

I must be swift in reaching out,
To those whose hearts are yearning;
O, swift indeed to love them much
Before the long road's turning!

Before a sudden summons comes,
I surely must be saying
The words that I have failed to say—
The prayers I should be praying.
—*Grace Noll Crowell.*

THE ANSWER—We will never get anywhere with our finances till we pass a law saying that every time we appropriate something we got to pass another bill along with it stating where the money is coming from.—*Will Rogers.*

ALL OTHER KNOWLEDGE is hurtful to him who has not honesty and good nature.—*Montaigne.*

STUDY THE PAST if you would divine the future.—*Confucius.*

"IMPROVE YOUR OPPORTUNI-TIES," said Bonaparte to a school of young men, "every hour lost now is a chance of future misfortune."

~

TOO LATE— The foolish virgins of Christ's parable faced the fact that there is a point in life at which no excuses will avail.

The door was shut. There is absolutely nothing to be done about it. All action should have been taken beforehand. Now it is too late.

But the important thing to remember is that the arrival at the inexorable point of hopelessness is always the culmination of what has gone before; and that this desperate plight is avoidable if we are continually ready.

Many of us are going to do great things —tomorrow. But tomorrow never comes. For the only day we have is today. And this corrupting habit of running behind schedule—even in small things—has for its inevitable result the bringing of us face to face with a shut door.

The demand that life makes on all of us is to be ready at all times, to live neither in the past nor in the future but in the present.

Until we learn that lesson we cannot escape the certain consequence that we shall one day stand, sorrowful but too late, before the one door through which we desire to enter but cannot—because it is shut.

~

ESSENTIAL — There can be no per-severing industry without a deep sense of the value of time.—*Mrs. Sigourney.*

~

DOST THOU LOVE LIFE? then do not squander time, for that is the stuff life is made of.—*Franklin.*

POSTPONED DUTIES—Tomorrow is never what we think it will be. In that sense tomorrow never comes. Today we think we will be happy and please our-selves. Tomorrow we will do our duty. But we only make ourselves wretched pleasure-seekers.

For human nature is fundamentally such that it can only find enduring glad-ness in the incidental accompaniments of duty performed today.

~

THE KEEN SPIRIT seizes the prompt occasion; makes the thought start into instant action, and at once plans and per-forms, resolves and executes.
—*Hannah More.*

~

A SECRET OF GREATNESS — "The flighty purpose never is o'ertook Unless the deed go with it."

Is this not one of the secrets of great-ness? Certainly it is not a common char-acteristic of men.

We have an impulse to send a note to a friend. But postpone it and perhaps forget it.

We encounter a noble idea in conver-sation or a book. But let it slide through our leaky minds.

We hear or read a strange word or idea. Instead of turning to the dictionary or other book of reference or making a note for later investigation, we let it go.

Is it any wonder that our minds grow dull or that we are oppressed with the sense of unfulfilled purposes? Greatness may not be within our reach, but mental growth is. And no one need be oppressed by the haunting memory of unaccepted opportunities.

~

PROGRESS is the activity of today and the assurance of tomorrow.—*Emerson.*

PARADISE—If the state of the dead until the resurrection morning be one of entire unconsciousness, our Lord's parable of the rich man and Lazarus is worse than unmeaning. It is untrue in a sense which we forbear here to characterize. Nor is this the only decisive statement of His. The promise to the dying thief, "This day shalt thou be with Me in paradise," would be worse than unmeaning if the dying man were to lapse that instant into unconsciousness and continue in that state till the moment of the general awakening.—*J. B. Heard.*

TIME IS PAINTED with a lock before, and bald behind, signifying thereby that we must take time by the forelock, for when it is once passed there is no recalling it.—*Swift.*

PUNCTUALITY is the stern virtue of men of business, and the graceful courtesy of princes.—*Bulwer.*

TIME! the corrector where our judgments err; the test of truth, and love; the sole philosopher, for all beside are sophists.—*Byron.*

INDEPENDENCE—It is a miserable thing to live a life of suspense; it is the life of a spider.—*Swift.*

SPEND YOUR TIME in nothing which you know must be repented of; in nothing on which you might not pray the blessing of God; in nothing which you could not review with a quiet conscience on your dying bed; in nothing which you might not safely and properly be found doing if death should surprise you in the act.—*Baxter.*

IT IS BETTER to be doing the most insignificant thing than to reckon even a half hour insignificant.—*Goethe.*

NOW — There is a time to be born, and a time to die, says Solomon, and it is the memento of a truly wise man; but there is an interval between these two times of infinite importance.—*Richmond.*

TO CHOOSE TIME is to save time.
—*Bacon.*

USE THE DAY — Keep forever in view the momentous value of life; aim at its worthiest use—its sublimest end; spurn, with disdain, those foolish trifles and frivolous vanities, which so often consume life, as the locusts did Egypt; and devote yourself, with the ardor of a passion, to attain the most divine improvements of the human soul. In short, hold yourself in preparation to make the transition to another life, whenever you shall be claimed by the Lord of the world.
—*J. Foster.*

TO KILL TIME is, by definition, to murder it.

SPENDTHRIFTS — If time be of all things the most precious, wasting time must be the greatest prodigality, since lost time is never found again; and what we call time enough is always little enough. Let us then be up and doing, and doing to the purpose; so by diligence shall we do more with less perplexity.
—*Franklin.*

AFTER ALL—It's a great country but you can't live in it for nothing.
—*Will Rogers.*

XXX. TRIFLES

FRAGMENTS—Macaulay tells the story of a man who had the contract for putting in the stained windows for a great cathedral. He was much annoyed by the persistent request of his apprentice for the privilege of designing and arranging the glass, for just one window. He did not wish to discourage the young man's ambition, nor did he wish an experiment to be made with costly material. So he said to him, "If you will furnish your own material, you may try your hand on that window," pointing to one not very prominent. But what was his surprise to find him gathering up the little bits of glass that he himself had cut off and thrown away. He set to work with these, and suceeded in working out a design of rare beauty. When the doors were thrown open, and the people came to view the work, they stood in great groups before that window, admiring its charming excellence, until the master artist became exceedingly jealous of the rising reputation of his apprentice. So we may gather up the little bits of time, and influence, and money, and opportunity, which we generally throw away, and weave them into a life so pure and beautiful, that the angels will stand before it in admiration and praise.—*Moffitt.*

THE KEY—Study the big problems all the time, but never to skip a small task, for one of the simple duties may hold the key to the biggest problem.
—*John T. Faris.*

IMPOTENCY — Those who bestow too much application on trifling things become generally incapable of great ones.
—*La Rochefoucauld.*

LITTLE SINS — It is Satan's custom by small sins to draw us to greater, as the little sticks set the great ones on fire, and a wisp of straw enkindles a block of wood.—*T. Manton.*

A spark is the beginning of a flame; and a small disease may bring a greater.
—*Baxter.*

Small twigs will prove thorny bushes if not timely stubbed up.—*Swinnock.*

What great difference is there whether your eternal burning be kindled by many sparks, or by one fire brand? Whether you die by smaller wounds, or by one great one? Many little items make a debt desperate, and the payment impossible.
—*Hopkins.*

WASTE —"Do not waste five-dollar time on a five-cent job."—*John T. Faris.*

LITTLE THINGS

"Little words are the sweetest to hear; little charities fly farthest, and stay longest on the wing; little lakes are the stillest; little hearts are the fullest, and little farms are the best tilled. Little books are read the most, and little songs the dearest loved. And when Nature would make anything especially rare .and beautiful, she makes it little; little pearls, little diamonds, little dews. Agar's is a model prayer; but then it is a little one; and the burden of the petition is for but little. The Sermon on the Mount is little, but the last dedication discourse was an hour long. Life is made up of littles; death is what remains of them all. Day is made up of little beams, and night is glorious with little stars."

LITTLE THINGS — "A cup of cold water"—a little thing! But life is made up of little things, and he who would rise to higher usefulness is wise if he cherishes the loving yet seeming trifles of daily living.—*Floyd W. Tomkins.*

BEGINNINGS—Little sins, so called, are the beginning of great ones. The explosion is in the spark, the upas in its seed, the fiery serpent in its smooth egg, the fierce tiger in the playful cub. By a little wound death may be caused as surely as by a great one. Through one small vein the heart's blood may flow not less fatally than through the main artery. A few drops oozing through an embankment may make a passage for the whole lake of waters. A green log is safe in the company of a candle; but if a few shavings are just lighted, and then some dry sticks, the green log will not long resist the flames. How often has a character which seemed steadfast been destroyed by little sins. Satan seldom assails in the first instance with great temptations. Skilful general! he makes his approach gradually, and by zig-zag trenches creeps towards the fortress he intends at length to storm. Therefore watch against little sins.—*Newman Hall.*

A MEASURING ROD
That best portion of a good man's life,
His little nameless unremembered acts
Of kindness and of love.
　　　　　—*William Wordsworth.*

THE OBLIGATION — The million little things that drop into our hands, the small opportunities each day brings He leaves us free to use or abuse and goes unchanging along His silent way.
　　　　　—*Helen Keller.*

GOD SEES—Perhaps at the Last Day all that will remain worth recording of a life full of activity and zeal, will be those little deeds that were done solely beneath the eye of God.—*Gold Dust.*

MANY FACETS—If falsehood had, like the truth, but one face only, we should be upon better terms; for we should then take the contrary to what the liar says for certain truth; but the reverse of truth hath a hundred figures, and is a field indefinite without bound or limit.—*Montaigne.*

THE HOURS—The bell strikes one. We take no note of time, but from its loss. To give it then a tongue is wise in man. As if an angel spoke. I feel the solemn sound. If heard aright, it is the knell of my departed hours. Where are they? With the years beyond the flood. It is the signal that demands dispatch; how much is to be done!—*Young.*

MUCH MAY BE DONE in those little shreds and patches of time, which every day produces, and which most men throw away, but which nevertheless will make at the end of it no small deduction from the life of man.—*Colton.*

TRIFLES? — Sometimes when I consider what tremendous consequences come from little things—a chance word, a tap on the shoulder, or a penny dropped on a newstand—I am tempted to think . . . there are no little things.
　　　　　—*Bruce Barton.*

OBSTINACY AND CONTRADICTION are like a paper kite: they are only kept up so long as you pull against them.

KINDNESS AND LOVE — If you will study the history of Christ's ministry from Baptism to Ascension, you will discover that it is mostly made up of little words, little deeds, little prayers, little sympathies, adding themselves together in unwearied succession. The Gospel is full of divine attempts to help and heal, in body, mind, and heart, individual men. The completed beauty of Christ's life is only the added beauty of little inconspicuous acts of beauty — talking with the woman at the well; going far up into the North country to talk with the Syrophenician woman; showing the young ruler the stealthy ambition laid away in his heart that kept him out of the kingdom of Heaven; shedding a tear at the grave of Lazarus; teaching a little knot of followers how to pray; preaching the Gospel one Sunday afternoon to two disciples going out to Emmaus; kindling a fire and broiling fish that His disciples might have a breakfast waiting for them when they came ashore from a night of fishing, cold, tired, and discouraged. All of these things, you see, let us in so easily into the real quality and tone of God's interests, so specific, so narrowed down, so enlisted in what is small, so engrossed with what is minute.
—*Parkhurst.*

BE CAUTIOUS — Springs are little things, but they are sources of large streams; a helm is a little thing, but we know its use and power; nails and pegs are little things, but they hold the parts of a large building together; a word, a look, a smile, a frown, are all little things, but powerful for good or evil. Think of this, and mind the little things.—*Hillis.*

DISCRETION—We may outrun by violent swiftness that which we run out, and lose by overrunning.—*Shakespeare*

LITTLE BUT MIGHTY—Size is not always an indication of importance. We all stop to look at a big man walking in a crowd. But he is not always superior to his less noticeable companions. The giant Goliath was no doubt a splendid figure on the field of battle; but he was no match for the ruddy stripling David.

There are small things which wield a mighty influence.

A rudder is a small thing compared to to the ship which it steers. But who wants to be on a rudderless ship?

Your home may be very small and humble, but would you exchange it and all that it means for a residence in the biggest hotel in the world?

A man may be a very small creature, but would you rather be an elephant or the man who controls him?

Words are little things, but what tremendous power for good or evil they may exert!

DREAM PEDLARY

If there were dreams to sell,
  What would you buy?
Some cost a passing bell;
  Some a light sigh,
That shakes from Life's fresh crown
Only a rose-leaf down.
If there were dreams to sell,
Merry and sad to tell,
And the crier rang the bell,
  What would you buy?

A cottage lone and still,
  With bowers nigh,
Shadowy, my woes to still,
  Until I die.
Such pearl from Life's fresh crown
Fain would I shake me down.
Were dreams to have at will,
This would best heal my ill,
  This would I buy.
—*Thomas Lovell Beddoes.*

ANGER — When some of those cutting, sharp, blighting words have been spoken which send the hot, indignant blood to the face and head, if those to whom they are addressed keep silence, look on with awe, for a mighty work is going on within them, and the spirit of evil, or their guardian angel, is very near to them in that hour. During that pause they have made a step towards Heaven or towards hell, and an item has been scored in the book which the day of judgment shall see opened.—*Emerson.*

PRIME MOVER — Whosoever shall review his life will find that the whole tenor of his conduct has been determined by some accident of no apparent moment.
—*Johnson.*

TRUE GREATNESS—Johnson well says, "He who waits to do a great deal of good at once will never do anything." Life is made up of little things. It is very rarely that an occasion is offered for doing a great deal at once. True greatness consists in being great in little things.
—*C. Simmons.*

GIVE-AWAYS — Trifles discover a character more than actions of importance. In regard to the former, a person is off his guard, and thinks it not material to use disguise. It is no imperfect hint toward the discovery of a man's character to say he looks as though you might be certain of finding a pin upon his sleeve.
—*Shenstone.*

A STRAY HAIR, by its continued irritation, may give more annoyance than a sharp blow.—*Lowell.*

MEN are led by trifles.—*Napoleon.*

CONTRAST — There is a care for trifles which proceeds from love of conscience, and is most holy; and a care for trifles which comes of idleness and frivolity, and is most base.—*Ruskin.*

BUZZ BUZZ—The mind of the greatest man on earth is not so independent of circumstances as not to feel inconvenienced by the merest buzzing noise about him; it does not need the noise of a cannon to disturb his thoughts. The creaking of a vane or pulley is quite enough. Do not wonder that he reasons ill just now; a fly is buzzing in his ear; it is quite enough to unfit him for giving good counsel.—*Pascal.*

A LITTLE and a little, collected together, become a great deal; the heap in the barn consists of single grains, and drop and drop make the inundation.
—*Saadi.*

LOST—It is in those acts which we call trivialities that the seeds of joy are forever wasted.—*George Eliot.*

IN EVERYTHING—There is a kind of latent omniscience not only in every man, but in every particle.—*Emerson.*

GREAT MERIT, or great failings, will make you respected or despised; but trifles, little attentions, mere nothings, either done or neglected, will make you either liked or disliked in the general run of the world.—*Chesterfield.*

THE SUM — Trifles make perfection, but perfection itself is no trifle.
—*Michael Angelo.*

XXXI. WORK

CHOICES — All through life we must keep choosing. Destiny hangs on "yes" and "no." As we look back, it is to wonder what would have happened if we had gone the other way when the road forked.

On life's bargain-counter are wares piled up for the pleasing of all tastes. We marvel that some eagerly select what we contemptuously reject. * * * Our tastes are as various as our natures.

How can Nature originate so great a variety of patterns? We speak of the mass of mankind as if it was all one. But it presents a bewildering variation. Human beings are as different from one another as their parental influences and their environments and their personal natures are different. Flesh and blood can never be run in a mould of monotonous uniformity. The fascination of travel is in the endless variety of mankind that one encounters, more than in silent buildings or inarticulate scenery.

The choice of personal associates is the all-influencing choice. To go wrong here is the likeliest way to cripple one's chances of eminence or of plain, everyday success. A man goes into business with partners guilty of malfeasance, and they pull him down. A woman marries the wrong husband, and though her courage may keep her at the sticking point and may enable her to preserve the appearance of domestic felicity, all that makes for the ideal relationship is absent. The basis of happiness is not in things, but in people. Those of us who are thoroughly normal cannot get along without congenial society. The kind of persons we choose to be with is the first and surest indication of character. The worthiest must be uneasy and unhappy in the company of the worst; and the best will naturally seek the best. What a man chooses, he is.

—*Philadelphia Public Ledger.*

DOING—Whatever your hands find to do, that do with all the might that is in you. That is the lesson of all experience. Face every task with a determination to conquer its difficulties and never to let them conquer you. No task is too small to be done well. For the man who is worthy, who is fit to perform the deeds of the world, even the greatest, sooner or later the opportunity to do them will come. He can abide his time, can rest—"safe in himself as in a fate."—*G. W. Goethals.*

MY TASK

To love some one more dearly every
    day,
To help a wandering child to find his
    way,
To ponder o'er a noble thought and
    pray,
And smile when evening falls—
    This is my task.

To follow truth as blind men seek for
    light,
To do my best from dawn of day till
    night,
To keep my heart fit for His holy sight,
And answer when He calls—
    This is my task.

And then my Savior by and by to meet,
When faith hath made her task on
    earth complete,
And lay my homage at the Master's
    feet,
Within the jasper walls—
    This crowns my task.

                MAUDE LOUISE RAY.

WEEDS come of themselves; flowers require cultivation. There is depravity in the soil, a tendency to thorns and thistles. It is under the curse. Good things are brought out of the soil, like good things out of the human heart, only as the result of much labor. It takes no pains to produce a harvest of weeds, nor to produce the harvest that the thief or the drunkard reaps—no more effort than is required to float down stream. This is depravity.—*Gleanings for Sermons.*

FINDING ONE'S WORK—The desire to begin over again is one of those longings so common and universal that we may say it is a native instinct... that we have failed, and failed again and again, need not intimidate us for a new trial. Aspirations, imperfections, and failures are intimations of future achievements. Defeats foretell future successes. The sin to be dreaded is the unlit lamp and ungirt loin. Our light must be burning, however dimly, and we must keep on the right road, however often we stumble on the way. Under no circumstances can it be true that there is not something to be *done*, as well as something to be suffered. Let us sit down before the Lord and count our resources, and see what we are *not* fit for, and give up wishing for it. Let us decide honestly what we *can do*, and then do it with all our might.
—*Amelia E. Barr.*

Faith and Works

If faith produce no works, I see
That faith is not a living tree:
Thus faith and works together grow;
No separate life they e'er can know;
They're soul and body, hand and heart—
What God hath joined, let no man part.
—*Hannah More.*

THE COMMON TASK—It is not the straining for great things that is most effective; it is the doing the little things, the common duties, a little better and better—the constant improving—that tells.

We often see young people who seem very ambitious to get on by leaps and bounds, and are impatient of what they call the drudgery of their situation, but who are doing this drudgery in a very ordinary, slipshod way. Yet it is only by doing the common things uncommonly well, doing them with pride and enthusiasm, and just as well, as neatly, as quickly, and as efficiently as possible, that you take the drudgery out of them. This is what counts in the final issue. How can you expect to do a great thing well when you half do the little things? These are the stepping-stones to the great things.

The best way to begin to do great things is to improve the doing of the little things just as much as possible,—to put the uncommon effort into the common task, to make it large by doing it in a great way. Many a man has dignified a very lowly and humble calling by bringing to it a master spirit. Many a great man has sat upon a cobbler's bench, and has forged at an anvil in a blacksmith's shop. It is the man that dignifies the calling. Nothing that is necessary to be done is small when a great soul does it.
—*Orison Swett Marden.*

HIT IT HARD—The temper of life is to be made good by big, honest blows; stop striking and you will accomplish nothing; strike feebly, and you will do almost as little. Success rides on every hour—grapple it, and you may win; but without a grapple it will never go with you. Work is the weapon of honor, and who lacks the weapon will never triumph.—*Ik Marvel.*

DURABLE SATISFACTIONS — A great deal of the joy of life consists in doing perfectly, or at least to the best of one's ability, everything which he attempts to do. There is a sense of satisfaction, a pride in surveying such a work—a work which is rounded, full, exact, complete in all its parts—which the superficial man, who leaves his work in a slovenly, slipshod, half-finished condition, can never know. It is this conscientious completeness which turns work into art. The smallest thing, well done, becomes artistic.

—*William Mathews.*

RESOLVE—The "bull's-eye" may not be hit by the rifleman whose hand is uncertain, and his footing infirm. The goal will never be reached by the runner who swerves from a straight course, and wanders into a pathless wilderness. The student will accomplish nothing who flies from study to study with the restlessness of disease; and no man, whatever his condition or mental powers, will win or deserve success, unless he fixes upon some special object to be carried out, and through cloud and sunshine steadily perseveres in his settled purpose.

Purpose, indeed, is the very essence—the main element—of an heroic character. It was purpose which animated Ignatius Loyola in his ascetic labors; in persecution, and captivity, and physical suffering, still toiling at the fulfillment of his cherished design, the establishment of that "Society of Jesus," whose influence on the world's history has been so signal and remarkable. Martin Luther's "purpose" achieved the Reformation. Oliver Cromwell's "purpose" turned the tide of battle at Naseby, and placed him in the seat of the English kings. Mahomet's "purpose" built up a mighty empire, and fixed the firm foundations of a new creed.

The man who concentrates his energies upon the fulfilment of an unalterable design will assuredly wring success from the hands of a reluctant fortune. Such a man will take no heed of "impossibilities." "Impossible?" exclaimed Napoleon, "there is nothing impossible; it is a word only found in the dictionary of fools." The difference between genius and mediocrity lies chiefly in this matter of "purpose;" for true genius has, what mediocrity usually wants, the capacity of labor. "Work and purpose" is the moral of every heroic life.

—*Public Speakers Library.*

WANTED—Men,
Not systems fit and wise,
Not faiths with rigid eyes,
Not wealth in mountain piles,
Not power with gracious smiles,
Not even the potent pen—
Wanted: Men.

—*Anonymous.*

CARPENTER—"Is not this the carpenter?" As though no words of wisdom or works of power could come from a carpenter! If Jesus had been a rabbi, in a scholar's robe, it would have been another thing. Yes: and what another thing for us, and for all the world's workers! Celsus sneered at the carpenter, and said that word proved he was an impostor. How could God so demean Himself? But the world has left Celsus behind, along with the critics of Nazareth, and blessed God for the gentleness and comfort, the sympathy and hope, which were given to us by the hands of the Carpenter.

—*Vance.*

LABOR—Labor, the symbol of man's punishment; Labor, the secret of man's happiness.—*James Montgomery.*

ZEAL—If there was ever a man who seemed to spend his life for nothing, it was Henry Martyn—a man of an exquisite nature, great power, and a sweet and loving disposition. Taking the highest honors at the university, and having the best prospects in the Church, he was led by the Spirit of God to consecrate himself to the cause of foreign missions. For that object he sacrificed that which was dearer to him than life—for she to whom he was affianced declined to go with him. He forsook father, and mother, and native land, and love itself, and went an elegant accomplished scholar, among the Persians, the Orientals, and spent a few years almost without an apparent conversion. Still he labored on, patient and faithful, until, seized with a fever, he staggered. And the last record that he made in his journal was, that he sat under the orchard trees and sighed for that land where there should be sickness and suffering no more. The record closed—he died, and a stranger marked his grave. A worldly man would say, "Here was an instance of mistaken zeal and enthusiasm. Here was a man who might have produced a powerful effect on the Church in his own country, and built up a happy home, and been respected and honored; but, under the influence of a strange fanaticism, he went abroad, and sickened and died, and that was the last of him."
The last of him! Henry Martyn's life was the seed-life of more noble souls, perhaps, than the life of any other man that ever lived. Scores and scores of ministers in England and America, who have brought into the Church hundreds and thousands of souls, and multitudes of men in heathen lands, all over the world, have derived inspiration and courage from the eminently fruitful, but apparently wasted and utterly thrown away, life of Henry Martyn.—*H. W. Beecher.*

NOT KNOWLEDGE, BUT APTITUDE—It isn't what a man knows that matters, but how near to a straight line he can drive the processes of his mind; how near to a lean and useful muscle he can make that mind; how near he can come to lassoing a truth or method. No man should be judged by what he doesn't know; he should be judged only by how quickly and sensibly he assumes new duties.—*Struthers Burt.*

BUILDING CATHEDRALS—Three men, all engaged at the same employment, were asked what they were doing. One said he was making five dollars a day. Another replied that he was cutting stone. The third said he was building a cathedral. The difference was not in what they were actually doing, although the spirit of the third might quite possibly have made him the more expert at his task. They were all earning the same wage; they were all cutting stone; but only one held it in his mind that he was helping build a great edifice. Life meant more to him than to his mates, because he saw further and more clearly.

The farmer may be only planting seed, but if he opens his eyes he is feeding the world. The railroad man, the factory hand, the clerk in the store, likewise are building their cathedrals. The investors in stocks and bonds, the executives of great corporations — they are building cathedrals likewise, if only they can catch the vision. The housewife does not count the dollars she receives for her exertions. If she did, her life would be unhappy indeed. The rest of us, the great figures of the industrial world more than the humble ones, are thinking too much about such things as cutting stone and making profits, fully to be realizing the beauty of life.
—*Omaha Bee.*

DEEDS REMAIN—Life passes; work is permanent. It is all going—fleeting and withering. Youth goes. Mind decays. That which is done remains. Through ages, through eternity, what you have done for God, that, and only that, you are. Deeds never die.—*F. W. Robertson.*

FAITH and works are as necessary to our spiritual life as Christians, as soul and body are to our natural life as men; for faith is the soul of religion, and works the body.—*Colton.*

Faith without works is like a bird without wings; though she may hop with her companions on earth, yet she will never fly with them to Heaven; but when both are joined together, then doth the soul mount up to her eternal rest.
—*J. Beaumont.*

Christian works are no more than animate faith, as flowers are the animate springtide.—*Longfellow.*

Faith and works are related as principle and practice. Faith—the repose in things unseen, the recognition of eternal principles of truth and right, the sense of obligation to an eternal Being who vindicates these principles—must come first. Faith is not an intellectual assent, nor a sympathetic sentiment. It is the absolute surrender of self to the will of a being who has a right to command this surrender. It is this which places men in personal relation to God, which (in St. Paul's language) justifies them before God.—*Lightfoot.*

It is an unhappy division that has been made between faith and works, though in my intellect I may divide them, just as in a candle I know there is both light and heat; but yet, put out the candle and they are both gone; one remains not without the other. So it is betwixt faith and works.—*Seldon.*

No good thing is ever lost. Nothing dies, not even life which gives up one form only to resume another. No good action, no good example dies. It lives forever in our race. While the frame moulders and disappears, the deed leaves an indelible stamp, and moulds the very thought and will of future generations.
—*Samuel Smiles.*

WORK

Let me do my work from day to day,
In field or forest, at the desk or loom,
In roaring market-place or tranquil room;
Let me but find it in my heart to say
When vagrant wishes beckon me astray:
"This is my work; my blessing, not my doom;
Of all who live, I am the one by whom
This work can best be done in the right way."

Then shall I see it not too great, no small,
To suit my spirit and to prove my powers;
Then shall I cheerful greet the laboring hours,
And cheerful turn when the long shadows fall
At eventide, to play and love and rest,
Because I know for me my work is best.
—*Henry Van Dyke.*

SLIPSHOD METHODS — Do your best, not because your work is worth it, but because you are. Whatever you are doing, you are making manhood. Half-hearted work makes only half a man. Slipshod methods mean loose principles. The only way to keep character up to the standard is by continually living up to the highest standard in all that you do.
—*Young People's Weekly.*

MAKE A DUST—My son, remember you have to work. Whether you handle pick or wheelbarrow or a set of books, digging ditches or editing a newspaper, ringing an auction bell or writing funny things, you must work. Don't be afraid of killing yourself by overworking on the sunny side of thirty. Men die sometimes, but it is because they quit at nine p. m. and don't go home until two a. m. It's the intervals that kill, my son. The work gives you appetite for your meals; it lends solidity to your slumber; it gives you a perfect appreciation of a holiday. There are young men who do not work, but the country is not proud of them. It does not even know their names; it only speaks of them as old So-and-So's boys. Nobody likes them; the great, busy world doesn't know they are here. So find out what you want to be and do. Take off your coat and make dust in the world. The busier you are, the less harm you are apt to get into, the sweeter will be your sleep, the brighter your holidays, and the better satisfied the whole world will be with you.—Bob Burdette.

INSPIRE—Men cannot be made wise or strong or moral by exterior laws or agencies. There are two ways to help a thriftless man. One is to build him a house and place him therein. The other is to inspire in him the sense of industry, economy, and ambition, and then he will build his own house. All tools, books, pictures, laws, on the outside, begin with ideas on the inside. Inspire the reason, and man will fill the library with books. Wake up the taste and imagination in young men, and they will fill the galleries with pictures. Stir the springs of justice, and men will go forth to cleanse iniquities and right wrongs.—Parkhurst.

UPWARD—Infinite toil would not enable you to sweep away a mist; but by ascending a little you may often look over it altogether. So it is with our moral improvement; we wrestle fiercely with a vicious habit, which could have no hold upon us, if we ascended into a higher moral atmosphere.—Helps.

HEROES—"No man has earned the right to intellectual ambition until he has learned to lay his course by a star which he has never seen—to dig by the divining rod for springs which he may never reach . . . To think great thoughts you must be heroes as well as idealists. Only when you have worked alone—when you have felt around you a black gulf of solitude more isolating than that which surrounds the dying man, and in hope and in despair have trusted to your own unshaken will — then only will you have achieved. Thus only can you gain the secret isolated joy of the thinker, who knows that, a hundred years after he is dead and forgotten, men who never heard of him will be moving to the measure of his thought—the subtle rapture of a postponed power, which the world knows not because it has no external trappings, but which to his prophetic vision is more real than that which commands an army."
—Oliver Wendell Holmes.

LIVING — A life spent in brushing clothes, and washing crockery, and sweeping floors—a life which the proud of the earth would have treated as the dust under their feet; a life spent at the clerk's desk; a life spent in the narrow shop; a life spent in the laborer's hut, may yet be a life so ennobled by God's loving mercy that for the sake of it a king might gladly yield his crown.—Farrar.

PICTURES IN THE FIRE.—You can always see a face in the fire. The laborer, looking into it at evening, purifies his thoughts of the dross and earthiness which they have accumulated during the day.

—*Thoreau.*

ATTITUDES AND APTITUDES.— Have an apitude for the thing you do, and have an attitude of respect or reverence toward it.

Some people learn the motions of their work without ever bothering to study the meaning of those motions; such are doubtless working without an aptitude for their jobs. On the other hand, perhaps the great failures are the persons who, having an aptitude for their work, have the wrong attitude. They do a poor job, knowing it to be poor, but they lack respect for their own handiwork, and have so little thought for their fellow beings, that they are willing to waste their time doing something worthless.

In medieval times people approached their work with prayer. Whether it was ultimately viewed by the many or the few, it was all, no matter how it might be hidden, seen by God; and it was done primarily for God.

When we were knee-high to grasshoppers we were taught: "What is worth doing at all is worth doing well." All else is waste.—*Boston Herald.*

WORKINGMAN.—Jesus Christ was a workingman. His hands were fitted to labor as His voice was fitted to music. He entered into the condition of the great majority of mankind and became one of them in the fellowship of toil and from that time it has been hard for a man to get into better company than that of working people.—*George Hall.*

ENTHUSIASM makes men strong. It wakes them up, brings out their latent powers, keeps up incessant action, impels to tasks requiring strength; and these develop it. Many are born to be giants, yet few grow above common men, from lack of enthusiasm. They need waking up; if set on fire by some eager impulse, inspired by some grand resolve, they would soon rise head and shoulders above their fellows. But they sleep, doze, wait for public sentiment, cling to the beaten paths, dread sacrifices, shun hardships, and die weaklings.

—*Theological Framework.*

THE CURE — The most unhappy of all men is the man who cannot tell what he is going to do, that has got no work cut out for him in the world, and does not go into any. For work is the grand cure of all the maladies and miseries that ever beset mankind—honest work which you intend getting done.—*Carlyle.*

CONSCIENCE.—It is a great source of encouragement to man to feel that he has conscience on his side. He does not feel it necessary to stop at every stage that he may build up a labored argument as to the truth of the positions which he has laid down or announced; he is not compelled to be forever busy with the process of demonstration, as though what he uttered had no self-evidencing power, but must be fenced about with an array of credentials, or he could not otherwise look to gain assent to its truthfulness. He knows that the work which he does carries with it its own proof. It goes straightway into the recesses of the mind, and there enforces truth, however unwillingly recognized, and however speedily forgotten, of its being precisely such as the Almighty might be expected to send.—*Melvill.*

LASTING SATISFACTION—There is no truer and more abiding happiness than the knowledge that one is free to go on doing, day after day, the best work one can do, in the kind one likes best, and that this work is absorbed by a steady market and thus supports one's own life. Perfect freedom is reserved for the man who lives by his own work and in that work does what he wants to do.

—R. G. Collingswood.

A MAN is a worker. If he is not that he is nothing.—Joseph Conrad.

PAY ENVELOPE—Folks who never do any more than they get paid for, never get paid for any more than they do.

—Elbert Hubbard.

AS A CURE for worrying, work is better than whiskey.—Thomas A. Edison.

I BELIEVE in work, hard work and long hours of work. Men do not break down from overwork, but from worry and dissipation.—Charles Evans Hughes.

FOR ACTION—Not alone to know, but to act according to thy knowledge, is thy destination, proclaims the voice of thy inmost soul. Not for indolent contemplation and study of thyself, nor for brooding over emotions of piety—no, for action was existence given thee; thy actions, and thy actions alone, determine thy worth.

—Fichte.

GREASING THE SKIDS — They that do nothing are in the readiest way to do that which is worse than nothing.

—Zimmermann.

I LIKE WORK; it fascinates me. I can sit and look at it for hours.

—Jerome K. Jerome.

NO HOPE—In idleness there is perpetual despair.—Carlyle.

VITAL FUNCTION — Work is as much a necessity to man as eating and sleeping.—Even those who do nothing that can be called work still imagine that they are doing something.—The world has not a man who is an idler in his own eyes.

—Humboldt.

THE PLAN IS DIVINE — The moment a man can really do his work, he becomes speechless about it; all words are idle to him; all theories. Does a bird need to theorize about building its nest, or boast of it when built? All good work is essentially done that way; without hesitation; without difficulty; without boasting.—Ruskin.

BUDGETING—The more business a man has to do the more he is able to accomplish, for he learns to economize his time.—M. Hale.

THE ONE CAUSE—It is to labor and to labor only, that man owes everything of exchangeable value. Labor is the talisman that has raised him from the condition of the savage; that has changed the desert and the forest into cultivated fields; that has covered the earth with cities, and the ocean with ships; that has given us plenty, comfort and elegance, instead of want, misery, and barbarism.

—McCulloch.

186

XXXII. WORTHY THOUGHTS

PATIENCE — A certain lady met with a serious accident, which necessitated a painful surgical operation, and many months of confinement in bed. When the physician had finished his work and was taking his leave, the patient asked: "Doctor, how long shall I have to lie here helpless?" "Oh, only one day at a time," was the cheery answer. And the poor sufferer was not only comforted for the moment, but many times during the succeeding weary weeks did the thought, "Only one day at a time," come back with its quieting influence.—*The Free Churchman.*

CHARACTER — Build character for God. Make it four-square, with a spiritual side, a moral side, a mental side, and a physical side. On the spiritual side square it with Jesus Christ; let it be your ambition to be as spiritual as your Master; on the moral side be satisfied with nothing less than the standard set by Christ, Himself; on t he mental side let the thoughts of God rule, and on the physical side strive to make the body as clean as you believe was the body of the Lord Jesus Christ. Build the whole life for God.—*Speer.*

CHRIST'S STANDARD — Our nation has had heated political discussions as to what is the proper standard of value in the financial world. But in the spiritual realm the followers of Jesus Christ have no room for "difference of opinion" as to what is the standard of value. When His disciples were debating the question as to who should be the greatest in the kingdom of Heaven, Christ put before them a little child.—*Moore.*

KINDNESS — In a remote district of Wales a baby boy lay dangerously ill. The widowed mother walked five miles through the night in the drenching rain to get the doctor. He hesitated about making the unpleasant trip. He questioned "Would it pay?" He knew that he would receive little money for his services, and besides, if the child were saved, he would only become a poor laborer. But love for humanity and a sense of professional responsibility conquered, and the little child's life was saved. Years after when this same child became first Chancellor of the Exchequer, and later Prime Minister of England, the old doctor said, "I never dreamed that in saving that child on the farm hearth, I was saving the life of a national leader." God is constantly justified in the responsibilities He has placed upon us for preserving both material and spiritual life.—*Selected.*

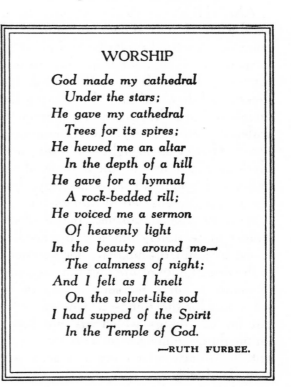

WORSHIP

*God made my cathedral
  Under the stars;
He gave my cathedral
  Trees for its spires;
He hewed me an altar
  In the depth of a hill
He gave for a hymnal
  A rock-bedded rill;
He voiced me a sermon
  Of heavenly light
In the beauty around me—
  The calmness of night;
And I felt as I knelt
  On the velvet-like sod
I had supped of the Spirit
  In the Temple of God.*

—RUTH FURBEE.

WHISPERS—There is hardly ever a complete silence in our soul. God is whispering to us wellnigh incessantly. Whenever the sounds of the world die out in the soul, or sink low, then we hear these whisperings of God. He is always whispering to us, only we do not always hear, because of the noise, hurry, and distraction which life causes as it rushes on.
—*Faber.*

Love's Garden

Love planted a rose,
    And the world turned sweet,
Where the wheatfield blows
    Love planted a rose.
Up the mill-wheel's prose
    Ran a music beat.
Love planted a rose,
    And the world turned sweet.
—*Katharine Lee Bates.*

Taken from THE RETINUE AND OTHER POEMS, by Katharine Lee Bates, published and copyright by E. P. Dutton & Co., Inc., 1918.

AMBITION — While visiting in a nearby city I was shown an unfinished mansion. A retired capitalist had planned to spend the remainder of his days in this luxurious home. But death ended his dream and deprived him of achieving his ambition. For eight years no workman had scaled the scaffolds; no sound of hammers heard. There was no sight of life save one black crow perched on the summit of an unfinished spire. What a tragedy, but one frequently enacted in human life.

And so that unfinished house stood amidst those stately pines as the symbol to me of unfilled ambition; a monument to the uncertainty of life and the certainty of death; a silent message urging us to strive not for the things which are seen, but for the things which are not seen; for the things which are seen are temporal; but the things which are not seen are eternal.—*Laws.*

AN ACRE of performance is worth the whole world of promise.—*Howell.*

UNIVERSAL—It has been said that Julius Caesar was the greatest man who ever lived. Ridpath says that he was head and shoulders above the age in which he lived. Did angels announce the birth of Julius Caesar? Did the sun refuse to witness his assassination in the senate chamber? Did Julius Caesar have the power to lay down his life, then take it up again? Was it at the name of Julius Caesar that apostles proclaimed and martyrs died? Caesar and his kingdom are things of the past, and were it not for history they would have been forgotten long ago. The name of Jesus is lauded today more than ever before. You may go to the remote isles of the sea and His name is there. You may sail the boundless ocean and His name is there. You may visit every land and clime and His name is there. His name spans eternity past and eternity to come. There have been great spirits in every race, but only one Great Spirit of the race.—*Lookout.*

THERE ARE THREE great principles in life which weave its warp and woof, apparently incompatible with each other, yet they harmonize and in their blending create this strange life of ours. The first is, our fate is in our own hands, and our blessedness and misery the exact result of our own acts. The second is, "There is a divinity that shapes our ends, rough-hew them how we will." The third is, "The race is not to the swift, nor the battle to the strong; but time and chance happeneth to them all." Accident, human will, the shaping will of Diety,—these things make up life.
—*Frederick W. Robertson.*

SAFEGUARDS OF YOUTH — I was standing in Tiffany's great store in New York, and I heard the salesman say to a lady who had asked him about some pearls, "Madam, this pearl is worth $17,000." I was interested at once. I said, "Let me see the pearl that is worth $17,-000." The salesman put it on a piece of black cloth, and I studied it carefully. I said, "I suppose Tiffany's stock is very valuable?" and as I looked around that beautiful store, I imagined them bringing all their stock up to my house, and saying, "We want you to take care of this to-night." What do you think I would do? I would go as quickly as I could to the telephone and call up the chief of police, and say, "I have all Tiffany's stock in my house, and it is too great a responsibility. Will you send some of your most trusted officers to help me?" You would do the same, wouldn't you? But I have a little boy in my home, and for him I am responsible. I have had him for nine years, and some of you may have just such another little boy. I turn to this old Book and I read this word: "What shall it profit a man if he gain the whole world, and lose his own soul?" or "What shall he give in exchange for his soul?" It is as if he had all the diamonds and rubies and pearls in the world, and held them in one hand, and just put a little boy in the other, and the boy would be worth more than all the jewels. If you would tremble because you had seventeen thousand dollars' worth of jewels in your house one night, how shall you go up to your Father and the lad be not with you?

—J. Wilbur Chapman.

IMPOSSIBILITIES—Law never does anything constructive. We have had enough of legislators promising to do that which laws can not do.—Henry Ford.

STRENGTH — I wonder if you remember the story that Carlyle tells about the dying of Oliver Cromwell. If ever there was a big man and a strong man in the place of ruler in Britain, it was Oliver. His chaplain had been reading to him, and amongst other sentences he had read this: "I can do all things through Christ which strengtheneth me," — all things, even die triumphantly. It was a great word, and the Protector for a time stumbled at it. And in a moment he was heard saying to himself: "Paul's Christ is my Christ. What Christ would help Paul to do, He would help me to do." And he faced that last fight and won it by the grace of Jesus Christ.—J. D. Jones.

From Gray's ELEGY

The boast of heraldry, the pomp of power,
    And all that beauty, all that wealth
      e'er gave,
Awaits alike the inevitable hour:—
    The paths of glory lead but to the grave.
Can storied urn or animated bust
    Back to its mansion call the fleeting
      breath?
Can Honor's voice provoke the silent dust,
    Or Flattery soothe the dull cold ear of
      death?

Full many a gem of purest ray serene
    The dark unfathomed caves of ocean
      bear;
Full many a flower is born to blush
    unseen,
    And waste its sweetness on the desert
      air.

GENERAL OBSERVATIONS drawn from particulars are the jewels of knowledge, comprehending great store in a little room.—Locke.

USE THE FRAGMENTS — Regret for time wasted can become a power for good in the time that remains. And the time that remains is time enough, if we will only stop the waste and the idle, useless regretting.—*Arthur Brisbane.*

CONFESSION

Last night my little boy confessed to me:
Some childish wrong;
And kneeling at my knee
He prayed with tears—
"Dear God, make me a man
Like Daddy—wise and strong,
I know you can."
Then while he slept
I knelt beside his bed,
Confessed my sins,
And prayed with low-bowed head.
"Oh God, make me a child
Like my child here—
Pure, guileless,
Trusting Thee with faith sincere."
—*Andrew Gillies.*

UNPREPARED — There is a legend of an oriental king, whose servant was also his personal friend and favorite. The king, one day, impatiently presented him with a golden bell, saying, "If ever you find a greater fool than you are, give this to him." Years passed and the king lay on his dying bed. To his servant the king said, "I am going on a long journey, and alas, am ill prepared." "Is it an unexpected journey?" "No, on the contrary, I have been forewarned these many years; but so engrossing have been the cares of government and the pleasures of court that I have given this matter little attention." Whereupon the servant silently handed him the golden bell. He had found a greater fool than himself at last. —*Selected.*

ONWARD — We are never present with, but always beyond ourselves.— Fear, desire, and hope are still pushing us on toward the future.—*Montaigne.*

THE ABIDING PRESENCE — The Lord Jesus Christ was here long enough to remove all doubt as to His personal identity, yet He withdrew Himself immediately. He had secured for His personality an unquestioned place in human history. Nothing more was to be gained by His visible continuance on earth; His bodily mission had been wholly fulfilled, and therefore He vanished out of the sight of men. But what of the future of His work? Then, according to Christian teaching, was to come manifestation without visibility; instead of bodily presence, there was to be a new experience of life, spirituality, insight, sensibility, and sympathy almost infallible in holy instinct. In one word, the Holy Man was to be followed by the Holy Ghost. As the disciples were to be sent abroad into all coasts, to be scattered all over the earth to preach the gospel, and not to stay together still, in one place, Christ's corporeal presence would have stood them in small stead. He could have been resident but in one place, to have comforted some one of them. . . The Spirit, that was to succeed, was much more fit for men dispersed. He could be, and was, present with them all, and with every one by himself, as filling the compass of the whole world.—*Andrews.*

FIRST — The greatest prayer is patience.—*Buddha.*

TO HIM who harkens to the gods, the gods give ear.—*Homer.*

SEVEN WONDROUS WORDS—

Last words are precious words; how we cling to them, and let them gently stir through the memory and persist through the years. Men build about them great paeans and songs.

The last words of Jesus, matchless for pathos and forgiveness and trust, form a garland of seven flowers that shall never fade while the world lasts. There are three before the darkness; one during the darkness, and three after the darkness. The first is the word of intercession: "Father, forgive them, they know not what they do." These hired soldiers, who are driving the nails and raising the cross, He would forgive them.

The second word is the world of hope beyond death, spoken to the young thief: "This day shalt thou be with Me in paradise." The third word is one of loving provision, "Woman, behold thy son." One of the tenderest acts in all history. Jesus did not forget His mother; He was a son as well as a Saviour; a Son to the last. The fourth: "Why hast thou forsaken Me?" spoken in the awful darkness, we shall never understand. It is the word of loneliness. The first three were spoken for others: He cared for others before He thought of Himself. The great heart broke and He cried, "My God." He lost His sense of God for a moment but not His trust. As the darkness passes He speaks three more words—"I thirst!" "It is finished," the word of victory. The seventh word is the word of trust—"Father, into Thy hands." Father! a precious word for God. The word of supreme confidence, of assurance, of victory.—*A. E. Gregory.*

HABIT — The diminutive chains of habit are generally too small to be felt, till they are too strong to be broken.

READY—Robert Hardy had a dream, and in that dream he thought he was to live only seven days. If you had only seven days to live, how would you live them? How did Robert Hardy begin? He began to study. He began to get ready. Did all in his power each day. He came to the seventh day; and he came near the end of the day. But all at once it was made known to him that he wasn't to die. He looked around and was glad, but he said, "Some seven days will be my last seven," and he lived every day as though he were in his last. You will be in your last seven days soon, and may be even there now.
—*Scoville.*

WHO IS EDUCATED?—There are five tests of the evidence of education—correctness and precision in the use of the mother tongue; refined and gentle manners, the result of fixed habits of thought and action; sound standards of appreciation of beauty and of worth, and a character based on those standards; power and habit of reflection; efficiency or the power to do.

PROTECTION—Dr. Forsyth has told how a friend of his was on a sheep farm in Australia and saw the owner take a little lamb and place it in a huge enclosure where there were several thousand sheep whose bleating, together with the shouting of the sheep-shearers, was deafening. Then the lamb uttered its feeble cry, and the mother sheep at the other end of the enclosure heard it and started to find her lamb. "Do not imagine that you are beyond the reach of the Good Shepherd," said the preacher. "He sees you, He hears you, every good desire of yours is known to Him, and every secret longing for better things. He sees you as if there were no other child in the whole world."

GENERAL INDEX